Educational Evaluation:
Classic Works of Ralph W. Tyler

Educational Evaluation:
Classic Works of Ralph W. Tyler, *Winfred*, 1902 –

Compiled and Edited
by
George F. Madaus and Daniel L. Stufflebeam

Kluwer Academic Publishers
Boston Dordrecht London

Distributors

for the United States and Canada: Kluwer Academic Publishers, 101 Philip Drive, Assinippi Park, Norwell, MA 02061.

for the UK and Ireland: Kluwer Academic Publishers, Falcon House, Queen Square, Lancaster LAI IRN, UK.

for all other countries: Kluwer Academic Publishers Group, Distribution Centre, P. O. Box 322, 3300 AH Dordrecht, The Netherlands

Library of Congress Cataloging in Publication Data

Tyler, Ralph Winfred, 1902-
    Educational evaluation: classical works of Ralph W. Tyler/
edited by George F. Madaus and Daniel Stufflebeam.
       p. cm. — (Evaluation in education and human services)
    Bibliography: p.
    Includes index.
    ISBN 0-89838-273-4: $45.00 (est.)
    1. Educational tests and measurements—United States—
Collected works. 2. Students—United States—Rating of—
Collected works.
    I. Madaus, George F. II. Stufflebeam, Daniel L. III. Title.
IV. Series.
LB3051.T93 1988
371.2'6—dc19   88-833
                                                          CIP

PRINTED IN THE UNITED STATES

Contents

Foreword

I personally learned to know Ralph Tyler rather late in his career when, in the 1960s, I spent a year as a Fellow at the Center for Advanced Study in the Behavioral Sciences at Stanford. His term of office as Director of the Center was then approaching its end. This would seem to disqualify me thoroughly from preparing a Foreword to this "Classic Works." Many of his colleagues and, not least, of his students at his dear *Alma Mater*, the University of Chicago, are certainly better prepared than I to put his role in American education in proper perspective. The reason for inviting me is, I assume, to bring out the influence that Tyler has had on the international educational scene. I am writing this Foreword on a personal note. Ralph Tyler's accomplishments in his roles as a scholar, policy maker, educational leader, and statesman have been amply put on record in this book, not least in the editors' Preface. My reflections are those of an observer from abroad but who, over the last 25 years, has been close enough to overcome the aloofness of the foreigner.

Tyler has over many years been criss-crossing the North American continent generously giving advice to agencies at the federal, state, and local levels, lecturing, and serving on many committees and task forces that have been instrumental in shaping American education. Several years ago, Tyler's famous student, Benjamin Bloom, told me that he and a group of colleagues had ventured a guess of how much of his life Tyler had spent in airplanes. They came up with an estimate of two years! One Saturday morning in the mid-1960s when I drove up to the Stanford Center I ran across Ralph whom I had not seen for the whole week. I knew that he — as usual — had been busy with many things at many places, but in particular with the preparatory work for the National Assessment of Educational Progress. I asked him: "Ralph, how often do you cross the American continent?" With the typical sense of humor pouring through his peering eyes he replied: "I am trying to keep it down to one tour per week."

Ralph Tyler's fellow countrymen are perhaps less familiar with his international than his national impact. As a graduate student in the early 1940s (during the war when scholarly communications were scarce) I obtained a copy of a report from the Eight-Year Study that, along with his subsequent book on the basic principles of curriculum and instruction, soon began to be regarded as a classic. These and other publications from the 1940s provided a solid empirical foundation for those of us who conducted studies in educational psychology.

During the early stages of his career, Ralph Tyler was instrumental in developing relevant examinations in specific subject matter fields and he laid the ground for better methods of achievement testing. Psychometricians had, around 1930, developed techniques of measuring certain psychological traits, but Tyler adapted these techniques to suit achievement testing. He widened the horizon with his famous rationales for both evaluation and curriculum construction. It was certainly part of the logic of the events that he was the one who, in due time, provided the rationale for a national assessment of educational progress.

What strikes me, both in reading this book and in reflecting on my close contacts with American educators, is how seminal Tyler has been with his ideas, not least through his own students. Tyler's bibliography at the end of this book carries a large number of articles in a variety of professional journals (educational and others) in which he acts as a builder of bridges between theory and practice. No wonder, then, that he has been a much sought after consultant and has been asked to nominate superintendents, deans, and other leading people in the educational enterprise.

To me — and, I think to many of my colleagues around the world — Ralph Tyler stands out as the leading figure in American educational research and evaluation — indeed as Mr. Education himself. During the "classical period" epitomized in this book, he advanced his evaluation theory and its applications as well as the principles of curriculum and instruction. It was therefore no surprise to me during my first year at his Center to find that he was the central figure and the idea injector in the enterprise later known as the National Assessment of Educational Progress. Apart from the intellectual leadership required to establish this new system of national evaluation, he had to develop a skillful diplomacy in order to overcome the deep suspicion that many people held against centrally organized assessment. It smelled of federal intrusion.

Neither was it a surprise to me to learn that Tyler emerged as the leading figure in the establishment of a U.S. National Academy of Education. He served as its president for quite some time and his contribution gave it a high status both within and outside the educational community. As a Foreign Associate of the Academy, I had ample opportunity to observe how, in conducting business during our meetings, he could draw upon an inexhaustible body of experience and could sprinkle the sessions with his witty remarks and anecdotes.

The International Association for the Evaluation of Educational Achievement (IEA), on Ben Bloom's initiative, decided in 1971 to organize an international seminar in Sweden on curriculum development and evaluation. The seminar went on for six weeks with some 125 participants from more than 23 nations. Ralph Tyler was the self-evident choice as the key lecturer. We succeeded in holding him for the whole 6-week period in the little town of Gränna in Sweden. This was, indeed, quite an achievement. I wondered whether Ralph had stayed for such a long time at the same place at any time in his adult life!

When a person comes to our mind, we tend to imagine him or her in concrete situations. In my case, what particularly stands out in recalling encounters with Tyler is a walk with him late one evening from the International House to the Quadrangle Club (where we were both staying) at the University of Chicago — that great institution where Tyler had spent so many productive years and had been instrumental in bringing its Education Department to the forefront, not only in the United States but in the whole world. I heard him often use the expression "cutting edge." He wanted to be part of it. As we passed Judd Hall that evening, Ralph gave me a detailed and vivid account of how education was established at the University during the Dewey era around the turn of the century. This was a fascinating piece of history of education.

Hardly have we on many occasions seized on any topic of conversation before Ralph's immense knowledge of individuals and his interest in their biographies flourished. He is a living *Who's Who* in American education, and has an encyclopedic grasp of the educational enterprise. Many of us have experienced how he, without even a piece of paper with its main points in his hands, could give a well-structured lecture on almost any topic in education. The Annual Meeting Programs of AERA still carry Tyler's name in several sessions and symposia. He is, indeed, a great generalist in a field where short-sighted specialization, as in other scholarly areas, is gradually creeping in.

We are all, to varying degrees, prisoners of prevalent "paradigms," a term that (it is well known) was coined at the University of Chicago in the early 1960s. Ralph Tyler's contributions to modern thinking in education as epitomized in this volume have, in a remarkable way, survived the change of time and paradigms. He has been able to cut through generations of educational scholars, which is no surprise to those of us who have seen the rapport that he is able to establish with young people. This timelessness is, in my view, the main reason why it has been considered fitting to collate his lasting contributions to educational scholarship. They have, indeed, withstood the test of time.

The emphasis in the present collection is naturally on publications from Tyler's early and mid-career — periods when he apparantly had more time to devote to the writing of major, monographic pieces. He had not yet been submerged in the many activities that took him around his home country and the world at large. His creativity and accomplishments as an innovator did by no means diminish after he left Chicago for the Stanford Center in the early 1950s. The Bibliography attached to this book bears witness to this.

American public education has been intermittently under fire and subjected to severe criticism during the post-war years. Those of us on the other side of the Atlantic who in various capacities have been involved in reforming the school systems in our home countries have, since the 1940s, been looking at the American public school as a model because of its role as a pillar of American democracy. Ralph Tyler has, during his entire career, always held a strong commitment to free public education that takes care of all children from all walks of life and all ethnic backgrounds — a school providing the same conditions and having them under a common roof. Tyler has seen his task as one of giving service to that school.

Dr. Tyler now lives in Milpitas, California. When I last visited California, somebody gave me a clipping from the *San José Mercury News* of an article published on his 85th birthday. He was presented as a person whose "main problem" since he was young had been "excess energy," something that was behind the opposition that brought him into trouble in high school. He is quoted as saying, after consulting his doctor, that as long as he is active he has no reason to worry about health. He has kept so much of his youthfulness and a combination of seriousness and levity of mind that has been behind his inspiring achievements.

Dr. Torsten Husén, President
International Academy of Education

Preface

For nearly 60 years, Ralph W. Tyler has been one of the most influential figures in education, at all levels both nationally and internationally. He has made substantial contributions to the fields of curriculum, testing, evaluation, and educational policy. Directly through his work, and indirectly through his many famous students, he has deeply influenced many noteworthy developments in education, including objective-referenced testing, objectives-based program evaluation, mastery learning, achievement test construction, item banking, the taxonomic classification of educational outcomes, and cooperative test development. He has been instrumental in the development of several national testing programs including the General Educational Development Program, the Cooperative Testing Program, and the National Assessment of Educational Progress.

During the past half-century, Tyler's role in education may easily be labeled that of educational statesman. He has been an advisor to presidents, legislators, and national and international commissions. He has helped local schools, school districts, colleges and universities, and state departments of education in the United States and in numerous overseas countries. His work and influence have always been grounded in practical experience, oriented to service, and dedicated to improvement and progress in education. His work reflects his brilliance and vision. His life's work has been governed by a keen sense of values, equity, and fairness. Throughout his career his work shows his humility and sense of humor — the latter often at his own expense.

Tyler's writings chronicle his ideas and projects over the years. His writings are filled with rich and instructive examples that still illuminate many contemporary theories, practices, and policies in education. Students of education can greatly increase their understanding of education's history and progress since the 1930s through a review of Tyler's work. Some of his writings address issues in important debates that have occurred during the past 60 years in education. For example, in the early thirties he directly challenged the ideas of the most prominent figure in testing, Ben Wood. Wood argued that it was sufficient to limit testing to measures of recall and recognition of facts and knowledge. If students had the necessary knowledge, they could apply it to solve problems. Tyler argued and then demonstrated that measures of higher order objectives such as application did not correlate highly with measures of mastery of factual knowledge. He concluded that if higher order cognitive skills were the objectives of instruction they had to be measured directly. His ideas about this — excerpted here in Part I — have influenced achievement test construction to the present day.

Another example of Tyler's past work that still influences the fields of curriculum development and program evaluation is his work in the Eight-Year Study. The Eight-Year Study, as its name suggests, was a longitudinal assessment of students from thirty progressive and traditional high schools through four years of secondary school and four years of college. The very existence of private and public progressive schools was threatened in the mid-thirties when many prestigious colleges changed their entrance requirements. They began to require courses in specified subjects like American History and Physics. Since the progressive schools were not organized around courses but around learner outcomes, this new requirement posed a real difficulty for them. Under a grant from the Carnegie Corporation, the comparative Eight-Year Study was undertaken. Tyler's work on the study is still the best available description of how evaluators can work cooperatively with teachers to clarify instructional objectives and develop indicators of students' continuous progress toward the mastery of a whole range of learning outcomes. His description of what was done — excerpted at length in Part II — is a model of sound practical advice for those interested in improving teaching and learning at the classroom level.

Still another example of Tyler's foresight is his persuasive argument against the practice employed in developing many norm-referenced achievement tests of discarding test questions that fail to discriminate among examinees. Tyler recognized that items that were answered by most students as well as those missed by most could, if they were good items to begin with, provide valuable information about instruction and student progress. Information of this kind was more valuable than including items for the sole purpose of differentiating among examinees in order to rank them. Items selected to meet an individual differences model, using technology originally developed in intelligence testing, typically did not provide the necessary information needed to evaluate the full range of educational objectives.

Today, the objectives-referenced testing movement owes a debt to Tyler for his observations about item selection criteria.

Unfortunately, however, the vast majority of Tyler's writings are out of print, and not easily accessible in libraries. The difficulty of getting at this important source of information is the main reason we are bringing out this collection of the classic contributions of Ralph Tyler. But there is another important reason for this book. Tyler's ideas still influence many people in testing, evaluation, and curriculum development. However, all too frequently his ideas have been misinterpreted or misapplied. Unwittingly or not, some interpreters have translated and applied his ideas with a simplicity and expediency he never intended.

For example, some educationists have imposed a rigid and mechanistic construction on his recommendations for defining course objectives. They have often assessed course outcomes too narrowly and have not sought to define or assess the full range of educational objectives. They have directed teachers to write hundreds of behavioral objectives without the benefit of discussion with the constituents of educators about the purposes of schooling. They have gravitated to the paper-and-pencil, multiple-choice standardized test and have not realized the essential need for more direct measures or indicators of student progress. They have lost sight of the centrality of the classroom teacher in defining, teaching, and assessing student outcomes. They have advocated evaluating student performance only at the end of courses, avoiding implementing programs that continuously monitor student progress. Unfortunately, Tyler has often been blamed for these kinds of misapplications of his ideas.

Still another reason for this book, perhaps less important than those described above but nevertheless we feel important, is that many recent innovations in curriculum, testing, and evaluation have not been properly associated to the degree they deserve with Tyler's seminal ideas. It is our belief that Tyler's ideas helped motivate and spawn many developments by others. Some investigators, of course, have acknowledged their great debt to Tyler and have built on and expanded his ideas. For example, ideas such as the taxonomic classification of learning outcomes, the need to validate indirect measures against direct indicators of the trait of interest, the development of scoring techniques that provide teachers with information that is helpful in directing instruction, the concept of formative evaluation, content mastery, decision-oriented evaluation, criterion-referenced and objectives-referenced tests, and criticisms of standardized testing all owe a debt to Tyler's influence.

Others coming out of a different tradition have not realized that what they suggest as new or innovative had already been described sometimes in great detail by Tyler. An example is Mortimer Adler's call in the *Paideia Proposal* for the development by teachers of different types of learning objectives and of direct indicators of their attainment. These ideas are explicated in great detail in Tyler's work in the Ohio State Service Studies and in *Appraising and Recording Student Progress*. Here we need to point out that Tyler's ideas were, of course, influenced by his predecessors and mentors including, among others, Percy Bridgeman, John Watson, John Dewey, E. L. Thorndike, C. H. Judd, and W. W. Charters.

One other example of how contemporary educators could benefit from reading Tyler should suffice. Currently there is intense interest in teaching, and in evaluating students' higher order thinking skills (euphemistically referred to as HOTS). The work of Tyler and his colleagues in the Eight-Year Study in defining and developing indicators of what they called critical thinking skills should provide a rich source of ideas about HOTS and their measurement. We feel that at the very least Tyler's early writings provide an extensive set of advance organizers for developments that are commonly attributed to more recent authors.

Depending on one's values and philosophy of education, a few of Tyler's ideas are viewed as having led education in the wrong direction. For example, there was always a tension in his writings between effectively serving local needs for data and finding efficient ways to serve broad societal needs for accountability. His contribution to testing served the latter but probably detracted from localized internal evaluation services such as those illustrated in his service studies at Ohio State and in the Eight-Year Study. In those cases there was a realization of the idiosyncratic nature of instruction and learning. Tyler worked closely with instructors in team efforts to use testing and evaluation to improve their courses and ultimately student learning. But the classroom and school were the units of interest. Unfortunately, we feel — and this, of course, is a value judgment on our part — the approach was not sustained, possibly due in part to its high costs. His later influence and leadership was in the direction of developing efficient national tests, such as the National Assessment of Educational Progress (NAEP). NAEP has cost the American public heavily. Unfortunately, while the results have been used extensively for accountability and to inform public policy debates — legitimate societal concerns — they have not yet impacted on instruction at the classroom level.

Our aim in this book is not to critically evaluate the works of Ralph Tyler. That requires a different kind of volume. In fact, our comments have necessarily been kept to a minimum so that we could include as much of Tyler's work as possible within the page limitations. Therefore, what we have attempted to do is to set the record straight by presenting large excerpts from a select body of his extensive works. By and large, we present a small, but what we feel is an important, sample of Tyler's writings over the last 55 years. Tyler's bibliography spans 60 years and hundreds of works. Obviously we had to be very selective when choosing among Tyler's writings, as well as editing within a particular work. We were guided by several criteria in this selection process. First, we wanted the sample to be representative of his major involvements in testing and evaluation. Second, we tried to use works that Tyler himself recommended be included. Third, we chose to excerpt from works that are generally thought of as classic but difficult to find, e.g., *Appraising and Recording Student Progress*, or what we felt was the best brief description available of an important contribution of Tyler's, e.g., the early descriptions of National Assessment. Finally, we must confess that we gravitated to works that we read as graduate students and that influenced our careers and thinking, works we have recommended to our students over the years but which they found difficult, if not impossible, to obtain. Therefore, we readily admit that what follows is our subjective judgment of what was important to include and what had to be edited out because of space limitations.

Readers interested in Tyler's complete works are referred to the Ralph Tyler Project of The National Foundation for the Improvement of Education of the National Education Association. The purpose of that project was to document and archive all of Tyler's work.

The book is divided into six sections. Each section is prefaced by a brief description of its importance and the major points the reader should look for. We hope you will see the richness, the concreteness, and the creativity that we have found in the writings. Those who contribute to advancements in any profession must stand on the shoulders of giants; clearly Ralph Tyler is a giant in the fields of educational testing, curriculum development, and evaluation.

In preparing this book we owe a great debt of gratitude to many people. First, we would like to thank our editors at Kluwer-Nijhoff, Jeffrey Smith and Zachary Rolnik, for their vision in agreeing to publish this collection of Tyler's work and for their support and patience during the project. Second, our thanks to Helen Kolodziey of the Ralph Tyler Project for her suggestions and for sending us copies of hard-to-obtain articles for consideration, and for the Tyler bibliography. Sandra Ryan of Western Michigan University, and Amelia Kreitzer and Katherine Spinos of Boston College, read drafts and gave us their impressions from a student's view of the material. Sally Veeder, of Western Michigan University helped produce and proof the final manuscript. Finally, we will never be able to thank Ralph Tyler sufficiently for his permission to undertake the work, his encouragement and suggestions during the process, and for the influence he has had on our careers.

Educational Evaluation:
Classic Works of Ralph W. Tyler

I THE SERVICE STUDY YEARS: 1929 TO 1938

1 OVERVIEW

Between 1929 and 1938 Ralph Tyler served in the Bureau of Educational Research and Service at The Ohio State University. One of his major activities involved assisting professors throughout the University to evaluate their courses with the aim of improving instruction and ultimately student learning. We thought it was essential to give the reader a flavor for what that work entailed and how it influenced his later work. We selected from the 1932 Ohio State publication, *Service Studies in Higher Education* by Tyler and others, the Introduction and a chapter entitled, "The Construction of Examinations in Botany and Zoology," both written by Tyler. The reader will recognize that Tyler's ideas about test construction contained in the selection from *Service Studies in Higher Education* are incorporated in our next selection, *Constructing Achievement Tests* (Tyler, 1934; The Ohio State University). Nonetheless, we have included it to give the reader an appreciation for his early involvement in evaluation and an appreciation of his keen realization of the necessity of including teachers in the systematic process of course planning, development, and evaluation. *Service Studies in Highter Education* outlines the roles of teachers and evaluators in course improvement.

The second selection in Part I, largely excerpts from *Constructing*

Achievement Tests, grew out of Tyler's experience with the Service Studies. As the name implies, it presents a generalized approach to the construction of achievement tests, an approach followed to this day by those who teach measurement courses in the Tyler tradition. In this approach test construction involves clearly defining important learning outcomes, collecting the most direct indicators of these outcomes, recording the outcomes, improving the reliability of the indicators, and validating indirect measures of these outcomes against direct indicators of them. The essential validity question of the correctness of the inferences made from a test is answered through a demonstration of the test's correspondence with direct indicators of the trait in question.

Constructing Achievement Tests also synopsizes the results of the Wood/Tyler debate over the necessity of measuring all outcomes of learning. It includes reference to the results of a number of applied research studies from the *Service Studies in Higher Education* book. Finally, these selections offer an excellent description of the process of constructing what contemporary measurement people like to call criterion-referenced or objective-referenced tests. The examinations Tyler describes are not norm-referenced standardized achievement tests.

Key Points

- The construction of examinations should be a cooperative process involving five key steps. There are at least ten types of educational objectives instructors should consider. Here one can see some of the seminal ideas that later led to the development of *The Taxonomy of Educational Objectives*.
- Ongoing course improvement requires continuous evaluation of student progress toward the realization of educational objectives. This idea foreshadows by 30 years Scriven's distinction between formative and summative evaluation, and the development of systems of continuous achievement monitoring (CAM) used today by some school districts.
- Educational measurement up to that time had been dominated by three major influences: (1) the late nineteenth century comparative studies of spelling by Rice and the early twentieth century attempts to measure outcomes of arithmetic; (2) the studies by Starch and Eliot and others of the unreliability of essay exams; and (3) the profound impact of the development during World War I of the first group-administered, easily scored intelligence test — the Army Alpha, and the work on early commercial standardized norm-referenced achievement tests after the war by those pioneer psychologists that developed the approach.

- All methods of evaluating human behavior involve four technical problems: (1) defining the behavior to be evaluated; (2) determining situations where the behavior can be observed; (3) recording the behavior; and (4) evaluating the recorded behavior.
- Requirements of sound evaluation by instructors includes: (1) working from unambiguous definitions of student behaviors that specify what a student who has attained the objective can do or produce; (2) specifying the situations where, or ways in which, students can demonstrate the behaviors of interest; (3) determining appropriate standards; (4) using multiple approaches to measurement; (5) assessing all types of behaviors that are significant in the educational development of students; (6) keeping records of student progress; and (7) developing scales and scoring schemes that convey useful information.
- Instructors should strive to assess all the important objectives of the course, not just those involving mastery of the knowledge and facts associated with the course.
- Separate tests are needed for different objectives as the correlation between measures of recall or recognition of facts and higher order skills is low.
- Different kinds of indicators should be employed to measure student outcomes, not just paper-and-pencil tests. Indirect measures of outcomes must always be validated against the most direct measures possible.
- Instructional objectives should be defined in terms of observable student behavior and course content.
- Well-defined objectives form the domain of the test, the blueprint for test construction.
- There should be an ongoing examination of objectives, course materials, learning experiences, and student outcomes so that both the course and student learning can be improved.
- The assumptions underlying standardized norm-referenced testing should not be taken for granted.
- Tests should not be uniform across schools but should reflect the diversity and pluralism that exist in education.
- Statistical and social significance are not the same.
- Units of measurement should be expressed in terms that are easily understood by classroom teachers.
- The evaluator's repertoire should include observational techniques, written tests, self-report instruments, interviews, and examples of student products.

2 SERVICE STUDIES IN HIGHER EDUCATION

Introduction

Service studies made by members of the faculty and administrative staff offer a promising means for improving the work of colleges and universities. Reports of such investigations are particularly appropriate at this time, since we are now witnessing an extraordinary interest and activity in the attempts to make higher education more effective. Criticism of the college is not new, and various modifications of practices in an effort to meet these criticisms have been known for generations. The extensive character of the present attempts to improve higher education and the greater use of empirical evidence especially characterize the critical attitude of the present. Purpose, curriculum, instructional methods, organization, materials, selec-

Service Studies in Higher Education was published in 1932 by the Bureau of Educational Research at The Ohio State University, Columbus. Tyler's collaborators in this publication were Homer C. Sampson, Lewis H. Tiffany, William M. Barrows, Blauche B.M. Meyer, Marion E. Griffith, Robert E. Monroe, Walter Gausewitz, Floyd C. Dockeray, H.W. Nisonger, Huntley Dupre, Sada A. Harbarger, David F. Miller, John W. Price, John A. Miller, Arthur H. Noyes, Eve E. Turnbull, and Charles Wells Reeder.

tion and treatment of personnel, all have been modified at some point by some institution of higher learning. More than ever before are the tangible results of these innovations being critically examined.

This critical activity directed toward the practices of higher education makes it increasingly apparent that there is no single solution to any one of the more significant problems which would be wholly satisfactory to each instructor or to each college. The effectiveness of any solution depends upon the purpose of the college and upon its student body, faculty, and facilities. Therefore, if the problems confronting the college instructor and administrator are to be solved, much work must be done by the members of the faculty and the administration of the individual college or university. In such an investigation of college and university problems service studies have a place. Educational research is essential, but it is concerned with investigations which are small enough in scope and adequately enough controlled so that there will be few untested assumptions. The findings of research are of necessity obtained slowly. In the meantime, the college is running, and it becomes necessary for the programs to be outlined and the instructional plans to be developed pending research findings upon many vital current problems. As a method for obtaining preliminary evidence on problems in higher education and as a means of adapting fundamental generalizations to particular classroom situations, the service study is most useful. A service study lies between the offhand attempt to solve a problem and the research study of it. Because the service study is not primarily concerned with results of wide application but rather with the best solution to the problem for a particular situation, it does not require as extensive investigation as does the research study. Because the instructor or administrator is giving conscious attention to the problem to be solved and is using all of the devices for its solution for which he has time, facilities, and ability to apply, the result of a service study is generally far better than would have been a casual attempt to solve the problem.

This volume describes service studies conducted by various staff members of Ohio State University. Although the book was open to all who had carried through such studies, many staff members who had conducted fruitful investigations were unable to report due to lack of time or because of other reasons. These descriptions should all be conceived as progress reports. While the fiindings may not be directly applicable to other institutions under other conditions, the methods and results should prove suggestive to readers who are interested in investigating similar problems. These studies were conducted by persons who, although their major responsibilities were teaching and administration, yet sensed the importance of the problems and were not content with casual solutions but took the effort and the thought to attack them systematically. They have made an important contribution to higher education. The real improvement of the college or the university rests upon the productive study of its interested faculty and administrative staff.

The Construction of Examinations in Botany and Zoölogy*

Purpose of the Examinations

The Department of Botany [at The Ohio State University] has been improving its examinations and developing objective tests for nearly ten years, but until three years ago this had largely been incidental to the revision of the elementary courses. In the autumn of 1929, as the reorganization of the elementary courses in zoölogy was begun, Mr. Barrows requested the writer to assist the members of the Department of Zoölogy in making better examinations. Shortly thereafter, the instructors in elementary botany began a concerted program of examination improvement in which the Bureau of Educational Research was asked to help. This chapter describes principles which have been adhered to and the procedures which have been followed in these co-operative projects of examination construction. . . .

Most of the service studies described in this volume represent attempts to improve instruction. An essential part of such improvement is the evaluation of every important step taken in terms of the improved learning of the students. Definite evidence of what students have learned and how much they retain becomes a necessity. Accordingly, it is important to develop examinations which can be used in evaluating the various experiments which are being undertaken with the purpose of improving instruction.

When examinations are needed for this purpose, it becomes necessary for most persons to enlarge their conception of what constitutes an examination. It is traditional to conceive of an examination as consisting of a series of questions or exercises to which the student writes answers. When the purpose is to determine as accurately as possible what students have learned, we may think of the examination as any means of obtaining valid evidence of the degree to which students have attained the desired objectives of instruction. Hence, the fundamental task in constructing tests of student achievement is to make certain that all the important objectives of the subject and course are adequately measured.

---

* This section originally comprised Chapter 2 in *Service Studies in Higher Education*.

Defining the Objectives of the Course

The first step in the task of constructing examinations in botany and zoölogy was to define the objectives which students were expected to attain as a result of instruction in these subjects.[1] . . . For purposes of examination construction the statements of the objectives were expressed in terms of the behavior expected of students as a result of instruction in the course; for example, one objective expected of students is an ability to recall important facts, principles, and technical terms. A second is an ability to formulate reasonable generalizations from the specific data of an experiment; a third is the ability to plan an experiment which might be used to test a given hypothesis in botany or in zoölogy; a fourth, the ability to apply general principles to new situations; a fifth, skill in the use of the microscope; and so on. The nature of these objectives determines the variety of achievement tests to be constructed. Measurements of the information which a student recalls may be made with a paper-and-pencil examination, while a test of skill in the use of the microscope would require a different set-up.[2] There are many types of examinations required in college achievement tests as indicated by the projects in examination improvement which are in progress in several departments of the University. Thus far these departments have formulated at least ten major types of objectives each of which will probably require different types of examinations. . . . It has been necessary to develop new types of examinations for many of the objectives. . . .

Collecting Test Situations

To build tests for those objectives which were not adequately covered by previous examinations, samples of specific situations in which the student could be expected to express each of these types of desired behavior were collected. A fundamental assumption in all testing is that a sampling of a student's reactions will give a measure of his reactions in a much larger number of situations. Thus, for example, for the objective, ability to use the microscope effectively in botany, a number of situations in which the student was expected to use the microscope were collected; these situations were presented to the student; and the degree to which he was able to use the microscope effectively in these test situations was used as an index of his general ability to use the microscope in botany. To measure attainment in each of the objectives of the course the collection of an adequate sample of situations representing each objective was needed.

The sources for these situations depend upon the nature of the objective.

In the case of one of the objectives proposed for zoölogy, the ability to draw inferences from experimental data, the most productive source of situations, was current research in zoölogy. The results of new experiments obtained from this source may be presented to students as a test of their ability to interpret experiments. Since they are new experiments, the student cannot interpret them from memory using textbook interpretations. The following are examples of the data from new experiments which were collected to test this objective.

1. Some ants were observed running along a wall. The rates of movement of 49 ants were measured under various conditions. The average speed of travel of the 49 was found to be:

3.8 cm. per second at 40°C.

2.9 cm. per second at 35°C.

2.0 cm. per second at 26°C.

2. A buzzing fly struck a spider's web. The spider rushed toward the fly and seized it. A vibrating steel tuning fork held against the web was seized in the same way.

A productive source of situations to test the objective, the ability to propose ways of testing hypotheses, was found in the problems proposed for investigation by various research workers in the field. Since these problems have never been investigated, the student cannot depend upon his memory of the method of attack used by others. Such situations as the following were collected from this source:

1. How could you discover whether or not the rate of movement of the potato beetle increases with increase in light intensity?

2. How could you discover whether or not immunity to hoof and mouth disease is inherited in cattle?

The most productive source of situations for testing the student's ability to apply principles of botany or of zoölogy to new situations was a series of conferences with the instructors, during which the important principles of the courses were formulated, and concrete illustrations of these principles were selected. The illustrations chosen were those which did not appear in the testbooks or reference books and were not presented in class. Such situations as the following were obtained to test the student's ability to apply principles in explaining zoölogical phenomena:

1. Explain why a fish living in water has a temperature higher than the surrounding water.

2. Explain why meat digests in the stomach of a cat in two or three hours,

while in the stomach of a frog it takes much longer although the enzymes in the digestive juices in the two animals are similar.

Before it was possible to test the student's attainment of a given objective, it was necessary to collect many appropriate situations in which the student would be likely to express the behavior represented by the objective. The ingenuity of the instructors and of the test technician was required to find productive sources of tests for each objective.

Presenting the Situations to Students

After selecting the situations, methods of administration were devised by which it was possible to present these situations to the students and to get records of their reactions. Accuracy of observation was tested by experiments which were observed by each student, and his observations were recorded by him on a blank specially prepared for the purpose. A check list of students' reactions was devised to test skill in the use of the microscope, and the observer used it to make a record of each student's actions when using the microscope. Situations which were verbal in character, such as the memory of important principles, were easily presented to the students in the form of written examinations.

Evaluating Students' Responses

After a record of the student's behavior had been made, the next prerequisite was to evaluate his reactions in the light of each objective. For illustration, the test of the interpretation of experiments might be described. In this test the results of experiments were presented to the students, and they were asked to write down the most reasonable generalization which could be drawn from each set of data.

After such an examination had been given, the important question at once arose as to the degree of objectivity in grading the answers. If instructors varied widely in their marking of any particular answer, the scoring of such an examination would be so subjective that the results would be of little value. In a previous article the writer has described an experiment in which the scoring of these answers was tested. It was found that when the answers were evaluated independently by each instructor the average of the ratings given any answer by three instructors chosen at random was almost identical with the average rating given the answer by all the instructors in the Department. In no case did the evaluation of any question by the three instructors differ more than 3 from the average evaluation of all the instructors.[3] Apparently, then, these answers could be marked by three instructors and would give results which were almost identical with those obtained by having the members of the entire Department evaluate the student's responses. This indicates that, although to determine how well a student has drawn a reasonable inference from specific data is a matter of judgment, this judgment is not wholly subjective varying widely with individual biases, but rather it is exact enough to yield a fairly accurate score for each student.

In tests for measuring several of the other forms of achievement many of the evaluations of the student's behavior were not wholly objective; but when any significant variation in the evaluation from one instructor to another was found, it was usually possible to develop a method for judging or scoring reactions which largely eliminated the individual biases in judgment. Several of these procedures have been described in a recent article.[4]

Developing More Practicable Tests

Sometimes an examination prepared in this way is difficult to administer and is expensive in time and in facilities for scoring. In such cases the development of more practicable methods of measurement becomes a problem of some importance. To illustrate the development of such methods, in case the original test is more or less impracticable, the test of ability to draw inferences in zoölogy might again be used.

The preliminary test of drawing inferences required the typing of the inferences on cards and their evaluation by three instructors. This was an expensive and a time-consuming process so that a more practicable test was needed. An attempt was made to use a multiple-response form of test since this could be quickly scored by clerks. The behavior to be measured, however, was the student's ability to formulate for himself a reasonable inference, so that a test which required him only to select the best inferences from a given list could not be used unless we could show that this latter type of test was highly correlated with his ability to formulate his own inferences. After we had found that the students' answers could be scored with some precision, a test of the type described was constructed containing so large a sampling of test situations that its reliability was .94. Using this test we wished to find out whether a simple multiple-response test would give identical results. The procedure followed was first to give the test requiring students to formulate their own generalizations. These papers were taken up, and the students were given the same test situations, but, instead of being asked to formulate their own generalizations, a series of five possible generalizations followed each test exercise. The student was asked to check the best generalization of the five. This multiple-response test was scored, and the results correlated with the results obtained from the original test giving a coefficient of correlation of only .38. Hence, it was clear that this multiple-response test could not be used in place of the original test which required the students to formulate their own generalizations.

A new test was then constructed in which the alternatives used were arranged from those generalizations which have actually been proposed by students who took the preliminary examination. Each test situation was followed by five of these students' responses. Each student was asked to check the generalization which he thought was the best and also the one which he thought was the poorest of the five. This new test was scored by giving the student a certain value for each alternative checked as the best and a value for each alternative checked as the poorest. These values were obtained by having the alternative generalizations judged by three instructors independently and using the means of their ratings. The student's response for each item, then, was not counted as either right or wrong, but his score might be anywhere from the highest to the lowest value. This new test was administered to a new group at the same time that the original test requiring the students to propose their own generalizations was given. The scores on the new test were correlated with the scores on the original test giving a coefficient of .85. This new test has higher validity than the simple multiple-response test and is more practicable than the original examination.

Co-operative Nature of the Project

This brief description of techniques in use in construcing examinations in botany and zoölogy suggests clearly the co-operative nature of the enterprise. No test technician alone, unless he is an expert in the field of subject-matter, can construct an achievement test which is certain to be valid. The members of the department concerned should formulate the course objectives, define the objectives in terms of student behavior, collect situations in which students are to indicate the presence or absence of each objective, and provide the method of evaluating the students' reactions in the light of each objective. The test technician sets up the specifications for the course objectives and for the definition of objectives in terms of students' behavior. He assists in the collection of test situations, formulates a plan for presenting the situations to students, sets up specifications for the

evaluation of student reactions, determines the objectivity of the evaluations, develops a plan for improving objectivity when necessary, determines
the reliability of the test, and improves the reliability when necessary. The
department concerned and the test technician together attempt to develop
more practicable methods of measurements when necessary, while the test
technician determines the validity and reliability of these proposed practicable methods.

Distinctive Features of the Techniques

This brief description should also have revealed certain features in these
techniques of test construction which are different from those usually
followed. The first of these is the analysis of objectives in place of the
analysis of content alone. This reveals a much wider field for objective
testing than is likely to occur to the test constructor who depends upon an
analysis of content. For example, certain test technicians recently have been
publishing articles dealing with such questions as, "Is the true-false test
superior to the multiple-response test?" "Should the true-false test or the
essay-type test be used?" It is obvious that these questions cannot be
answered in general terms. The real question is how to measure particular
objectives, not how to measure student reactions in general. The true-false
test may be a superior method for testing the student's memory of information, yet it might be quite inferior as a means of testing his ability to
organize ideas effectively for presentation.

The second difference between this technique and the usual method is
that the test situations used are not selected from a few general types of tests
now in use, but are obtained directly from the analysis of the course objectives in terms of student behavior. This permits the development of
diagnostic tests measuring each objective separately. It gives a criterion of
validity which is probably more valid and certainly more exact and reliable
than teachers' marks.

Characteristics of the Tests

Finally, this description should make clear the general nature of the examinations used to measure the effectiveness of instruction in botany and
zoology. They provide evaluations of student achievement representing a
variety of objectives, and are not restricted to tests of facts remembered.
All of the tests now in use in these courses can be scored with a high degree

of objectivity, and none of them have coefficients of reliability less than .94. The examinations have been refined through continuous trial and revision so as to give as exact a measure of student progress in learning as possible. In general, it has been found that such small increases in achievement as those resulting from only three days of instruction can be measured by these tests; hence, they can be used to evaluate with some accuracy the results to improve instruction. This program of examination building and the use of the tests to judge the effectiveness of instruction has just begun and is projected as a continuous task.

3 CONSTRUCTING ACHIEVEMENT TESTS

Measuring the Results of College Instruction

It has become almost a tradition to consider as the only necessary equipment for one engaged in educational measurement some ingenuity in translating subject-matter content into short-answer forms of questions and familiarity with the statistical methods of computing central tendencies, percentiles, the standard deviation, and the coefficient of correlation. Probably this conception has developed because of the types of problems which historically have received the focus of attention in the construction of tests for elementary and secondary schools.

Three avenues of influence have largely dominated educational measurements. The effectiveness of a comparison of results obtained by using the same test in several grades, in various schools, and in different cities, was shown by the spelling investigation of Rice and by the pioneer survey at Cleveland. The result of this influence has been to emphasize standardization of test items and testing conditions. Since spelling and arithmetic were the first subjects to be used in such tests, the problem of validity was concealed by the very nature of the subject-matter. The assumption that a pupil's ability to spell a given list of words was a valid test of his spelling ability was accepted without extended consideration of the psychological nature of the outcomes to be expected, while his response to the request that he perform indicated arithmetic operations upon a given list of numerical exercises was thought to be a valid test of his ability in the fundamental operations of arithmetic. Much study has been given to such problems as the words to be used in the spelling list and to the numerical exercises to be included in the arithmetic test, but the types of mental reaction which should be expected of pupils in a valid test of these subjects has rarely been considered.

A second major influence in educational measurement has been the intelligence-testing movement. Since many persons who had constructed intelligence tests were asked to build educational tests, and because most of the other educational testers were profoundly impressed by the intelligence-test program, certain techniques used by the intelligence testers naturally dominated the procedures in making educational tests. Intelligence tests for school children were commonly validated by getting a fairly high correlation between the test results and the teachers' judgment of the children's brightness, or between the test results and their school marks. Surprisingly enough, educational testers, who are continually criticizing the lack of validity and reliability of teachers' marks, frequently use these same marks as the criteria of good tests for measuring the results of instruction. Another method of intelligence testers has been to validate individual items by their relationship to the total test score. This has been done by calculating biserial r or by determining the difference between the percentage of correct responses among the pupils who made high total scores on the test and those who made low total scores. This method, too, has been taken over by those making educational tests. Probably because of this influence of the intelligence-testing movement, when the question of the validity of an educational measurement has been raised, a fairly high correlation between the test results and teachers' marks has been accepted as an assurance for the validity of the test, while a high relation between the response on an individual item and the total test score has been accepted as a guaranty of the validity of the item. Obviously, however, this procedure cannot guarantee a total test which is more valid than the teachers' judgments and can only assure homogeneity of items rather than validity.

The evident lack of objectivity and of reliability in traditional examinations has perhaps been the most potent influence. It was easy to show that the same examination paper when marked by a large number of teachers was given a variety of marks, ranging in some cases from 25 to 95. It was also simple to collect evidence that the same person when marking a set of examinations a second time assigned different marks to many of the papers. The accumulation of such evidence made it clear to those interested in examinations that the mark a student received on a paper was not only a matter of the quality of his answers but it also depended upon the judgment of the marker, which varied among individuals and varied at different times with the same individual. This criticism of the subjectivity of traditional examinations caused test-builders to give prime consideration to examinations that could be scored objectively. They ignored, however, the fact that the selection of the form of the test and of the test items is a highly subjective process which greatly influenced the test results.

The other deluge of examination criticism was concerned with the adequacy of the sampling of test questions, often called "reliability." The typical examination with five, ten, or twenty questions did not give an adequate sample of the student's responses to serve as a basis for a dependable estimate of his attainments. When the student was given a second set of questions covering the same material, his mark was often widely at variance with that obtained from the first examination. Because this fact was brought home so forcibly, educational testers gave careful study to reliability. Reliability was measured by the correlation between the two sets of scores obtained from two similar tests covering the same field. Measured in this way, reliability was quite distinct from validity.

The accepted techniques used by educational testers have been the translation of subject-matter into forms of questions which may be scored objectively, the standardization of the test items in terms of the percentage of pupils who answer items correctly, the computation of the coefficient of correlation between the test results and the teachers' marks, the determination of the relation between the response on an individual item and the total test score, and the computation of the coefficient of correlation between the results obtained from two similar forms of the test. Obviously, then, in the past the desirable training for one engaged in constructing educational measurements was conceived in terms of these techniques.

The extension of the problem of measuring the results of instruction to the college level is changing the conception of the type of training appropriate for educational testers. An analysis of the mental processes characteristic of a given subject assumes an importance heretofore unrecognized. Many college instructors are suspicious of the so-called "objective examinations," and not without reason. Not only are many objective tests quite different from the examinations to which they are accustomed, but it is also difficult for them to determine whether the tests provide a measure of the objectives of the subject they are teaching. It is, therefore, natural that they should be cautious in relying upon such examinations. Hence, a fundamental task in constructing achievement tests which will be used by college instructors is to make certain that the important objectives of the subject and course are adequately measured.

A Generalized Technique for Constructing Achievement Tests

...This is so obvious a requirement for a valid examination that there is nothing new in the suggestion that it is the essential criterion for validity. However, techniques of test construction in which test items are consciously derived from the specific objectives of the course are much more rare. Thus, Ruch in his recent text on building objective examinations covers the derivation of the test items in two steps, drawing up a table of specifications, and drafting the items in preliminary form.[5] The first step covers the relation of test items to objectives, but the assumption commonly made by the reader is that the table of specifications is merely a topical outline and not an outline of objectives. That there are other objectives to be measured besides information is not adequately emphasized.

Similarly, in an earlier book, Wood, describing the achievement tests used in Columbia College, recognized that the test items were derived directly from an analysis of the informational content of the course only. However, he stated that every experimental study thus far made and reported has shown a very high relationship between measurements of information in a field and intelligence or ability to think in the material of that field.[6] This has not been found true in the elementary biology courses at The Ohio State University. We found the correlation with the scores on information tests of tests of application of principles to be only .40; of tests of interpretation of experiments to be only .41; and of tests of the formulation of experiments to test hypotheses to be only .46.

In defense of Mr. Wood's position, it may be pointed out that these correlations are higher in advanced courses. Nevertheless, in elementary courses, the correlations are all too low for one to obtain valid measurements in these classes by use of an information test only. Tests need to be constructed for each of the important objectives in a course.

Peters in analyzing the methods employed in validating standard tests showed that few tests were validated against educational objectives, and suggested that tests should be derived on this basis.[7] Unfortunately, he does not describe a technique which could be generally followed in deriving test items from objectives. It, therefore, seems apparent that although some college instructors are properly demanding tests which measure the attainment of each of the objectives of their courses, the usual method of test construction based upon an analysis of informational content alone will not meet this demand. Accordingly, we have been using a general technique for achievement-test construction which involves these steps:

1. Formulation of course objectives
2. Definition of each objective in terms of student behavior
3. Collection of situations in which students will reveal presence or absence of each objective
4. Presentation of situations to students
5. Evaluation of student reactions in light of each objective
6. Determination of objectivity of evaluation
7. Improvement of objectivity, when necessary
8. Determination of reliability
9. Improvement of reliability, when necessary
10. Development of more practicable methods of measurement, when necessary

The task of formulating objectives is a necessary first step in any case where no curricular study has previously been made. Obviously, the step can be omitted when objectives have previously been formulated. The character of these objectives is illustrated by those formulated by the Department of Zoölogy for the elementary courses. These were presented recently.[8]

The nature of these objectives determines the variety of the achievement tests to be constructed. It is obvious that the measurements of the information which a student possesses may be done with a paper-and-pencil examination, while a test of skill in use of the microscope would require a different set-up. The variety of examinations required in college achievement tests is indicated by our work with several departments of the University. Thus far we have found at least eight major types of objectives. These are:

Type A, Information, which includes terminology, specific facts, and general principles

Type B, Reasoning, or scientific method, which includes induction, testing hypotheses, and deduction

Type C, Location of Relevant Data, which involves a knowledge of sources of usable data and skill in getting information from appropriate sources

Type D, Skills Characteristic of Particular Subjects, which includes laboratory skills in the sciences, language skills, and the like

Type E, Standards of Technical Performance, which includes the knowledge of appropriate standards, ability to evaluate the relative importance of several standards which apply, and skill or habits in applying these standards

Type F, Reports, which include the necessary skill in reporting projects in engineering or reporting experiments in science and the like

Type G, Consistency in Application of Point of View, which is most apparent in courses in philosophy

Type X, Character, which is perhaps the most inclusive, involving many specific factors

This first step, formulating course objectives, is necessary in order to indicate what the tests are to measure and thus to define the variety of tests essential for an inclusive measurement of student achievement. When present standard tests are compared with this list of types of objectives large areas are found which are as yet untouched.

The second step is to define each objective in terms of student behavior. This is most useful because it suggests the set-ups required for the preliminary test. How this differs from the analysis-of-content method usually used in test construction may easily be shown by illustration. Textbooks in zoölogy describe certain experiments that have been performed which show that a frog responds to light stimuli in his feeding reactions. A textbook analysis would include the description of these experiments, but on the usual basis of test construction it would be assumed that the student is expected to remember these descriptions. A test would then be constructed which would disclose whether or not the student remembers the details of these experiments. In contrast, a definition of objectives in terms of student behavior does more than indicate the content to be covered. It defines the reactions which a student is expected to make of this content. Thus the Department of Zoölogy defined their third objective, the ability to draw inferences from facts, by stating that students should be able to observe such experiments as those dealing with the feeding reactions of frogs, or to read the results of experiments and from the facts thus obtained propose hypotheses which would constitute reasonable inferences from these experiments. It is not expected that a student will remember the details of an experiment, but upon being given the details will be able to interpret the experiment for himself. Obviously, with the same content it makes a great deal of difference whether the test is to measure the student's memory of the facts or to be able to interpret them when they have been presented to him.

Each of the eight objectives set up for elementary courses in zoölogy was defined in terms of the behavior expected of students. In defining the first objective, a fund of information about animal activities and structures, the specific facts and general principles which the students should be able to recall without reference to textbooks, or other sources of information, were indicated. The second objective, an understanding of technical terminology, was defined by listing the terms which the student himself should be able to use in his own reports, and another list of terms which he would not be expected to use, but should be able to understand when he finds them in zoölogical publications. The third objective, an ability to draw inferences from facts, that is, to propose hypotheses, was defined by describing the types of experiments which an elementary student should be able to interpret. The fourth objective, ability to propose ways of testing hypotheses, was defined by listing the types of hypotheses which an elementary student should be able to validate by experiment, or to propose ways of validation. The fifth objective, an ability to apply principles to concrete situations, was defined by listing the principles which elementary students should be able to apply, and types of concrete situations in which the student might apply these principles. The sixth objective, accuracy of observation, was defined by listing the types of experiments in which elementary students should be able to make accurate observations. The seventh objective, skill in use of the microscope and other essential tools, was defined by describing the types of microscopic mounts and types of dissections which elementary students should learn to make. The eighth objective, an ability to express effectively ideas relating to zoölogy, was defined by indicating the nature of the reports, both written and oral, which zoölogy students are expected to make and the qualities demanded for these reports to be effective.

The mere enumeration in this way of data obtained by this second step suggests the large amount of raw material thus made available which will form a direct basis for test construction. It is, of course, true that these first two steps are largely curricular problems and must be a function of the department concerned. Neither of the steps could be done by the technician in test construction. He can only outline the specifications demanded, while the formulation of objectives and their definition in terms of student behavior must be done by the department concerned.

The second step has served to define the types of situations in which students will reveal the presence or absence of each of the objectives of the course. The third step is undertaken to collect samples of specific situations which belong to each of the types. A fundamental assumption in all testing is that a sampling of student reactions will give a measure of his reactions in a much larger number of situations. So it is necessary to collect a sampling of situations which might be used to test each of the objecitvies formulated for the course. The sources for these situations depend upon the nature of the objective. In the case of the third objective proposed for zoölogy, the ability to draw inferences from facts, the most productive source of situations was the current research in the field of zoölogy. From this source the results of new experiments can be obtained which can be presented to students to test their ability to interpret these experiments. Since they are new experiments the students cannot interpret them from memory of textbook interpretations. Similarly, productive sources for the fourth objective, the ability to propose ways of testing hypotheses, was found in the problems proposed for investigation by various research workers in the field. Since these problems have never been investigated the student cannot depend upon his memory of the method of attack used by others. For each objective the ingenuity of the test maker and of instructors in the department concerned is required in order to find productive sources of test situations which are available.

The fourth step, presenting the situation to the students, is primarily the function of the test constructor. He must develop a method of administration which makes it possible to present these situations to the students and to get a record of their reactions. In the case of accuracy of observation it was necessary for us to have experiments performed which could be observed by every student in the group and then to develop a record blank upon which the student could record his observations. In testing skill in use of the microscope it was necessary to develop a check list of student reactions so that an observer could make a record of the actions of each student in his attempt to use the microscope. Those situations which are verbal in character, such as the memory of important principles, are easily presented to students in written examinations.

The fifth step, evaluating the student reactions in the light of each objective, is essentially a co-operative one in which the department has certain functions and the test technician certain other functions. The technician sets up specifications for the standards to be used in evaluating students' reactions and specifications relative to the objectivity required. The instructors in the department concerned formulate the standards to be used in evaluating reactions and they make those evaluations which are not wholly objective in character. In the case of tests of information, the department can prepare a key which is wholly or almost wholly objective and clerks can score the students' reactions. In the case of tests of ability to draw inferences from facts it was necessary for the department to set up standards to be used in evaluating students' inferences and for the instructors to evaluate the responses since these standards were not wholly objective.

After the preliminary evaluation of students' reactions it is necessary to take the sixth step for those evaluations which are not wholly objective. The method followed in determining the objectivity of the evaluations of students' inferences was to have these inferences judged by several instructors in the department independently, and then to determine the variations in the evaluations of each paper. When there is found to be any significant variation in the evaluation from one instructor to another the seventh step improving objectivity, is necessary....

After a satisfactory degree of objectivity has been obtained the next step is to determine the reliability; that is, the adequacy of the sample of test situations used to measure that particular objective. This can be done by the usual method of submitting a second random sample of test situations to the same students and correlating the scores from the two samples. When the correlation coefficient has been calculated, it is possible to determine the number of test situations required to obtain any satisfactory degree of reliability. In case the reliability of the preliminary test is too low the ninth step is necessary. To improve the reliability of the preliminary examination the provision of a larger sampling of test situations is usually sufficient since the final test will often be quite different.

If the first nine steps have been carried through to completion an objective, reliable, preliminary test for each of the course objectives has been obtained. Very often this preliminary test may be difficult to administer and expensive of time and facilities in scoring. Hence the development of more practicable methods of measurement becomes a problem of some importance. The preliminary test now serves as a criterion against which the proposed practicable form of test may be checked. It seems to me that this preliminary test is a much more adequate criterion of validity than the usual set of teachers' marks. Not only are teachers' marks somewhat unreliable but they are often not diagnostic; that is, they do not distinguish between the student's attainment of different objectives separately. Our work to date has shown quite clearly that the correlation between the student's attainment of one objective and his attainment of another may be quite low. Thus we found a correlation between skill use of the microscope and memory of information to be only .02, between an understanding of technical terms and ability to draw inferences from facts only .35, between information and ability to apply principles to concrete situations only .40. These correlations are so low that we are justified in preparing separate tests for each of the objectives so that the instructor may diagnose the difficulties of students in achievement with reference to each objective separately. These preliminary tests give criteria for validating diagnostic tests....

Formulating Objectives for Tests

The current literature on constructing examinations deals almost wholly with questions concerning the form of the examination. This is an unfortunate emphasis, for the problem of first concern to teachers is to obtain tests which really show how well the students are progressing in their school work. Hence, a satisfactory test or examination must first be one which actually gives us evidence of the amount of progress which students are making.

What constitutes progress in school work? It is certainly true that every change which takes place in a student during the time he is in school cannot be considered progress. During that time he may grow taller, he may get fatter, he may acquire a new slang vocabulary, his voice may change, but we do not consider these as evidences of progress in his school work. Each subject which is taught is offered with the expectation that each student who takes it will undergo certain desired changes as the result of the course. In algebra, for example, it is expected that students will acquire a certain understanding of the meaning of abstract numbers, and that they will become somewhat skillful in solving numerical problems. These changes which we expect to take place in the student are the objectives of the subject. It is apparent that a satisfactory test in algebra is one which shows us the degree to which students are reaching these objectives; that is, the degree to which they have acquired an understanding of the meaning of abstract number, and the degree to which they have become skillful in solving numerical problems.

In similar fashion every subject offered involves certain objectives which we hope students will reach as the result of instruction in this subject. A satisfactory test or examination in any subject is an instrument which gives us evidence of the degree to which students are reaching the objectives of the subject. One major defect of typical examinations has been the fact that these examinations have given evidence with reference to only a limited number of objectives and have not been adequately indicating the degree to which students are attaining all of the important goals which instructors are trying to reach in a given subject.

The importance of covering all of the significant objectives in a total examination program can best be shown by illustration. In chemistry the objectives which instructors are commonly trying to reach include teaching students: to acquire a fund of important facts and principles, to understand the technical terms commonly appearing in chemical publications, to be able to apply important chemical principles to appropriate situations, to express chemical reactions by means of equations involving chemical symbols and formulas, and to be skillful in certain laboratory techniques. Any adequate examination program for chemistry will provide means for discovering how far each of these objectives are being attained. Tests need to be included which will indicate how well students are acquiring these important facts and principles, how well they understand the technical terms commonly appearing in chemical publications, how able they are to apply important chemical principles to appropriate situations, how satisfactorily they can express chemical reactions by the use of equations, and how skillful they are in the essential laboratory techniques. Obviously, evidence of all of these attainments cannot be had from a single examination, but an inclusive examination program should cover all of the important objectives. Some of these attainments can be determined by means of paper-and-pencil tests with which everyone is more or less familiar. Others would need to be tested by different devices. To discover how skillful the students have become in the essential laboratory techniques it is probably necessary to set the students at work on certain laboratory problems and to evaluate their skill by means of observation and by checking the outcome of the laboratory exercises.

The variety of examinations necessitated by a variety of objectives may also be illustrated in the subject of English. Without attempting to list all of the objectives which English teachers consider important it is probable that among these would be included teaching students: to use correct English, to write effectively, to be familiar with significant literature, to be able to evaluate various types of literary productions, and to appreciate good literature. A satisfactory program of examinations in English will therefore include tests which reveal the student's ability to use correct English, his ability to write effectively, his familiarity with significant literature, his skill in evaluating literary productions, and how well he has learned to appreciate good literature. This means again that the examination program involves a variety of testing techniques. Skill in written composition can be judged by the use of paper-and-pencil tests; the use of correct oral English may need to be evaluated by a different device. To discover how well they have learned to appreciate good literature would probably require still other devices, as, for example, one which would indicate the literary preferences of students.

These subjects are but illustrations of the situation prevailing in every field. Because of the importance of having an examination program which gives evidence of the degree to which students are reaching each of the significant objectives of the subject an essential step in planning an examination program is to formulate in a clear and understandable fashion the important objectives which the instructor is trying to reach. This formulation then becomes the comprehensive plan against which the various tests are checked to be sure that the total examination program includes devices for determining the degree to which students are attaining each of these objectives.

Two problems are usually involved in formulating the objectives of a particular course. One is to get a list of objectives which is reasonably complete; that is, which includes all of the important objectives to be reached. The other is to state the objectives in such clear and definite terms that they can serve as guides in the making of the examination questions. Many statements of objectives are so vague and nebulous that, although they may sound well, they prove to be glittering generalities which are of little value as guides in teaching and useless in making examinations.

In making a list of objectives for a course, one procedure commonly followed is to begin with the general function or purpose of the subject and to analyze this into its several aspects or subfunctions. Another method is to begin with the content of the course and with reference to each topic ask the questions: What is the purpose of this topic? What do I expect students to get from this topic? In most cases it is necessary to use a combination of both procedures in order to get a relatively complete list of important objectives and in order to clarify the meaning of each objective. The validation of these functions and of the course content is an important step in curriculum construction but is not treated here since it is assumed that this curriculum problem has been attacked before beginning to build examinations.

This combination of methods can be illustrated by the procedures followed by the Department of Zoölogy in The Ohio State University in formulating the objectives for the elementary course. This Department recognized two major functions or purposes of the elementary course. One of these was to teach the student a fund of important zoölogical information; the other was to teach the student to use scientific method in zoölogy. Beginning with these accepted major functions the instructors in the Department first analyzed these into several subfunctions; that is, they broke up the general objectives into the several more definite objectives which these general objectives included. Upon analysis the fund of important zoölogical information was subdivided into recalling important specific facts, remembering general zoölogical principles, and recognizing the meaning of common technical terms found in zoölogical publications. The use of scientific method, the instructors decided, meant the ability to formulate reasonable generalizations from experimental data, the ability to plan satisfactory experiments to test promising hypotheses in zoölogy, and the ability to apply significant zoölogical principles to situations new to the students. By means of an analysis of the two general objectives the department was thus able to formulate these six more definite objectives.

To check the completeness of these six objectives the instructors then took up, topic by topic, the content of the elementary course, asking themselves in connection with each topic what they expected students to get from the topic. In most cases the answers to these questions represented objectives already obtained by the method of analysis; however, in examining the topics dealing with the structures of a frog which were studied by means of dissection, the instructors decided that one of the purposes of this laboratory work was to teach the students to make certain typical dissections. In examining the laboratory units involving microscopic work they decided that one of the things which the student should get from these units was skill in the use of the microscope. Hence, they added another major objective to the list, namely, skill in the laboratory techniques of dissection and use of the microscope. In going over these laboratory units another purpose which appeared to be significant was to teach students to report the results of their experiments in effective English. In examining topics in the course involving library reading another purpose was to teach students to be familiar with sources of information on zoölogical problems. The final list of important objectives accepted by the Department of Zoölogy for its elementary course included the six in the original list and the three additions obtained by checking the content of the course. Thus, by a combination of procedures, going both from the major functions by means of analysis to the more definite objectives involved, and going from the specific content of the course back to the purposes for which this content was used, a list of objectives was obtained which serves to guide the Department in formulating its program of examinations. By various means throughout the course an effort is made to get evidence of the degree to which the students are reaching each of these nine major objectives.

In order to make a list of major objectives usable in building examinations further analysis is also necessary. Each objective must be defined in terms which clarify the kind of behaviour which the course should help to develop among the students; that is to say, a statement is needed which explains the meaning of the objective by describing the reactions we can expect of persons who have reached the objective. This helps to make clear how one can tell when the objective is being attained since those who are reaching the objective will be characterized by the behaviour specified in this analysis. Behaviour is here used in the broad sense to mean any sort of appropriate reactions of students, mental, physical, emotional, and the like. For example, in the case of the objectives for the zoölogy course, the first one was to teach students to recall important specific facts. This objective was analyzed by defining the behaviour expected of students who are reaching the objective in the following terms: To remember and state these facts without having to look them up at the time, and to recognize misconceptions which are commonly mistaken for zoölogical facts. The analysis of this objective also required a definite statement of what the important zoölogical facts are which students are expected to remember and what are the misconceptions which are often mistaken for zoölogical facts.

Similarly, in analyzing the second objective, remembering general zoölogical principles, the behaviour expected was defined as the ability to remember and state these principles without having to look them up at the time, and to recognize misconceptions which are commonly mistaken for zoölogical principles. The analysis of this objective also required a formulation of the list of general zoölogical principles which students are expected to remember. The third objective was defined as the ability to formulate an appropriate definition or description of the common technical terms in zoölogy. A collection was then made of the common technical terms which students should be able to understand. For each term, a statement was made of the sort of definition or description which would be expected from elementary students. This was necessary since some terms were so complex that only certain ideas about them would be understood by elementary students, while for other terms a very exact definition would be expected.

The fourth objective was defined as the ability to formulate in his own words as complete a generalization as is justified by the data presented, when the student is given the results of a zoölogical experiment. As a further step in the analysis it was necessary to collect typical experiments which were new to the students yet which they should be able to interpret in this way. The experiments should be new to the students so that they cannot depend upon their memory of the interpretations which have been made by others.

In analyzing the fifth objective it was defined as the ability to determine what facts would need to be established in order to substantiate a given hypothesis and the ability to plan an experiment to establish or disprove these facts. A list was then made of hypotheses new to the student and yet for which they should be able to plan satisfactory experiments. It was necessary to have hypotheses which were new to the students so that they could not depend upon their memory of the experiments proposed by others to test these hypotheses.

The sixth objective was defined as the ability to predict the outcome of a situation involving one or more of the zoölogical principles included in the course and the ability to use these principles in explaining why this outcome could be expected. The analysis also required the collection of situations new to the students which would give them a chance to apply the important zoölogical principles taught in the course and previously formulated in connection with the second objective. The situations should be new to the students so that they cannot depend upon their memory of the explanations made by others.

For the seventh objective, skill in certain significant laboratory techniques, it was necessary to list the types of dissections which students should be able to make, the kinds of microscopic mounts which they should be able to prepare, and typical objects which they should be able to find under a microscope. For the eighth objective, the ability to report the results of experiments in effective English, specifications were drawn up to guide the instructors in their evaluation of the English used by the students in writing up their experiments. The ninth objective was defined as the ability to state the sources which were most likely to give dependable information on specific kinds of zoölogical problems. A list was made of the sources of information with which elementary students should be familiar and the types of zoölogical problems in connection with which they would be expected to consult the sources of information.

When these definitions of objectives in terms of behaviour have been formulated, and the necessary lists of facts, principles, terms, experiments, and the like have been made, the instructors have all of the basic material which they need in constructing examinations to cover the major objectives of the zoölogy course. Some time is required to collect these basic materials, but when they have been assembled they serve as a reservoir for making new examinations and ultimately save a great deal of time. Furthermore, many of these lists are helpful means of checking the content of the course and are useful as guides in preparing lectures, planning laboratory work, and in outlining other class assignments.

Many subjects, especially the sciences, are constantly changing with the discovery of new facts and principles. Hence, it is necessary to prevent the reservoir of basic materials from becoming static, thus crystallizing what ought to be a developing course. It is, therefore, desirable to provide for an annual review of each of the basic lists by instructors in the department. As each list is examined, items are deleted which have been rendered obsolete by the new developments in the field, and other items are added to cover these new developments. The revision requires relatively little time and helps to insure a continuously appropriate set of materials from which examinations may be quickly made.

This illustration taken from the work in zoölogy is suggestive of the value of formulating and analyzing the objectives of a course in order to make examinations which are satisfactory and relatively complete. Similar procedures can be appropriately used in other fields of subject-matter. In a foreign-language course, for example, the objectives might include the ability to comprehend the meaning of selections written in the foreign language; the ability to understand oral expression in the foreign language; the ability to pronounce orally words, sentences, and paragraphs in the foreign language; the ability to compose effective oral expression in the foreign language; knowledge of the grammar of the foreign language; an understanding of the important vocabulary in the foreign language; and a knowledge of the art, literature, and customs of the people whose language is being studied.

In analyzing the first objective, the nature of the reading ability could be defined, and a collection could be made of selections written in the foreign language which are new to the students and which they should be able to comprehend. This collection would serve to define the kinds of reading material to be covered in the examinations in terms of narratives, expositions, descriptions, and the like. In making the collection, care should be exercised to have appropriate vocabulary included and to obtain selections involving ideas of the appropriate difficulty for the class. To analyze the ability to understand oral expression the objective could be defined in terms of the behaviour which characterizes understanding of oral expression, a statement of the kinds of oral expression which students are expected to understand could be formulated, and a collection made of examples which are of the appropriate difficulty. In analyzing the ability to pronounce orally a statement could be made of the kinds of material which the students should be able to pronounce fluently, and a collection made of typical words, sentences, and paragraphs which involve the variety of pronunciation skills which the students are expected to acquire.

The analysis of the ability to compose effective written expression in the foreign language could include a statement of the kinds of expression which the students are expected to compose, a collection of typical examination projects which would require these kinds of written compositions, and a statement of the specifications to be used in evaluating these compositions. The complete list of projects should include all of the various kinds of compositions which the students are expected to make. Each examination project should make clear the nature of the compositions to be written by stating the purpose which the writer needs to keep in mind and the type of readers for whom the composition is to be written. For example, one such project might be to compose a description of an American high school to be prepared for French students who have no acquaintance with any American schools. Correspondingly, the analysis of the ability to compose effective oral expression could include a statement of the kinds of oral expression which the students are expected to use and a collection of examination projects which would require the students to make these oral compositions. In analyzing the grammar objective, the kinds of behaviour which represent an understanding of grammar could be defined, a statement could be made of the grammatical principles which the students are expected to understand, and a collection could be made of typical situations in which these grammatical principles are involved. The analysis of the objective concerned with an understanding of the important vocabulary could include a statement of the behaviour which characterizes understanding of vocabulary, and a list could be made of the important words, terms, and idiomatic expressions which the students are expected to understand. In analyzing the objective of knowledge of the art, literature, and customs of the people, the sort of behaviour which shows whether or not the student has this knowledge could be defined, and a list could be made of the kinds of art, the characteristics of the literature, and the particular customs which the students are expected to know. By carrying through these analyses of the objectives of the foreign-language course, these basic materials are obtained from which examinations can easily be made. It is readily apparent that the procedures of formulating and analyzing the major objectives are desirable for any course and are invaluable when making a comprehensive program of examinations.

These illustrations demonstrate the fact that the first steps in examination building are those involved in determining objectives. It is usually necessary to consider first the major functions or purposes of the course, breaking those up into several more definite major objectives. To make this list of major objectives more nearly complete, the content of the course is then examined, topic by topic, to discover why the topic has been included in the course; that is, or state the things which students are expected to gain from studying the topic. This examination of individual topics usually suggests additions to the list of major objectives. The purpose of these steps is to obtain a relatively complete list of the most important objectives. After the list has been formulated, an analysis is then made of each objective to give it definite meaning by defining it in terms of the behaviour expected of students, and to obtain a comprehensive statement of the specific elements involved in the objective. This analysis provides the basic material from which a complete program of examinations may be constructed. Finally, a plan of periodic review and revision of these basic materials prevents crystallization of the course and of the examinations.

Ability To Use Scientific Method

One of the most difficult problems in the construction of achievement tests is the development of objective examinations which will measure the student's progress toward the wide range of important educational objectives. A rather high degree of skill in testing the amount of information which a student prossesses has already been attained. Methods have been developed by which these tests of information may be made objective and highly reliable. Unfortunately, the same degree of development has not taken place in the measurement of other objectives. To develop examinations which might be used in determining the progress of students toward a variety of educational objectives is the purpose of the work being carried on with a number of subject-matter departments of The Ohio State University. The general procedure followed in constructing these examinations has been described previously.[9] Certain of the new examinations will be described in more detail in this paper.

One of the objectives considered important by every science department in the University is "to teach students to use scientific method." The instructors in these departments believe that their courses should train students who are able to go beyond the information and opinions of the day and, by applying scientific method to new problems, to gain new knowledge. Because this is considered such an important objective it is exceedingly necessary that examinations be used which will indicate whether or not the students are actually attaining this goal. Such examinations to be good tests should be as valid, as objective, and as reliable as possible.

The first step we have used in constructing an examination for a given course has been to define each objective of the course rather specifically in terms of student behavior. The next step is to collect situations in which the students will have an opportunity to express this behavior. These situations can then be used as the preliminary test situations. The assumption involved in this method is that the student's behavior in a sampling of these situations is an index of the degree to which he has attained the desired objective. Thus, for example, if the objective is "ability to use the microscope effectively in botany," we would collect a number of situations in which the student would be expected to use the microscope, we could present these situations to the student, and the degree to which he was able to use the microscope effectively in these test situations would be an index of his general ability to use the microscope in botany.

When this method is applied to the objective "ability to apply scientific method" it is first necessary to analyze this objective in terms of the student behavior desired. When this has been done by the instructors in the departments concerned, we find at least three types of student behavior involved in scientific method. The first of these is the ability to formulate a reasonable generalization from specific experimental data. The second type of behavior is to plan an experiment which could be used to determine whether or not a proposed hypothesis is true, and a third type of behavior is to apply general principles to concrete situations. A valid test of the student's ability to use scientific method must then consist of situations which require the student to do these three sorts of things.

After the objective has been defined in terms of specific student behavior, we must collect samples of situations which could be used for the examinations. This means for the first type, a collection of situations which requires a student to draw reasonable generalizations from specific experimental data. In botany, for instance, such exercises as follow are examples.

A number of barley plants were grown in soil low in nitrates. It was found that the tops weighed five times as much as the roots. At the same time similar barley plants were grown in a soil containing an abundance of nitrates. In this case the tops weighed nine times as much as the roots.

A coleus plant exposed to full sunlight became green. A similar coleus plant exposed to only red rays of light became green. A similar coleus plant exposed to only orange and yellow rays of light became green. A similar coleus plant exposed to only green rays of light became green. A similar coleus plant exposed to only blue-violet rays of light became green.

When a number of tobacco plants were grown in the sun, it was found that the average dry weight of each plant was 31.4 grams, the average amount of water absorbed from the soil by each plant was 7.7 liters, and the average amount of salts absorbed from the soil by each plant was 3.04 grams. When similar tobacco plants were grown in the shade, it was found that the average amount of water absorbed in the soil by each plant was 6.0 liters, and the average amount of salts absorbed from the soil by each plant was 3.51 grams.

These are samples of test situations collected by Professor Sampson, of the Department of Botany. The students were asked to read each exercise and then to write beneath it the generalization which they thought could most reasonably be made from the data given. Similar exercises were developed by other science departments. It is obvious that these are quite different from the usual information type of examination questions. The essential facts are given to the student; the test determines whether he is able to relate these facts and to draw a reasonable generalization from them....

Up to this point I have been describing the development of an objective method of testing the ability of the student to draw generalizations from specific data. The second type of behavior involved in scientific method is to plan experiments to determine the truth or falsity of certain hypotheses. A student who has been trained in botany, for example, when asked whether ultra-violet rays stimulate the growth of vegetative organs of the plant should be able to say how the answer to this question might be found out; that is, he should be able to plan experiments which would determine whether or not ultra-violet rays do stimulate the development of vegetative organs in a given plant. The proper test situations for this type of behavior are hypotheses which have not been tested or which elementary students would not know about before. In connection with each such hypothesis, the student would be asked to describe an experiment which could be used to determine whether or not this hypothesis were true. As examples of hypotheses, these have been used by the Department of Zoölogy.

1. The hibernation response of the frog is the result of low temperature and not the particular season of the year.
2. Temperature of the external atmosphere affects the rate of heartbeat in the frog.
3. Lizards breathe through their skins as well as through their lungs.
4. The action of ptyalin in changing starch to sugar is most rapid at 80 degrees F.

Similar tests situations were developed in other science subjects. It was found that reports of recent research studies which indicated the problems yet unsolved constituted an excellent source for hypotheses which have not already been tested and which would require the students to use their own originality in planning appropriate experiments.

These tests were administered by presenting the hypotheses to the students and asking them to describe an experiment which could be used in testing these hypotheses. As in the case of the generalization, the student's answers were typed upon cards and evaluated by each instructor independently. In this case, too, it was found that the evaluations were so much alike that the mean ratings of any three instructors chosen at random could be used to represent the ratings of the entire group of instructors.

After developing this rather exact method of grading the answers, enough exercises were chosen to make an examination which had a reliability coefficient above .90. We then attempted to construct an examination which would give results similar to those obtained when the students were asked to plan original experiments yet which might be scored easily and administered quickly. Following the suggestion of the generalization tests, a number of the experiments proposed as answers by students who took the original examination were selected as alternatives for a multiple-response test, consisting of a series of hypotheses each of which was followed by a description of five possible experiments. The student was asked to check the experiment he thought the best to find out whether the hypothesis was true and the one which he thought the poorest. This test was administered to a new group at the same time as the one in which the student was asked to formulate his own experiment. The correlation between the two tests was .63. This means that the multiple-response test gives somewhat similar results to those obtained by the original test but hardly close enough so that one could be used entirely in place of another.

Next, we experimented with a multiple-response test constructed in the same way that one mentioned in the preceding paragraph was built; that is, a number of experiments which had been proposed as answers by a group of students were selected as alternatives for the test which consisted of a series of proposed hypotheses each of which was followed by a description of five possible experiments. In this case, however, the student was asked to mark with the figure 1, the experiment which he thought the best way of verifying the hypothesis, with the figure 2 the second best, with a 3 the third best, with a 4 the fourth best, and with a 5 the poorest. This test was administered to an entirely new group at the same period but immediately after the students had been given the test in which they were asked to formulate their own experiments. The correlation between these two tests was .79. This means that this new test gives results still closer to those obtained by the original test. We are still experimenting upon other methods of examination with the hope of finding a simple and easily administered method of measurement which will give even more valid evidence of the ability of the student to plan an experiment to evaluate an hypotheses. Until such a device is developed, we shall continue to use for a portion of our measurements the original method of having the student propose his own experiment and to evaluate the answers by three or more instructors independently.

A third aspect of scientific method is the ability of the student to apply principles to new situations. To develop such a test requires the formulation of a set of important principles taught in the given science subject. After this has been done we are ready to collect situations which require the student to apply one or more of these principles. In the case of principles which involve definite mathematical relationships, the application of the principle requires the solution of a mathematical problem as in the case of applying Boyle's Law in physics or chemistry. There is nothing new in testing mathematical principles in this fashion except that we can separate the measurement of the student's memory of the principles from his ability to apply them by providing for the memory questions in the first part of the test, then taking up these papers and giving the student a list of the important principles, together with a series of situations requiring the student to apply the principles. The student shows his ability to apply mathematical principles by solving the mathematical problems. For principles that are not mathematical in character, the student shows his ability to apply them by formulating an explanation of the specific situations given in terms of the general principles which have also been given him. These explanations can then be evaluated by several instructors independently as was done with the other exercises.

This test may be set up in much more objective form by asking the student to write below the situation the numbers of the principles given in the accompanying list which explain the situation described. An example of this sort of test is the following prepared by D. F. Miller, of the Department of Zoölogy.

EXPLANATION TEST

Directions. — Each of the following exercises consists of a statement of an observed fact. You have been given a list of important zoölogical principles which have been treated in the course. You are asked to read the observed fact, and then explain it by selecting the principles from the list which help to explain the fact. List the numbers of the principles in logical order below the fact as in the sample.

SAMPLE

Statement. — A person in an anaemic condition, that is, with a deficiency of red corpuscles in the blood, is not usually physiologically active.

3, 12.

Principles. — Note that if principles 3 and 12 are read in order, one gets a logical explanation for the inactivity of the anaemic person. Remember to select the principles which help to explain the statement. Then write the numbers of these principles in logical order so that reading the principles in the order you have listed them will give a logical explanation.

EXERCISES

a. Salivary digestion is not as effective in an acid mouth as in one which is alkaline.

b. Two animals of the same size and kind are fed upon the same quantity of food although the food is different. One animal excretes 2 grams of urea per day, while the other excretes 40 grams.

Along with these exercises the student is given a leaflet in which the important principles of the course are stated and numbered to facilitate reference. The results of this latter test were correlated with those in which the student formulates his own explanation from the principles given. The coefficient of correlation of .87 thus obtained indicates that the second type of test gives almost identical results with those obtained by the first type. Since this second test can be easily administered and is objectively scored it is feasible to use it as a fairly valid measure of the student's ability to apply principles.

In summarizing, may I say that the results thus far obtained justify the belief that scientific method may be measured directly with some degree of precision even though the task of scoring the answers is time-consuming and a bit tedious. In cases where it is desirable to use easier and more practicable methods of testing, types of tests have been developed which give results corresponding quite closely to those obtained from direct measurement as a means of determining the student's ability to formulate generalizations from specific data and his ability to apply general principles to concrete situations. We have not yet developed a wholly satisfactory simple device for testing the student's ability to plan experiments for testing hypotheses which correspond closely with the direct method. This is a problem upon which we are still working.

Measuring the Ability To Infer

The necessity of having objective evidence as to the degree to which students are attaining each of the important objectives of education is stressed in an editorial in this issue of the Bulletin. This need has been recognized in several departments of The Ohio State University. The work in the Department of Zoölogy may serve to illustrate the general program now under way in several other departments.

As a result of considerable deliberation, the instructors in zoölogy have set the following goals toward which students should progress in elementary courses:
1. A fund of information about animal activities and structures
2. An understanding of technical terminology
3. An ability to draw inference from facts, that is, to propose hypotheses
4. An ability to propose ways of testing hypotheses
5. An ability to apply principles to concrete situations
6. Accuracy of observation
7. Skill in use of the microscope and other essential tools
8. An ability to express effectively ideas relating to zoölogy

There were already available techniques which are apparently valid for measuring the degree to which students have attained Objectives 1, 2, and 8. A test for microscope skill is described elsewhere in the Bulletin, while ways of measuring 4, 5, and 6 will be presented at a later date. In this article will be described a method of measuring the ability of a student to draw inferences from the facts which have been presented.

By drawing inferences from facts is meant the ability to propose reasonable inferences which serve to interpret the related zoölogical facts obtained from observation, reading, or listening. It is essential in any such test that the student be presented with the necessary related facts which he is asked to interpret. Furthermore, in order that this may not be a measure of memory, it is necessary that these related facts be new to the student. If he previously has heard these facts interpreted or has read an interpretation, his response is likely to represent his memory of the interpretation made by someone else, which, of course, would not give a measure of his own ability to infer.

For an elementary class, the most productive source of new related zoölogical facts is the current research work in this field. A brief description of a recent experiment and its results presents material which is typical of the data which the student is expected to learn to interpret. Since the facts are new, successful performance is not a matter of mere memory. Hence, a series of such descriptions was prepared for use as test items. An illustration of one of the simpler items is:

> In autumn, when the pond is cold, frogs hibernate by burrowing into the bottom of the pond. In the spring a frog put into a tank of water goes to the bottom and attempts to burrow into the bottom of the tank.

After formulating a series of such items of varying difficulty, the next problem was the method of making the test objective. The ability to propose his own inferences without suggestion was desired for the student. It was hoped, however, that this ability might be highly correlated with the ability to select the best inference from a series of alternatives, which could easily be measured objectively by a multiple-response test. To learn whether the two abilities were highly correlated a group of sixty-six students was given two tests on the same day. The first test consisted fo a series of items preceded by the following directions:

> Suppose in each of the exercises which follow that the facts given were observed or known to be true. Write in the space below the facts, the one inference which seems to you most reasonable in attempting to interpret the facts. The sample illustrates this procedure.
> SAMPLE
> *Facts.* — Starch when treated with iodine solution gives a blue color. When saliva is mixed with starch and left for a time the mixture no longer turns iodine solution blue.
> *Inference.* — Saliva produces a change in starch.
> Remember to write down the inference which seems most reasonable from the facts given.

These papers were then taken up and the students were given the same items in a multiple-response form. The following directions were used in this second form:

> In each of the exercises below several facts are given. After the facts are suggested a number of inferences. Supposing these facts are true, select the inference which seems to you most reasonable and place a check mark in front of it as in the following sample.
> SAMPLE

Starch when treated with iodine solution gives a blue color. When saliva is mixed with the starch and left for a time the mixture no longer turns iodine solution blue.

    a. Saliva turns starch to sugar
    b. Saliva turns iodine blue
  √c. Saliva produces a change in starch
    d. The color of saliva destroys the blue color
    e. Saliva has no effect on grape sugar

Remember to check the inference which seems most reasonable from the facts given.

The test items were the same in both tests, but the difference was in the ability required of the student. In the first test, he had to propose his own inferences; in the second, he had to select the most reasonable inference from a list of alternatives. A correlation between the results of these two tests shows whether the multiple-response test, which is much more easily scored, could be used in place of the first test as a measure of the ability to propose inferences. The method of scoring the first test will be described presently, showing that its score is highly reliable. The multiple-response test was scored in the usual manner. By the split-half method its reliability was found to be .90. However, when the results of the first test were correlated with the results of the second, the coefficient obtained was only .38. This indicates that there is some relationship between the tests, but by no means high enough for the multiple-response test to be used in place of the first test. The ability to select the most reasonable inference from a given list is not the same as the ability to propose an original inference.

Since the objective multiple-response test could not be used to measure the ability to propose inferences, it became necessary to develop a reliable method of scoring the original inferences proposed by the students. To this end, several devices were tried. Each different inference proposed was typed upon a separate 3-inch by 5-inch card. No names were placed on the cards in order that the instructor might not be influenced. A set of these cards was given to an instructor in zoölogy who was asked to take each test item in turn and to sort the inferences into as many different levels of quality as he could identify, placing the best pile at the right and the poorest at the left. A record was made of the instructor's sorting, the cards were then shuffled and given to each of the other instructors in turn. The number of different levels of quality recorded varied from four in the case of one instructor to eleven in the case of another.

A given instructor's judgments were given numerical scores by assuming that all of the responses, if accurately measured on a scale of merit, would be normally distributed. By this means a value for each judgment can be obtained in terms of the standard deviation of this distribution, using the formula:

$$\frac{M_s}{\sigma_s} = \frac{Y_1 - Y_2}{F}$$

When

$\dfrac{M_s}{\sigma_s}$ ▬ the mean value of a given judgment expressed in σ units,

Y_1 ▬ the left ordinate of the normal curve under consideration,

Y_1 ▬ the right ordinate,

and

F ▬ the fractional part of all the cards which were placed in a given pile.

The values Y_1 and Y_2 may be quickly obtained from published tables of the normal curve.

After the scores had been calculated for each student on the basis of each instructor's judgment separately, the objectivity of the method was determined. It was found, if the ratings made by any three instructors chosen at random were used and each student's score obtained by averaging the scores given by the three instructors, that none of these scores differ more than .3° from the scores obtained by using the ratings of all the elementary instructors in the department. The ratings of three instructors, then, can be used to represent the combined judgment of the entire department as to the quality of the original inferences which have been proposed by the students.

Another device for evaluating these inferences, which is much simpler to use, was tried. Each instructor was given the set of cards and asked to place them in five piles according to merit, No. 5 representing the best inferences and No. 1 the poorest, attempting to place the cards so that the average quality of pile No. 5 was as much better than the average of No. 4 as No. 4 was better than No. 3, as No. 3 was better than No. 2, and as No. 2 was better than No. 1. This is the method of equal-appearing intervals. In scoring, an inference placed in pile No. 5 was given five points; one placed in No. 4 was given four points, and so on. The average scores obtained by this method were then correlated with the average scores obtained by the method previously described, giving a coefficient of .98. The simpler method of equal-appearing intervals, therefore, can be used in place of the σ method.

A final check on objectivity was made this Autumn Quarter. Several new instructors had been added to the department, none of whom had seen the set of inferences or had any idea as to their placement by the instructors last year. Three of these instructors were given the shuffled cards, and were asked to place them by the method of equal-appearing intervals. The average scores given by these three new instructors were correlated with the average scores given by the instructors the year before. The resulting correlation coefficient of .96 indicates that the scoring by three zoölogy instructors is not likely to vary from year to year nor to depend upon the particular personnel of the staff, and that the merit of an inference is not the purely subjective quality often claimed.

In addition to making certain of the objectivity of the scoring, it is necessary to know whether the number of test items is adequate for the determination of the student's ability or the interpretation of zoölogical facts. Since the items used represent only a sample of all the facts which he might conceivably be expected to interpret, the reliability of the test depends upon the adequacy of this sample, and was determined by the split-half method and the use of the Spearman-Brown formula. The reliability coefficient thus obtained was .95. It thus appears that the test is both reliable and objective.

Several persons who have constructed tests have maintained that all of the important objectives were so closely correlated with information that an information test was all that was necessary in measuring achievement. This is not true in zoölogy. The correlation between a test covering the important zoölogical information and this test of proposing inferences was found to be only .29, entirely too low to justify the use of the information test alone as a measure of both objectives. If the ability to propose inferences is an important objective of zoölogy, we must have a measure for it, for we cannot depend upon information tests to indicate the student's attainment of this objective.

A final problem is now under investigation. It is very necessary that this method of measurement does not become a test of memory, hence the items must always be new to the students. This is only possible by selecting new items from current research for each new test. If new items are continually used, there is a danger that they will be of differing difficulty from those used previously, resulting in the condition that no evidence of student growth in this function will be obtained. We are now trying to formulate a method by which the difficulty of a new item can be predicted accurately in advance in order that the test may consist of new items while at the same time it can be used to measure student progress.

A Test of Skill in Using a Microscope

Adequate and reliable methods for testing the amount of information which a student remembers have been developed recently in many fields of subject-matter. Equivalent progress in developing other types of measurements has not been made. Few tests are yet available for measuring the degree of laboratory skill attained by the students, yet in the natural sciences one objective is to develop certain laboratory skills which are essential for getting first-hand contact with scientific phenomena.

The necessity for a test in microscope skill in botany and zoölogy classes at The Ohio State University became apparent when it was found that some students in advanced classes were unable to use a microscope effectively. These students had taken two courses in which they had been expected to use the microscope, yet a few of them were totally unable to manipulate the instrument. They had been unable in these two courses to make any first-hand observations of the minute structures in which most of the life processes of plants and animals take place. To discover these students who are not learning to use the microscope early, to determine the nature of their difficulties, and to provide the necessary remedial instruction so that they may gain in the essential proficiency it was necessary to devise a test of skill in using the microscope.[11] Such a test should be administered after the students had been given the usual class training in using microscope, in order to identify those who had not attained the desired skill.

The writer made a series of observations of the reactions of individual students for the purpose of determining the types of difficulties students encounter in using the microscope. Thirty-three students in Botany 402, the second half of the elementary course, were selected for observation. Using a room which was unoccupied for the day, two microscopes were placed on a table together with yeast culture, slides, covers, cloth, and lens paper. The writer placed himself in a position which gave him a good view of the actions of anyone at the table. The instructor, Miss Pearle Williams, then called in from the laboratory one student at a time. When the student came in she told him that the bottle contained some yeast culture and asked him, as quickly as he could, to find a yeast cell under the microscope and to show the cell to her when he had found it.

As each student began, the writer noted the time and made a record of the sequence of actions. When the student finished, the time was recorded together with a brief characterization of the quality of the student's mount. From these thirty-three observations a preliminary list of actions, both desirable and undesirable, was obtained. This preliminary list was supplemented by more than fifty additional observations. A portion of the final form of the check list is shown in figure 1.

STUDENT'S ACTIONS	Sequence of Actions
a. Takes slide	*1*
b. Wipes slide with lens paper	*2*
c. Wipes slide with cloth	
d. Wipes slide with finger	
e. Moves bottle of culture along the table	
f. Places drop or two of culture on slide	*3*
g. Adds more culture	
h. Adds a few drops of water	
i. Hunts for cover glasses	*4*
j. Wipes cover glass with lens paper	*5*
k. Wipes cover with cloth	
l. Wipes cover with finger	
m. Adjusts cover with finger	
n. Wipes off surplus fluid	
o. Places slide on stage	*6*
p. Looks through eyepiece with right eye	
q. Looks through eyepiece with left eye	*7*
r. Turns to objective of lowest power	*9*
s. Turns to low-power objective	*21*
t. Turns to high-power objective	*8*
u. Holds one eye closed	
v. Looks for light	
w. Adjusts concave mirror	
x. Adjusts plane mirror	
y. Adjusts diaphragm	*10*
z. Does not touch diaphragm	
aa. With eye at eyepiece turns down coarse adjustment	*11*
ab. Breaks cover glass	*12*
ac. Breaks slide	
ad. With eye away from eyepiece turns down coarse adjustment	
ae. Turns up coarse adjustment a great distance	*13, 22*
af. With eye at eyepiece turns down fine adjustment a great distance	*14, 23*

STUDENT'S ACTIONS (Cont'd)	Sequence of Actions
ag. With eye away from eyepiece turns down fine adjustment a great distance	*15*
ah. Turns up fine adjustment screw a great distance	
ai. Turns fine adjustment screw a few turns	
aj. Removes slide from stage	*16*
ak. Wipes objective with lens paper	
al. Wipes objective with cloth	*17*
am. Wipes objective with finger	
an. Wipes eyepiece with lens paper	
ao. Wipes eyepiece with cloth	*18*
ap. Wipes eyepiece with finger	
aq. Makes another mount	
ar. Takes another microscope	
as. Finds object	
at. Pauses for an interval	
au. Asks, "What do you want me to do?"	
av. Asks whether to use high power	
aw. Says, "I'm satisfied"	
ax. Says that the mount is all right for his eye	
ay. Says he cannot do it	*19, 24*
az. Told to start new mount	
aaa. Directed to find object under low power	*20*
aab. Directed to find object under high power	

NOTICEABLE CHARACTERISTICS OF STUDENT'S BEHAVIOR	
a. Awkward in movements	
b. Obviously dexterous in movement	
c. Slow and deliberate	✓
d. Very rapid	
e. Fingers tremble	
f. Obviously perturbed	
g. Obviously angry	
h. Does not take work seriously	
i. Unable to work without specific directions	✓
j. Obviously satisfied with his unsuccessful efforts	✓

SKILLS IN WHICH STUDENT NEEDS FURTHER TRAINING	Sequence of Actions
a. In cleaning objective	✓
b. In cleaning eyepiece	✓
c. In forming low power	✓
d. In forming high power	✓
e. In adjusting mirror	✓
f. In using diaphragm	✓
g. In keeping both eyes open	✓
h. In protecting slide and objective from breaking by careless focusing	✓

CHARACTERIZATION OF THE STUDENT'S MOUNT	Sequence of Actions
a. Poor light	✓
b. Poor focus	
c. Excellent mount	
d. Good mount	
e. Fair mount	
f. Poor mount	
g. Very poor mount	
h. Nothing in view but a thread in his eyepiece	
i. Something on objective	
j. Smeared lens	✓
k. Unable to find object	✓

Figure 1. Check List of Student Reactions in Finding an Object Under the Microscope

The check list, as it is now used, requires little writing. The arrangement is substantially the same as when it was first developed. A botany student is asked to find a yeast cell, whereas a zoölogy student is asked to find a blood cell. A record of the time is kept, but instead of writing down his actions the check list contains all of the actions both desirable and undersirable which have been observed thus far. The observer records the sequence of actions by placing the figure *1* after the description of the student's first action, a figure *2* after his second, and so on. The sample reproduced here has been filled out for illustration. By reading the actions in the order they are numbered one gets a detailed description of the student's procedure in finding an object under the microscope.

An examination of the sample will serve to indicate the usefulness of the test. It is clear that this student is very deficient in microscope skill. He used eleven minutes without finding the cell, whereas the better students find an object in approximately two minutes. He does not adjust mirror nor diaphragm, he closes one eye and turns down the coarse adjustment, while his eye is at eyepiece — all habits which must be remedied before he can use a microscope skillfully. As would be expected, he has poor light on the object, has a smeared objective, and is unable to find the object. He needs training in each of the specific phases of microscope skill. Hence, this test record gives the instructor an analysis of the student's behavior which permits the selection of the individual students who need training and a determination of the specific phases of training which each student needs.

The most promising part of the procedure is the discovery that students deficient in microscope skill can be quickly trained to reasonable proficiency. Miss Blanche B. Montgomery has had charge of the remedial training in the Department of Zoölogy. She has been giving the test followed by remedial instruction to a large number of students. She finds that ten minutes of her time on the first day for instruction, followed by five minutes for a check a week later, will provide the necessary guidance for more than half of the students. After the ten minutes of instruction the student spends several periods in practice, with a result that more than 90 per cent of the students have become sufficiently skillful to use the microscope effectively.

This microscope test is, of course, an individual test which requires a certain amount of the instructor's time. Ordinarily, ten to twelve students can be tested in an hour, but to use such an individual test with each of the seven hundred students in Botany 401 would require nearly two weeks for one instructor. Only the persons who are having difficulty in using the microscope need to be observed. By means of an easily administered group test those who should take the individual test may be selected. In the group test, the entire section is in the laboratory seated at microscope tables each of which is provided with the necessary materials. The instructor informs the class that they are to see how rapidly they can find an object under the microscope. They are all to commence when he gives the signal and to stop when he gives the second signal.

The second signal is given at the end of three minutes, and the instructor quickly passes from microscope to microscope noting those students who are unable to find the object in three minutes. This same group test is given a second time several days later. Those students who were not able to find an object in three minutes in both tests are then given the individual test. This group test requires only ten or fifteen minutes to administer, but by means of it the instructor identifies about three-fourths of the class who are already proficient with the microscope. This means that in a class of forty only ten need to be given the individual test. These ten tests can be given in an hour, which is not a heavy burden on any instructor.

The microscope test is not a paper-and-pencil test, but it is an objective device for determining the degree of skill possessed by students in biology. By its administration a record is obtained which permits the instructor to determine the type of remedial training needed and to give that training with a minimum expenditure of time and effort. The student thus trained has acquired skill in the use of an essential tool of biology.

The Master-List as a Device

Recently the writer examined samples of a large number of objective achievement tests which had been constructed by high-school, college, and university instructors and used by them in their courses. These tests fell into three classifications, true-false, multiple-choice, and completion. The reliability of the majority of these tests was low, partly due to the fact that they were so worded that clues to the right responses could often be obtained without having any real knowledge of the subject.

The undesirable characteristics found in these tests are largely due to the difficulties in constructing them. Some of the problems involved in formulating the common types of objective tests have been discussed recently by various writers. In general, it may be said that valid and reliable tests of these types are much more difficult to construct than is commonly realized. For example, a true-false statement must be so carefully worded that the necessary judgment of its truth or falsity will depend upon an understanding of the idea to be tested and may not be surmised from the peculiarities of expression. The statements which are only partly true present another limitation of the true-false test, for the student is directed to mark "false" any statement which is partly false, as well as those which are entirely false. In most subjects it is hard to put some of the significant ideas into such form that they are not partly false. When the statements are so carefully made that they are entirely true, their guardedness often furnishes a clue to the student who then can mark the statement correctly although he may have no knowledge of the idea being tested.

In formulating a multiple-choice test it is very necessary to have alternatives which are plausible and commonly confused with the right answer, otherwise the student can choose the right response because the wrong responses are not plausible. The formulation of these alternatives is often difficult.

The problem in constructing completion tests is to provide blanks, each of which may be properly filled in by only one correct response, without making the test more a measure of intelligence or of ability to manipulate words than a measure of the knowledge of the idea being tested. Students who do not know the idea itself are sometimes given clues by the sentence structure. Other students who know the fact itself may fail on the test because they are unable to manipulate their language to fit the blanks.

The mere enumeration of the difficulties involved in constructing these three types of tests would suggest the desirability of developing other supplementary types. The need for such tests is enhanced by the fact that many kinds of abilities are not easily tested by the true-false, the multiple-choice, or the completion test. In the social studies the ability to evaluate persons, events, and institutions is quite significant, but the usual types of objective tests do not readily lend themselves to the testing of the student's ability to judge these social data. The ability to appraise literary selections with reference to elements of style and qualities of content is another example of an objective not readily tested by the usual types of tests.

The need for types of objective tests which might be used as measures of abilities not readily tested by the usual tests, and which might be more easily constructed led the writer to experiment with various types of tests for college courses. In this experimentation frequent use has been found for a type of objective test which might be called a "master-list test."

The nature of the test is best described by illustration. Let us suppose a test is to be constructed to determine the student's understanding of the important technical terms used in college botany. A single technical term in many cases has several different meanings each of which the student should know. Thus the term "carbon dioxide" has the chemical meaning "a compound composed of carbon and oxygen in the proportion of two atoms of oxygen to one of carbon." It also has the everyday significance "a gaseous product formed when carbon is burned in air," and it has the botanical meaning, "one of the products formed in the cells by the oxidation of carbohydrates." There may be other meanings for the term which are significant for the botany class, but these will do for illustration. Similarly, other important terms have various meanings. "Protoplasm" might be thought of as "the material basis of all living things," "the material of which cells are made," "the living material composed of carbon, hydrogen, oxygen, nitrogen, phosphorus," and so on. It is highly desirable, therefore, to construct a test to determine which of these meanings the student associates with the term.

The master-list test has two significant divisions. One part is a comprehensive list or master-list of the terms which are significant for that course. If the list is not too long, it may be printed at the right-hand edge of the test sheets in alphabetical order, as in the accompanying example, A Terminology or Vocabulary Test, which is given on the page which follows. If the list is too long to appear at the side of the page, it may be printed upon a separate sheet of paper which is detached from the rest of the test to facilitate effective use. In any case, each term is numbered (*see* Exhibit 1).

EXHIBIT 1

A TERMINOLOGY ON VOCABULARY TEST*

Directions. — Following are several definitions or descriptions of geographic terms. Many of them are not exact definitions, but they are the definitions given in certain high-school textbooks. On the right-hand side of the sheet is a numbered list of geographic terms arranged in alphabetic order. Read each definition or description, decide what term answers the definition, then place the number of the term in front of the definition or description as in the sample.

SAMPLE

1 The actual amount of water vapor which is held by a certain body of air. Note that this is a definition for the term *absolute humidity*. In the list on the right *absolute humidity* is No. 1, so the figure *1* is placed in front of the definition. Remember that the list of terms at the right of the page is arranged in alphabetic order so that you may quickly find a term. For your convenience the numbered list is repeated on the next sheet so that you need not turn back to find a term.

1. ...The distance expressed in degrees north or   1. absolute humidity
    south of the equator.   2. alluvial plain

---

*This is a section of a pre-test in general geography for freshman students. It was given the first day of the quarter and used for judging the student's background.

2. ..The distance expressed in degrees east or west of the prime meridian.
3. ..A large region of ascending air.
4. ..An area in which the atmospheric pressure increases toward the center.
5. ..Ratio between the distance on the map and the distance in the field.
6. ..The average of weather conditions over. a long period.
7. ..As area in which the atmospheric pressure decreases toward the center of the region.

3. altitude
4. barometer
5. climate
6. coastal plain
7. doldrums
8. erosion
9. fiords
10. "high"
11. horizontal scale
12. isobars
13. isotherms
14. latitude
15. longitude
16. "low"
17. map projection
18. regular coast line
19. relative humidity
20. standard-time belt
21. Trades
22. vertical scale
23. Westerlies

The second part of the test contains the test items themselves which are a series of definitions or descriptions; for example, one item might be "the material of which cells are made." The student reads each definition or description in turn, decides upon the term to which the item refers, finds the term in the master-list, and places the number of the term in the blank space provided in front of the test item. For illustration, suppose that the student is reading one of the descriptions which applies to carbon dioxide. As he reads he thinks, "This refers to carbon dioxide." Because the master-list is arranged in alphabetical order he can find the term quickly, notes, for example, that it is number 9, and then writes "9" in the space provided. A little later he may come to another test item which describes another significant meaning for carbon dioxide. Again, he uses the figure "9" placing it in front of this other test item. When he reaches the third description, "one of the products formed in the cells by the oxidation of carbohydrates," he should place two numbers in front of the test item, figure 9 for carbon dioxide and also the number given to water in the master-list, since water is also one of the products thus formed in the cells.

From this description it is clear that the master-list test is a matching test with several important modifications. The three modifications emphasized in the foregoing illustrations are: the use of an element in the master-list more than once, using more than one element for one test item, and the arrangement of the elements of the master-list in a form which makes it easy to find the number of an element if the meaning is already known to the person taking the test.

The possibility of using an element from the master-list more than once is of especial value when it is important to find which of several significant meanings for a term the student understands. If "protoplasm," for example, has various meanings to students, as many different meanings as are important may be included in the test. The possibility of using more than one element for certain test items is, also, of value. Thus, a test item, "materials from which plants make carbohydrates," permits the student to place the number of each such material in the proper blank space. In this way meanings shared in common with other terms may be tested. The arrangement of the elements of the master-list in alphabetical or logical order to facilitate the finding of the numbers is no less important. The ordinary matching test usually requires that the student re-read the entire list for each test item. In the master-list test, if he knows the correct answer, he can find the number of the proper element in an instant.

Another example may serve to illustrate that the test has a wider range of use than has previously been implied. Suppose a zoölogy test is to be constructed in which it is desired to determine the student's familiarity with the habitats of certain important animal forms. In this case, the test items will contain the names of various animal forms, while the master-list will consist of the types of habitat in which animals are found, such as "fresh-water swamps," "warm sea water near shore," "dry soil," and so on. In this example, the alphabetic arrangement would not facilitate finding the numbers as much as would a logical arrangement. If the list were classified logically so that all marine habitats came first, then all fresh-water habitats, then land habitats, the student could easily find the item desired. For example, the student could quickly find the numbers of the habitats in which the hydra, the frog, the amoeba, and other animal forms are commonly to be found, and could place the proper numbers in the blank space provided before the name of the animal without the loss of time involved in searching for the item and its number. An example of a master-list arranged in logical order is given in Exhibit II.

This example should serve to illustrate another important difference between the master-list test and the typical homemade matching test. The number of items in the master-list need have no relation to the number of test items, whereas, commonly in the homemade matching tests there is the same number of items in the two lists which are to be matched. Where there is the same number of items in the two lists it is possible to get some of the items right by elimination, that is to say, the student reasons that the two items belong together because they are about the only items left. Hence, some of the brighter students get credit for more items than they really know. With a master-list containing more elements than the number of test items, this type of elimination cannot avail the student.

To illustrate still further the wide range of use to which the master-list is adapted, let us consider the construction of tests of the student's ability to make certain pertinent judgments or evaluations. The master-list form is especially effective as an evaluation test. We shall first consider a type of evaluation in which there are but two categories of judgment. In the social sciences, historical events, persons, and institutions may need to be evaluated to indicate whether they contributed to certain significant criteria such as "development of industry," "settlement of the west," "promotion of slavery," "promotion of good will between north and south," and so on. This is a case where the evaluation may require just two categories; that is, the event, person, or institution either did or did not contribute to "promotion of slavery," or to "development of industry," or to "promotion of good will between north and south."

EXHIBIT II

A MASTER-LIST ARRANGED IN LOGICAL ORDER*
   Directions. — The titles of several curriculum studies, together with certain questions about these studies, follow. You have, also, been given a sheet which contains a list of sources from which the data for many studies have been obtained. Answer each question on the line following it by writing the number of the sources used in the study as in the sample.
SAMPLE
Ayres' study of spelling vocabularies of letters. What sources were used to obtain the word list? 20, 21
In the Ayres' study referred to personal and business letters of adults were used as the source of words. These are numbers 20 and 21 in the list of sources. Hence, the figures *20* and *21* have been placed on the blank line to answer the question. Remember that one or more numbers may be required for the answer.
   1. The mathematics needed in freshman chemistry at Illinois—
      What sources were used to obtain the mathematical terms and operations?
   2. The *Commonwealth Teacher Training Study*—
      What sources were used to obtain the traits of high-school teachers?
   3. Bobbitt's Los Angeles curriculum study—

*This is a portion only of a test used in a course in curriculum construction. The complete test included twelve items together with a master-list of 29 sources.

What sources did he use to obtain specific objectives?
4. Study of secretarial duties and traits—
From what sources were the activities of secretaries obtained?

LIST OF SOURCES

PERSONS

1. Pupils or students in school or college
2. Teachers in school or college
3. School and college officials
4. Authorities in subject-matter fields
5. Experts in educational techniques
6. Members of the vocation concerned
7. Experts in the vocational fields concerned
8. Employers in the vocation concerned
9. Parents of pupils or of students
10. Laymen

RECORDED MATERIAL

11. Publications for teachers
12. Textbooks for pupils or students
13. Reference books for pupils or students
14. Tests and examinations for pupils or students
15. Exercise books and laboratory manuals for students
16. Papers written by children for school subjects
17. Published statistics dealing with social, economic, health, and political activities and agencies
18. Books for the general reader
19. Periodicals and newspapers for the general reader
20. Business letters written for adults
21. Personal letters written by adults
22. Letters written by children
23. Records required in the vocation concerned

LOCAL ENVIRONMENT

24. Homes
25. Museums
26. Industrial plants
27. Natural surroundings
28. Playgrounds
29. Stores

EXHIBIT III

AN EVALUATION TEST IN EUROPEAN HISTORY

Directions. — Following are the names of several historical events, persons, and institutions which are significant in European history. You have also been given a separate sheet of paper upon which is listed and numbered some of the major factors in European development. You are asked to evaluate the significance of each of the events, persons, or institutions by placing in the first blank column on the left of this sheet the numbers of the major factors to which the event, person, or institution did not directly contribute; by placing in the second column the numbers of the major factors to which the event, person, or institution made a moderately important direct contribution; and by placing in the third column the numbers of the major factors to which the event, person, or institution made an important direct contribution, as in the sample.

SAMPLE

First Column	Second Column	Third Column	Historical Events, etc.
1, 2, 4	5	3	Galileo

Notice that No. 3, *The development of the natural sciences*, is placed in Column 3 since Galileo exerted a great influence upon this factor. No. 5, *Promotion of exploration*, is placed in Column 2 since Galileo made a moderate direct influence upon this factor. The other factors are placed in Column 1 since Galileo bad no direct influence upon them. In the same manner evaluate each of the persons, events, or institutions listed in the following table by placing the numbers of the factors in the appropriate columns.

First Column	Second Column	Third Column	Historical Events, Persons, or Institutions*
No Direct Influence	Moderate Direct Influence	Great Direct Influence	
			Peace of Westphalia
			Edict of Nantes
			East India Company
			Colet
			British Parliament

Major Factors in European Development**

1. The development of absolutism in political government
2. The reformation of the Catholic Church
3. The development of the natural sciences
4. The promotion of nationalism
5. The promotion of exploration

The master-list test is easily used in such a case. The test items can consist of the historical persons, events, or institutions to be evaluated. The master-

---

*This is only a partial list of the events, persons, and institutions included in the complete test which contained forty items.

**This is only a partial list of the major factors in European development included in the complete test which contained twelve major factors.

list will then consist of the factors to be used in evaluating the items. Enough space should be left below or at the left of each test item so that the student may write in the numbers of the criteria which were promoted by the event, person, or institution. This use of the master-list is illustrated by an Evaluation Test in European History from which the directions and five items are listed in Exhibit III. Few objective tests have yet been devised for testing the ability of the student to evaluate data with reference to given criteria, hence the master-list test should be significant in this field.

As a final example, let us consider the use of the master-list test when the desired evaluation involves more than two categories. We shall take a course in English literature in which the student is expected to evaluate literary selections with reference to certain standards of style and content. In such a case, it is desirable to have more than two categories of evaluation; that is, one literary selection might fulfill a certain standard very well, another selection would fulfill the standard fairly well, while another might not fulfill the standard at all. This evaluation represents three categories: very well, fairly well, and not at all.

An evaluation requiring three or more categories permits the use of the master-list test, as well as does the evaluation requiring only two categories. In this case, however, there is a slight change in the left margin of the test paper. As in the previous example, the test items are the data to be evaluated, while the master-list contains the criteria with reference to which the data are to be evaluated. In the English illustration proposed, the literary selections to be evaluated would be the test items, while the standards of style and content would make up the master-list. In addition, three blank columns are provided at the left of the test sheet. The first column is headed "Standard not met at all," the second column, "Standard fairly well met," and the third column, "Standard very well met." If more than three categories of evaluation are desired, as many blank columns should be provided as categories desired.

The student reacts to this test by considering each literary selection with reference to each standard. The numbers of those standards which are not met at all he places in the first column opposite the name of the literary selection. The numbers of the standards which are very well met he places in the third column opposite the appropriate selection, while the numbers of the standards which the selection meets fairly well he places in the second column. The student with very little writing may thus express his best judgment in a form which is readily evaluated.

The advantages in the use of the master-list test are not alone in the wide use to which it may be put. Since the essential elements are already printed and placed before the student, he may react to a wide variety of test situations in a short time because of the minimum of writing required. With a rather comprehensive set of items in the master-list the opportunity for guessing is negligible. Spurious clues to the right answers are much less likely to exist than in the true-false, multiple-response, or completion tests. Furthermore, the scoring of the master-list is rapid and objective.

There are, of course, certain precautions to be observed in constructing the test, but these are not difficult to follow. They are concerned primarily with the formulation of a master-list which is sufficiently complete for the purposes of the test. Simple directions for constructing the master-list type of test will be given in a later article.

It has been suggested that the master-list test appears to have a wide range of use as a valid device for testing certain significant objectives of high-school and college courses. There remains the question of the test's reliability. The writer has obtained reliability coefficients for this type of test when used in college courses in zoölogy, geography, education, and statistics. In a zoölogy class of 68 students, a predicated reliability coefficient of .94 for a forty-five-minute test was obtained by using the split-half method. In a geography class of 250 students, the predicted reliability was .91 for the same length test. Using duplicate forms of the test in education and statistics, reliability coefficients of .89 and .91, respectively, were obtained for classes of 242 and 37 students. These coefficients indicate that the test may be made highly reliable.

In conclusion, it may be suggested that the master-list test deserves a trial by those who are constructing achievement tests. Table I is intended to present a summary of some of the uses to which the test seems adapted. The exhibits are presented to provide concrete illustrations of the form of the test and of the directions given to students.

Improving Test Materials in the Social Studies

The topic here discussed is so general that there are many phases which of necessity must be left untouched in this paper. I have chosen to discuss two aspects of the subject; namely, the adequacy of the commonly used tests in the social studies, and the steps that can be taken by the classroom teacher to improve the testing of the outcomes of instruction in this field. To discuss these two phases of the topic I shall take the risk of boring my readers by repeating facts which are probably familiar to all of us.

Human life has been and is becoming increasingly more complex. With the development of rapid transportation and communication, with the industrial life centering in cities, the very existence of human life depends upon an increasingly large degree of social contacts and social co-operation. The perpetuation and progress of society rest upon the development of

Table 1. Summary of Suggested Uses for Master-List Tests

Character of Objective to Be Tested	Nature of the Master List	Nature of the Test Items	Nature of the Test Set-Up	Nature of the Reaction to Be Made by the Student
A. Understanding of the significant meanings of the vocabulary used in the course..........	A numbered list of terms used in the course	Definitions or descriptions of the significant meanings of the terms	The terms are alphabetized at the right side of the test sheet or on a separate sheet	The student places the number of the term opposite the definition or description
B. A knowledge of the authors of important books, articles, and studies in the field covered by the course..........	A numbered list of authors' names	Titles or descriptions of the important books, articles, or studies	The authors' names are alphabetized at the right side of the test sheet or upon a separate sheet	The student places the number of the author opposite the title or description of the book, article, or study
C. A knowledge of the characters, plots, and significant events in literary selections..........	A numbered list of titles of literary selections	Names of characters, outlines of plots, description of events occurring in literary selections.	The titles are alphabetized or arranged according to the author at the right side of the test sheet	The student places the number of the title of the literary selection opposite the name of the character, outline of the plot or description of an event
D. A knowledge of the habitats in which certain animals or plants are commonly to be found...	A numbered list of habitats	Names of various plant or animal forms	The habitats are arranged in logical order at the right side of the test sheet	The student places the number of the habitat opposite the name of the plant or animal form
E. Ability to plan an investigation in the field covered by the course..........	A numbered list of methods of investigation	A description of a problem to be investigated	The methods of investigation are arranged in logical order on a separate sheet	The student places the numbers of the methods of investigation opposite the description of the problem
F. A knowledge of the elements of important investigations and studies in the field covered by the course..........	A numbered list of elements of investigations such as sources of data, methods of investigation	Titles of important investigations and studies	The elements are arranged in logical order on a separate sheet	The student places the numbers of the elements which were involved in the investigation or study opposite the title
G. Ability to evaluate data with reference to given criteria or standards..........	A numbered list of significant criteria or standards relevant to the data	The titles or descriptions of the data to be evaluated	Blank columns provided at the left of the test items. There should be as many columns as the number of categories	The student places in the appropriate columns the numbers of the criteria or standards which are met by the data

desirable social abilities and traits among people generally. This necessity places the social studies in the most vital part of the school curriculum.

On the other hand, the success or failure of the teaching of the social studies is largely dependent upon determinations of the shortcomings of the pupils within the class and upon measurements of the relative success or failure of different types of teaching. The testing of pupils' achievement in the social studies is as imperative as in any subject of the curriculum.

A test in any subject is a means for measuring certain qualities of the pupils either directly or indirectly. Thus, the speed or handwriting may be measured directly by counting the letters written in a specified time. On the other hand, such a complex quality as intelligence is measured indirectly and imperfectly by determining the relative success or failure in performing certain intellectual tasks. We assume that this success or failure is due to the relative degree of intelligence possessed.

Most of the more complex abilities and characteristic modes of behavior which we hope to develop in the social studies must be measured indirectly since our only contact with them is through their expression in the various activities of life. For example, such socially desirable modes of behavior as honesty, open-mindedness, considerateness, and the like are not measured directly, but are measured by the reactions of people to various situations which normally permit their expressions. The abilities and ideals demanded of the members of primitive tribes are relatively simple, and the presence or absence of these qualities is quite easily determined. In a complex society the problem of devising tests to measure social qualities becomes increasingly difficult as it becomes increasingly important that we know which desirable types of behavior each pupil lacks and how successfully we are teaching them. The development of good tests in the social studies is one of the essential steps in improving teaching in this field.

What are the characteristics of a good test? Aside from those of secondary importance, there are four criteria by which the value of a test should be judged — its validity, its reliability, its objectivity, and its accuracy of measurement. These criteria apply to tests prepared by the classroom teacher as well as to the standard tests which are sold on the market. We shall not consider the last three, but shall direct our attention to the question of the validity of tests.

When is a test valid? In other words, does it measure the essential qualities of the subject? Using an illustration from the physical world, an ordinary grocer's scale is a valid test of weight since it actually measures weight. On the other hand, a quart measure is not a valid test of weight since it measures the space occupied by material. A column of numbers to be added may be a valid test of addition, but it is not a valid test of total arithmetical ability since it only measures one phase of a subject which includes subtraction, multiplication, division, and problem-solving as well as addition. Whether a test is valid or not is determined by the usefulness of the test in measuring the degree to which the pupils have attained the objectives which are the true goals of the subject. The evaluation of tests cannot be made without considering the objectives which the school seeks to attain in this subject.

What are the objectives which it is hoped the social studies will attain? The national committee on the social studies reporting in the Fourth and Fifth Yearbooks of the Department of Superintendence states the following as the general goals which we hope to attain through the social studies: understanding of current political, social, and economic problems and principles; desirable emotionalized attitudes toward such problems (attitudes which arc social rather than antisocial); civic habits and ideals of civic conduct which promote progress and happiness. The further statement is made that social science is the science of getting along with people, not a study of rules and forms of social structure alone. Mere knowledge is less important than inclination based on understanding.

It is apparent that these objectives are general, and before we can use them in teaching or in constructing tests we shall need to analyze each to know what information pupils must have to understand current problems, what emotionalized attitudes they need in order to live with others happily, what habits and ideals promote progress and enjoyment of social life. These more specific objectives are being determined by those who are constructing curriculums in the social studies, and we shall not dwell at length upon them. What seems significant is that leaders in the field emphasize three types of development which the social studies should seek to promote, understandings, attitudes, and habits and ideals. To test achievement we must measure each phase and its integration.

Are tests actually constructed on the basis of these accepted objectives? When the tests developed by the committee of the American Historical Association, which is investigating social studies in the schools, are ready, improved tests will undoubtedly be available. Few tests, however, are based directly upon objectives, but most of them arc based upon the facts and principles common to a number of widely used textbooks. These are tests of information only. But what tests are made of the other aspects of understanding and of attitudes, habits, and ideals?

The Brown-Woody Civics Test consists of three parts: Civic Vocabulary, Civic Information, and Civic Thinking. The first part consists of a list of forty terms such as "statute," "thrift," "co-operation," "urban," "treason" after each of which are placed four words. The pupil is asked to select the word which is a synonym for the term. Most words are commonly used in books and articles dealing with civic problems. This is a test of the understanding of common civic terms. The second part is a test of information relating to the forms and rules of civic life. Such questions as the following are included:

Is the United States a democracy?
May any adult become a candidate for office, local or national?
As a general rule does ignorance of the law excuse its violation?

The third, a test of Civic Thinking, includes a number of problems, of which the following is typical:

Mr. L lives on a little farm just outside the limits of the city of X in the state of R. Mr. L wakes up one morning and finds that thieves have taken grain, chickens, and other possessions from his premises during the night. Mr. L wishes to bring the thieves to justice. To whom should be report his losses?
1. The chief of police of the city of X.
2. The chairman of the Board of Public Safety of city X.
3. The State Department of Justice in state of R.
4. The supervisor of his township.
5. The county sheriff.

This is a test of the application of information to civic problems.

The Hill Civic Tests consist of two parts entitled tests of civic information and of civic attitudes. The information test consists of definitions of terms widely used in civics, such as "wealth," "capital," "labor," "a bank," and "a boycott." The attitudes test consists of a number of common life situations and the pupils are asked to select the appropriate reaction. Thus:

You are playing ball with two friends. When you are "at bat" you knock the ball through a window. In this case:
a. knock at the door and offer to pay for the window.
b. run away as fast as you can so that no one will see you.
c. tell the tenant that one of your comrades hit the ball.
d. tell the tenant to call your father on the phone and talk to him.

In so far as the reaction to such a test represents the expression of a pupil's normal attitude the test is admirable, but in so far as the reaction is governed by the feeling that the school expects a certain type of response it does not measure attitude but knowledge. Both the Brown-Woody and the Hill are good tests for certain phases of civics, primarily informational.

The Columbia Research Bureau history test consists of four parts all of which are tests of information concerning American history. The Gregory test has five parts which are all primarily informational tests. The Pressey history tests are in four parts: Character Judgment, Vocabulary, Sequence of Events, Cause and Effect Relationship. In the first part a number of well-known historical names are given with a list of traits. The pupil is asked to indicate which traits best describe the character of each man. For many pupils this is more a test of understanding of trait names than of the character of historic figures. The second part is a typical test of history vocabulary. In Part III certain events are to be arranged in the order of the time at which they occurred. In Part IV the pupil is asked to select from a given list the most probable causes of certain events.

The Van Wagenen American History Scales consist of two parts: the information scale and the thought scale. The first contains such exercises as the following:

> Which two of these were the main means of getting farm work done during the colonial period? Oxen, horses, hand labor, gasoline engines. In which of these things have changes taken place since 1900? Treaty making powers; Elections of vice-president; Number of senators elected from each state; Function of the electoral college.

The thought scale contains such exercises as the following:

> A hundred years ago it took a letter several days to go from New York to Boston. Today it takes only a few hours. Why do you think it took letters so much longer to go from New York to Boston a hundred years ago than it does today?
> At the close of the Revolutionary War many of the people in America were driven from their homes by the official acts of a new state government, their property was taken and they were deprived of the right to vote or to hold public offices. How can you account for such actions?

These history tests are all measures of understanding or of information.

The geography tests commonly are place or location tests, although the Posey-Van Wagenen contains some thought questions. The Buckingham-Stevenson test is a good example of a typical test in place geography. It contains a list of important places which are to be located in various ways. For example:

> Indicate on which continent the following are found: Alps Mts., Canada, Italy, Ohio River, etc.
> Name the state which is next south of the following states: New Hampshire, South Carolina, Oklahoma, etc.

The thought tests measure understanding of geographic relations.

What conclusions can be drawn from these illustrations? These tests are good as far as they go, but the test constructors have concentrated most attention upon measuring information and the understanding of social facts and concepts. This criticism does not hold for those building tests for the study of the American Historical Association. Nevertheless, only a beginning has been made in testing social attitudes and habits. The very ease of measuring information as contrasted with the difficulty of measuring habits, attitudes, and ideals tends to cause us to judge the success or failure of our teaching by informational standards only, to set up the objective of information first and to neglect to develop the equally necessary habits, attitudes, and ideals required of socially effective citizens.

What can teachers do to improve the present situation? They can continue to use both standardized tests and tests of their own construction to determine the mastery of the desirable information. Moreover, they can begin to keep a record of the significant and characteristic acts of the pupils which indicate social habits. This will demand the observation of the reactions of pupils both in school and out, yet it is the only basis for getting material from which tests of habits and attitudes may be constructed.

In observing pupils' acts which indicate the presence or absence of those characteristic modes of behavior in certain situations which are called fairness, open-mindedness, thoughtfulness of others, sympathy, cooperation, honesty, and the like, we have begun to note those phases of social attainment which most need development in the school. At the same time, a description of these reactions of the pupils constitutes the beginning of the construction of tests for habits, attitudes, and ideals.

By keeping a record of these characteristic reactions of pupils, information is obtained which when interchanged among the teachers of the country would prove valuable. The materials could be organized by some interested group so as to formulate standard tests of the desirable modes of behavior which the social studies seek to develop in pupils. These tests would attempt to measure those phases of social living which are now neglected, based upon typical reactions of boys and girls.

The most important of all, the observation of pupils to determine the presence or absence of desirable social characteristics, however, stimulates the teacher to attempt the teaching of habits and attitudes as well as information. The very consideration of these qualities is a challenge to a good teacher to develop them within pupils who are notably lacking. The improvement of tests in the social studies goes hand in hand with the improvement of teaching.

Assumptions Involved in Achievement-Test Construction

Many people now distrust the soundness of educational research involving the use of educational tests because they had been led to believe that the development of tests meant the complete substitution of scientific method for personal opinion in education, that educational testing invariably meant objective and reliable data, and that unsound conclusions were no longer possible with these new instruments. This misplaced confidence has had harmful effects. In recent years the contradictory conclusions drawns by investigators using educational tests and the lack of agreement among testing experts have caused many teachers and administrators to believe that educational tests and educational research are no less fallible than opinion and therefore have little to contribute to the development of sound educational practice.

A new attitude toward educational testing is necessary. This attitude must avoid misplaced confidence, on the one hand, and cynical distrust, on the other. This new attitude should be guided by an intelligent understanding of the philosophy and methods of educational testing. This means that research workers and laymen alike should recognize the fundamental assumptions involved in the construction and use of achievement tests. Furthermore, if testing is really to contribute to educational theory and practice by developing a body of valid techniques, objective data, and sound conclusions, the progress of research in this field must be accompanied by the testing of one assumption after another so that progressively there will be fewer critical points which are not supported by adequate evidence.

The development of a science always involves a series of assumptions. The validity of the conclusions depends upon the validity of the assumptions. The science progresses both through the addition of new data and through the testing of previous assumptions, so that bit by bit the shaky scaffolding of untested assumptions is replaced by firm masonry. Educational research has been constantly in jeopardy through its failure to make explicit its fundamental assumptions. Each research worker either accepts the findings of previous investigators without examining their assumptions to determine their acceptability for the purposes of the new investigation, or makes a new investigation without reference to the implications of previous but related studies. Consequently, the body of findings and techniques is almost inextricably mixed up with a confused mass of assumptions and half-truths. Nowhere is this better illustrated than in educational testing.

Is it not time for us to pass from this adolescent confusion into the maturity of a carefully integrated science? Such an effort requires the recognition by each investigator of the fundamental assumptions involved in his study and the explicit statement of these assumptions. Each worker should be encouraged to strengthen the growing structure of research by testing certain of the assumptions previously made and by interpreting his findings with due regard for the pertinent assumptions involved in his own and in previous investigations.

Some of the major assumptions involved in achievement-test construction will be mentioned in this paper and possible procedures which might be followed in testing these assumptions will be mentioned. Several assumptions regarding the validity of achievement tests are common. It is generally assumed that a single test is a valid test of a school subject. Thus we speak of a test of arithmetic ability, or reading ability, or a test of American history. Now, a valid test of a subject implies that the test measures the student's attainment in all of the important phases of the subject, each of which is adequately and with proper emphasis represented in the test. A school subject, however, usually involves a variety of objectives. The objectives in reading commonly include: interest and enjoyment in reading about various topics, the ability to get the main idea from different types of selections, the ability to find and understand specific details, the ability to organize and to evaluate the ideas obtained from reading, the ability to catch the mood or feeling tone of certain types of reading selections, the ability to judge and appreciate the quality of various types of reading selections, and knowledge of standards which may be applied to reading materials. If a single test is to measure such a complex of outcomes, it must include exercises which adequately test the student's attainment of these various objectives and be so chosen as to give due weight to the various aspects of the subject. But there is no standardized weight to be given these different aspects of reading....

Fortunately, this assumption is not necessary in building educational tests. It is not necessary to attempt to construct a single test to cover a subject, but tests may be built to measure the student's attainment of particular objectives or of combinations of them. In place of a single test of reading there may be tests of the student's interest and enjoyment in reading about various topics, tests of his ability to get the main idea from various types of reading selections, and so on. This procedure has the added advantage that the tests may be used by schools having distinctly different evaluations for the particular objectives. The school which emphasizes interest and enjoyment in reading may give the results of the tests of this ability greater weight than schools not emphasizing this outcome, although both schools may be using the same instrument for testing.

A second major assumption often made when constructing achievement tests is that there exists a satisfactory criterion of validity with which a new test may be correlated. This gives rise to the concept of the coefficient of validity which frequently is the correlation of the test results with the marks given the pupils. This assumption is often not acceptable. The purpose of achievement tests is to give the teacher a more valid and accurate instrument for determining the student's achievement. Any test which correlates highly with the marks given by the teacher is not likely to be an improvement over the teacher's judgment. In place of this assumption, the criterion of a valid test should be the reaction of students in a variety of situations appropriate to the objectives of the subject. The essential assumption in achievement-test construction here is that the student's reaction in a sampling of the situations representative of the objectives is an adequate index of his characteristic reaction in all situations representing the objective. This latter assumption may be tested for each new test by extending the sample of test situations indefinitely and determining the effect.

Another assumption with reference to the validity of tests is that tests which do not directly evaluate the student's reactions in situations representative of the objectives are nevertheless satisfactory indexes of these reactions. For example, the objective to be measured by a vocabulary test is an understanding of the meaning of a variety of words. The type of understanding required will vary with the word, but in general it means that the word, as a symbol, will stimulate in the student certain appropriate reactions. The purpose of words used in the directions for making a radio is to stimulate the student to do certain operations; words used in describing a theory are to direct the development of ideas; words in poetry are to stimulate an emotional reaction. The ordinary vocabulary test, however, does not provide a means of evaluating such a range of reactions. The most common type of exercise in vocabulary tests requires the student to choose the nearest synonym for a given word from a list of four or five alternatives. This test may be a satisfactory index of all of the reactions expected in an adequate vocabulary test, but I know of no convincing evidence in support of it.

Test constructors have usually been content to set up a simplified device for testing purposes, but they have rarely attempted to determine the validity of these devices by correlating them against the results of the evaluations of the student's reactions in situations which are adequately representative of the objective to be tested. The assumption can and ought to be tested in any research program of test construction. There are times when a testing device which is not perfectly correlated with direct measurements of the student's achievement may be used because it is practicable to administer, whereas the direct measurement is not. It is, then, possible to recognize the rough character of the index by making due allowance for the variation in validity through the use of a standard error which has been computed on the basis of the correlation between the direct measurement and the more practicable device.

A second series of assumptions are concerned with the evaluation of test responses. It is commonly assumed that the method adopted for marking a given test will give a satisfactory evaluation of the student's responses in the light of the objective being measured. This assumption is rarely tested. For test exercises which cannot be scored by means of a key the marks assigned by one reader often differ from the marks assigned by another. Obviously, they cannot both be equally valid evaluations. In such a case, it becomes necessary to establish a criterion for evaluation against which any marking procedure may be checked. The most satisfactory criterion for reactions which must be evaluated by personal judgment is probably the composite evaluations of an infinitely large number of trained judges. Considering this large group as the total population in the statistical sense it is possible to determine the number of judges needed to give evaluations which are as close to the total composite as desired.

Even tests which are scored by means of a key ultimately depend upon personal judgment in determining the degree to which the possible responses represent the attainment or non-attainment of desired objectives. Consider a multiple-response test in which the alternative responses include true statements and misconceptions. Students may check true statements, leave statements unchecked, or check misconceptions. In the light of the objective being tested, what is the relative value which should be assigned to these three possible responses? In the opinion of instructors in certain sciences the student who has a misconception is more unfortunate than the student who knows that he does not know the answer. These instructors assign the highest value to those checking the true statement, the next highest value to those leaving the exercise unchecked, and the lowest value to those checking a misconception. On the other hand, I have known certain instructors in other subjects who express the belief that it is better for the student to try to formulate an answer even though it is a misconception than to make no response. These teachers give the highest value to those checking the true statement, the next highest value to those checking a misconception, and the lowest value to those leaving the exercise unchecked.

This variation in practice illustrates the fact that even a so-called "objective test" requires personal judgment in its evaluation. To check the assumption that a certain marking method gives a satisfactory evaluation of the student's reply it is possible to use as the criterion the composite evaluation of an infinitely large group of trained judges who are guided by clear statements of the objective being measured. Variations from this criterion on the part of any particular scoring method may be measured, and an estimate of the amount of error likely to be involved may be made.

A second assumption involved in the evaluation of responses is that the particular numerical values assigned to test responses provide a satisfactory scale for measuring the degree to which the students have attained the objectives. This assumption involves a number of related problems which have not been exhaustively investigated. Some test constructors give equal weight to each exercise in the test, others weight an exercise on the basis of the relative number of persons who answer the exercise satisfactorily. Some test scores are based upon a reference point which is the mean achievement of a group of students. Others attempt to express a reference in terms of an absolute zero. Some test scores are derived from the assumption that the quality being tested is normally distributed, others are derived from the assumption of equal-appearing intervals. These merely illustrate the variety of methods in use.

It is possible to test the validity of these various methods of assigning numerical values by establishing in each case the limits of possible error involved in these assumptions. This can be done by recalculating all the numerical values for the test responses using assumptions which are at the two greatest possible extremes from the assumptions used in the scoring of the tests. These two sets of values obtained from the extreme assumptions can each be correlated with the values originally used. This gives a means of estimating how widely different it is possible for the test results to become if the assumptions upon which the numerical values have been calculated are changed.

The major assumption relative to reliability in test construction is that the test provides an adequate and representative sample of the student's reactions to all the situations in which the desired objective may be expressed. There are two factors which through their variation affect the reliability of a given test. One of these is the range of situations in which the objective may be expressed, and the other is the variation in the reaction of the student to a given situation. A test of ability to multiply, for example, should adequately sample the range of situations in which the objective may be expressed. It should sample the different multiplication combinations; the different numbers of digits in the multiplier and multiplicand; the different situations in which multiplication may be used as, for example, buying situations, the making out of a budget, and so on. The test should also sample the varying reaction of the student to the same situation. The latter variation may be noted when the student, today, is able to multiply 7 by 8, and, tomorrow, fails to do this exercise correctly. The testing of the assumption of reliability is primarily a problem in sampling which may be attacked by the usual techniques of sampling, namely, by choosing samples which include all the known variables and selecting cases within the samples by some random method which is likely to include all pertinent variable not now known to effect the result. The size of the sample needed may then be calculated by the use of formulas for the standard error of the mean.

A final series of assumptions concerns the interpretation of test scores. It is assumed that the test scores provide measurements in fine enough units so that the student's progress may be noted and so that the tests may be used for experiments in methods of instruction. An examination of several wide-ly used standardized educational tests reveals the fact that measurements are being made in units so large that a single unit may represent the average progress in achievement which takes place during an entire semester. That is to say, the number of points of difference in the test score necessary to be statistically significant is no less than the average amount which a class gains in one half-year of study. It is apparent that such tests do not measure in fine enough units to show the student's progress from week to week, or month to month, nor to measure the differences between two months of in-struction used in a subject for one year or less. The situation is like trying to measure the progress of a baby's weight from week to week on a scale measuring in pound units.

The assumption that the test measures in fine enough units may be check-ed for any particular test by giving the test in various forms to the class at intervals of one week, or two weeks throughout the semester or year, and noting the changes in test score during the progress of the class. In case the test does not measure in units fine enough for the purposes intended it is possible to get more refined units of measurement by making a more detail-ed analysis of students' progress and providing test situations to cover these more detailed steps.

Concerning the units of measurement used in a test a second assumption is that any difference in test scores which is statistically significant is cor-respondingly of social value and desirable to have. The only way to test this assumption is to determine what the given units of measurement are equivalent to in terms of recognized social values. It might be discovered, for example, that a unit of improvement on a test is the equivalent of the progress made in ordinary class work during three days of instruction. The unit of improvement might be expressed in terms of its cost, or in terms of other equivalent values both material and non-material. When tests are be-ing used in educational research, it becomes increasingly necessary that the units of measurement be expressed in understandable terms.

These four types of assumptions which are involved in the construction of achievement tests are not exhaustive, but they are sufficient to represent the nature of the fundamental assumptions which are commonly untested. If test construction is to develop a sound body of philosophy, techniques, data, inferences, and principles, it is essential that these assumptions be tested one by one, so that we may be able to separate findings and methods which are based upon valid assumptions from those which are untenable because the assumptions underlying them are not true. This is a task which challenges all who work in the field of achievement-test construction.

What Is Statistical Significance?

The term "statistically significant" abounds in current reports of educational investigations. Two examples may serve for illustration. In Wood and Freeman's recent study of classroom moving pictures the results of an achievement test given to classes in general science which had utilized moving-picture films as a part of the teaching method were compared with the results obtained by classes not using the films. The differences were reported as statistically significant. In Hudelson's studies of class size, the achievement-test records of large classes in the University of Minnesota were compared with the results obtained from small classes, and the differences were said to be not statistically significant.

What is meant by statistical significance? Is a difference which is statistically significant necessarily of social significance? When a difference is reported as not of statistical significance, does it necessarily follow that there exists no difference of any importance? The interpretations which have commonly been drawn from recent studies indicate clearly that we are prone to conceive of statistical significance as equivalent to social significance. These two terms are essentially different and ought not to be confused.

The difference between the terms may, perhaps, be more clearly presented through illustrations chosen outside of the field of education. Suppose two herds of twenty-five cattle each were being fed two different diets, and were being weighed from time to time to determine which herd was gaining more weight. Let us present some hypothetical data to illustrate statistical significance. The total weights of the two herds at the beginning of the experiment were the same. At the second weighing some of the steers in the first herd had gained a great deal of weight, and others had gained but little. The same was true in the second herd. Nevertheless, the average gain in the first herd was 187 ± 1 pounds per steer, while the average gain in the second herd was only 181 ± 1 pounds. The difference in average gain between the two herds was 6 ± 1.4 pounds. By our usual criteria this is a statistically significant difference. We can be practically certain that with two other much larger herds chosen in the same way and fed the two diets, those fed upon the diet given the first herd would show greater gain.

The greater gain of the first herd is statistically significant, but is it significant for the cattle feeder? Here is an added gain of 6 pounds per steer. Applying the usual interpretation of probable error, we can be practically certain that other similar herds would not show less than .5 pounds nor more than 11.5 pounds greater gain per steer. Is this gain worth the cost?

Obviously, that is another question altogether, and cannot be answered in terms of statistical significance. We should need to know the cost of this diet which brings added weight, and the difficulties which might attend its use. The fact that the gain in weight made by the first herd is statistically significant does not prove that the gain is worth the cost.

This illustration serves equally well for the field of education. Scientific studies of learning and teaching which reveal statistically significant differences in the effects of various materials or methods should be continued or supplemented so as to indicate the social importance of a difference together with its social cost. For example, in a recent study we found that a definite program of conferences between instructors and students in The Ohio State University resulted in an increased achievement equivalent to 17 points on a comprehensive achievement test. Readers want to know, and the investigators should make it a point to report, how much this difference is and how much it costs. We discovered, for example, that the interviewed students accomplished as much in ten weeks as the others did in twelve, that the students liked the informal contacts with the faculty, and that to provide for conferences required one-third more instructors. This sort of information helps the readers to interpret and to utilize such investigations.

Differences which are statistically significant are not always socially important. The corollary is also true: differences which are not shown to be statistically significant may nevertheless be socially significant. Again, an example chosen from without the field of education may serve as a better illustration. Suppose that the gasoline consumption of two automobiles were being compared by running them both around a two-mile track, measuring the gasoline in the tank before and after the run. Suppose, further, that a quart measure were the only measuring device available. Ten times the gasoline consumption was measured, and each time the closest estimate which could be made with the quart measure was that each machine had consumed about a pint in running around the track.

If this were an educational investigation the difference in gasoline consumption of the two machines would be reported as "not statistically significant." Readers would interpret the report as showing that there was no difference in the gasoline consumption of the two automobiles. Would this be a valid interpretation? Certainly not. No difference was found, but it is apparent to us that the technique of measurement is entirely too crude for the purpose. Either a smaller gasoline measure should be used, or longer runs should be made. When the two automobiles were run for sixty miles, the first consumed only three gallons of gasoline, while the second consumed four. Here was a difference of real importance which, through lack of refined methods of measurement, failed at first to be revealed as statistically significant.

Similar illustrations are available in studies of learning and teaching. A recent investigation of large and small classes compared the gains made in one semester on a standard test. The average gain during the semester made by the large class was only 8.2 ± 1.5 points, and by the small class, 9.1 ± 1.6 points. It is evident that the difference between the gains made by the two classes is not statistically significant. Is there no difference of any social importance? This question cannot be answered by the use of a technique of measurement so unrefined. The probable error of the gain in each of these classes is approximately 1.5 points. Ordinarily, we demand a difference of at least 3 times the probable error to be certain that there is a real difference which is probably not due to the unreliability of the measurements. In this case, then, a gain of at least 4.5 points is required for the gain to be statistically significant. Since in the entire 18 weeks of the semester the classes gained only about 9 points, it is apparent that the test used was so crude a measuring instrument that for statistical significance a difference would need to be equivalent to nine entire weeks of instruction. Suppose one of the classes was actually superior to the other in attainment by an amount equal to four weeks of instruction. To be four weeks ahead at the end of a semester would certainly be important socially, but such a difference would not even be statistically significant with the crude measurements of this test. Really important differences may not be revealed as statistically significant when the methods of measurement are not sufficiently refined.

More refined tests for such purposes can be constructed by increasing their length and reliability. In the study at The Ohio State University, referred to previously, in which the effects of conferences between instructors and students were determined, we found that the first test used would not reveal a statistically significant difference which was less than that gained by a class during three weeks of instruction. By revising and lengthening these tests we are able to develop measuring instruments that would indicate differences which were statistically significant even when these differences were as small as the gain made by a class in one week of instruction. Most comparisons of teaching methods and materials require measurements correspondingly refined.

The implications of the distinction between statistical significance and social importance should be apparent to all research workers. Upon us is placed the responsibility, first, of determining whether real differences exist and then of indicating their social importance and their cost. When we fail to find any statistically significant difference, we are not justified in concluding at once that no real differences exist. We bear the responsibility for developing appropriate techniques of measurement, methods so accurate that if there are any real differences of importance they will be revealed with some precision. These measures must be so refined that we can determine differences which though small may be worth the effort to attain.

When we have measured differences with such precision, we need to be able to express them in terms of recognized social values. The research worker who reports his data in terms of abstract scores without further explanation is encouraging his readers to make gross errors in interpretation. The only way that the social significance of differences can be appreciated is for the research worker to show what these differences amount to in terms of weeks of schooling, hours of effort, depth of satisfaction, or other recognized social values.

Making a Co-operative Test Service Effective

There is danger that the value of standardized tests will be lost. Their development during the past thirty years has offered an opportunity for teachers to use tests more carefully prepared than the typical examination. Standardized tests have been given extensive trial so that many ambiguities and extraneous difficulties are removed. They can be more accurately scored and represent a wider range of content than the usual examination, and norms are provided so that the results obtained in a particular class may be compared with those of other classes and of other schools. Notwithstanding these characteristics, there are developments which threaten to cancel the values to be gained from the use of standardized tests.

Persistent attempts are made to construct one standardized test to cover an entire course or an entire subject. Exceptions to this method are the tests in arithmetic, reading, and language; but in the content subjects in high school and college, a single test often is made to cover an entire course. The author constructing such an examination is determining not only the particular objectives to be measured by the test, but also the relative emphasis to be assigned to each of these objectives. Consider, for example, some commonly used standardized test in American history. The author selects the items to cover each of the important aspects in the test, and he sets a certain relative value on them. Every teacher using this test is evaluating his instruction by an instrument which measures each pupil's achievement in terms of the emphasis judged important by the author of the test. From institution to institution and from teacher to teacher, we find differences in the relative importance attached to the various objectives to be reached through instruction in any subject. This is especially true in high school and college, and as a natural result, we find many teachers and administrators becoming critical of standardized tests. They make such comments as: "This does not measure the objectives which we are trying to attain in our classes," "This test mainly measures information, whereas we place major emphasis upon interpretation of facts and upon attitudes." Such criticism is often sound. Tests constructed in this way and used as they have been in the past may place a "strait-jacket" upon education. Legitimate differences in the emphasis placed upon the various goals to be reached in any school subject are to be expected with variations in environment, in types of pupils and in philosophy of education. No single test can be an equally valid measure of instruction for every school in the country or even for every school in a single state.

On the other hand, it would be unfortunate if every teacher in the state or country could depend only upon examinations or tests which he has constructed. Few teachers have the time to develop the refined measuring instruments necessary to make an exact evaluation of the results of instruction. Few institutions can afford the cost of special agencies devoting their time to the construction of improved examinations. Much of the promise of better tests disappears if complete reliance is placed upon examinations constructed by the individual teacher or institution. There is equally small promise of better tests if the objectives to be measured and the emphasis to be placed upon each objective are decided by a maker of standardized tests who makes no provision for the variations among institutions and instructors.

The choice in my opinion is not limited to these two possibilities. A cooperative program of test construction can be developed which provides for the differences in the objectives emphasized by different instructors and institutions and at the same time contains the advantages of the standardized test. This program is based upon the conception of an examination not as the device for measuring the subject, but as an instrument for measuring one of the objectives to be attained by the subject. An adequate measurement of results reached by teaching the subject would require a series of examinations testing each of the important objectives set for this subject. Thus, one examination in zoölogy is not enough, but a series of devices are needed for measuring such important objectives as the ability to draw reasonable generalizations from the data of experiments; the ability to propose experiments to test hypotheses; the ability to apply important zoölogical principles to new situations; the memory of the important facts, terms, and principles of zoölogy; and the like. When examinations are conceived in this way, it is possible to devise a measure of an important objective of zoölogy which may be used widely throughout the country, for wherever there is divergency of opinion as to the importance of this objective it can be given a different weight. A comprehensive examination under such a plan would consist of a series of tests measuring the objectives considered important by the institution in question. The results of each of these tests would then be weighted in accordance with the judgment of the institution as to the relative emphasis to be placed upon each objective.

Furthermore, when an institution can determine the relative value to be assigned to various objectives, it can then interpret the results of its own teaching in the light of pupils' attainment of these fundamental objectives. This procedure also provides a diagnostic instrument which can be used to guide remedial teaching. The development of tests to measure the attainment of the various specific objectives reduces the possibility of the serious neglect of the fundamental ones by a particular instructor.

The advantage of this procedure lies in the fact that a device for measuring a particular objective can be worked out carefully, can be given thorough trial, and can be used widely among many institutions so that classes may be compared with each other. Each instructor using the device, however, may interpret the measurement in the light of the emphasis he places upon that objective. The possibilities of this plan may be illustrated with the subject of college zoölogy.[12]

If a co-operative test service is to be provided for zoölogy, it will be necessary to develop devices for measuring the attainment of each of the objectives considered important by many teachers of zoölogy. The first step in a co-operative test project in this subject will be to make a survey of the objectives which need to be measured. Such a survey will give a list of objectives which would include the following:

1. A memory of important zoölogical information
2. An understanding of the common technical terms in zoölogy
3. An ability to draw reasonable generalizations from experimental data
4. An ability to plan experiments by which to test hypotheses
5. An ability to apply zoölogical principles to concrete situations
6. Accuracy of observation
7. Skill in use of the microscope and other essential tools
8. An ability to express effectively ideas relating to zoölogy[13]

It is apparent that if these eight objectives are measured separately we shall need as many tests or devices. Furthermore, because of possibly wide differences of opinion we shall need to break up certain of these objectives into more specific goals to be tested. The first and second objectives above will need to be subdivided. Some instructors in zoölogy place a great deal of emphasis upon information about the morphology of certain type forms of animals. Others are more concerned with the student's knowledge of animal physiology. Still others emphasize facts dealing with the classification of animals, while others may emphasize cytology and histology, heredity, evolution, ecology and distribution, and the history and scope of zoölogy. To have wide use tests of zoölogy which measure the two objectives, memory of important information and understanding of technical terms, must be subdivided into these eight parts. When this is done instructors who consider information about morphology especially important may weight the score accordingly since it is measured separately from information about animal physiology, about the classification of animals, or about any of these other aspects. Obviously, then, every objective must be analyzed to a point where there is little difference of opinion regarding the importance of outcomes classified under the specific objective.

This survey of the objectives reveals the types of student behavior for which separate measuring devices must be developed. The next step is to construct and to perfect devices for measuring each of the desired outcomes of the course. This is the point at which the importance of co-operative effort becomes apparent. To construct a valid and accurate device for measuring each of a dozen or more objectives requires the efforts of more than one person. A man may be found, however, who is especially interested in devising means for measuring the student's ability to draw generalizations from experimental data. Another may be willing to assume responsibility for developing procedures for testing the student's ability to apply principles to concrete situations. Still another may be eager to construct tests for measuring the information which a student possesses about morphology, and another may be willing to make an examination to test the facts of heredity. It is possible in this way to get the concerted efforts of a large number of interested persons in developing examinations which may be used widely in spite of differences in the emphasis placed upon various objectives of the course.

This plan provides another advantage not ordinarily obtained by the typical standardized test. Since it is a co-operative enterprise, the burden resting upon any individual is not so heavy but that a program of continuous test construction and improvement may be provided. One man in the field of zoölogy has been assuming responsibility for selecting materials to measure the application of principles. To keep this on a continuous basis he has agreed to spend a few hours each week searching the literature for new principles which may be developed from time to time and for new applications of these principles. After these have been submitted to representative zoölogists for criticism they will form the basic material for the new tests to be constructed each year to measure the student's ability to apply principles to concrete situations. Because new tests are continually prepared they can be used to test the student's ability to apply principles to new situations. A second man is responsible for going through the reports of current research in zoölogy and making a record of those experiments with which elementary students are not familiar but which they might be expected to interpret. He has agreed to carry this on year after year so as to provide materials for new examinations each year which measure the student's ability to draw generalizations from the data of new experiments. Since this provides experiments which are really new to the student, they can be used to measure his ability to interpret new experiments rather than to test his memory of the interpretation someone else has made of an old experiment. A third man is responsible for selecting the facts which are discovered from year to year with reference to animal physiology. After this material has been criticized it will form the basis for continually improved examinations covering the student's information about physiology.

A description of this plan should indicate its advantages. As long as we attempt to measure all of the outcomes of the subject by one examination which gives one score for the pupil's achievement, we are likely to place a "strait-jacket" upon education. As soon as we separate the objectives about which there is difference of opinion and measure each of these separately it is possible to develop examinations which can be used widely without solidifying educational procedures. It also makes it possible to obtain the assistance necessary to develop a valid and exact instrument for measuring a particular objective....

Techniques for Evaluating Behavior

Specialization in educational research so confines our thinking that various techniques for accomplishing the same purpose are commonly thought of as belonging to different fields of investigation and are rarely used by the same individual, yet many a problem is most appropriately attacked be several methods rather than by one. Especially is this true in that area called measurement, appraisal, or evaluation. The techniques of objective testing are differentiated from the methods of the psychological laboratory. The observation of child behavior is considered a distinct and separate field from mental testing, the analysis of pupils' written work is contrasted with personal-interview procedures, and the use of interest questionnaires is not identified with the collection of anecdotes.

Essentially, however, these techniques are methods for accomplishing the same purpose; they are all devices for evaluating human behavior. By isolating each device and making it a subject of special study we have probably improved the effectiveness of the device, but we have lost the value which comes from realizing the similarities in all of these procedures. The research worker, teacher, or school administrator confronted with the problem of appraisal is likely to think of one of these devices and fail to recognize that the choice of the particular method of evaluation should depend upon the effectiveness of that method for the particular problem under consideration. A clearer recognition of the common elements in all of these methods of evaluation is needed to provide a basis for choosing the techniques to use in a particular situation.

All methods of evaluating human behavior involve four technical problems: defining the behavior to be evaluated, determining the situations in which it is expressed, developing a record of the behavior which takes place in these situations, and evaluating the recorded behavior. Regardless of the type of appraisal under consideration, whether it be the observation of children at play, the written examination, the techniques of the psychological laboratory, the questionnaire, or the personal interview, these problems are encountered. The choice of the methods of evaluation rests primarily upon the effectiveness with which the methods solve the particular problems.

To define the behavior to be evaluated is essentially to determine all of the kinds of behavior which are particularly significant for the purposes under consideration. The reactions of any human organism are so many and varied that it is necessary to isolate the particular reactions which are significant for a given purpose. For example, during the process of instruction in a subject such as arithmetic, pupils are reacting in many different ways, some are talking, some are smiling, some are moving about in their seats; but these are probably not significant kinds of behavior from the standpoint of the purposes of arithmetic instruction. In making an appraisal of value in the field of arithmetic it is necessary to define the kinds of behavior which are significant in arithmetic so that we may discover whether the pupils are reacting in desirable ways. This definition would probably include behavior such as the ability to determine the total amount of an itemized grocery bill, a feeling of the importance of accurate numerical computations, the ability to determine the arithmetic processes to use in solving typical problems which are encountered in everyday life, and so on. Similarly, one must define social adjustment in order to evaluate the effectiveness of a child's adjustment in a social group. There are many reactions which the child makes when in a social group. Some of these reactions are random and of little or no significance from the standpoint of social adjustment, while others are vitally related to social adjustment. It is therefore necessary to identify the significant behavior so that the evaluation will concern itself with the significant rather than the irrelevant kinds of behavior.

A chief defect in defining behavior for educational evaluation has been the failure to indicate all of the types of behavior which are significant in the educational development of boys and girls. We have defined the reactions involved in recalling information; we have concerned ourselves with the overt behavior involved in spelling and handwriting. We have characterized somewhat accurately the behavior expected of pupils in locating places on maps. Much less frequently have we defined the emotional reactions, the attitudes, and the interests of boys and girls which are of educational significance. Nevertheless, these latter kinds of behavior are fully as significant in the complete development of boys and girls as are the kinds more commonly defined for purposes of measurement.

A satisfactory definition of behavior to be evaluated will indicate all of the kinds of reactions which are significant for given educational purposes. For example, in connection with the Payne Fund study of motion-picture appreciation conducted by Mr. Dale, an effort is being made to evaluate the progress children are making in appreciating motion pictures. When we begin to define the behavior to be evaluated in this project, we find that there are many kinds of reactions which are significant in connection with motion-picture appreciation. We are concerned with the likes or dislikes which children have for particular motion pictures, with the standards which they customerily use in judging motion pictures, with the abilities which they possess for applying these standards to particular motion pictures, with the sources to which they ordinarily turn for information about the motion pictures that they might possibly attend, with the attitudes which they have toward the importance of the motion picture as an agent for social education, and so on. It is clear that many of these types of behavior are not ordinarily recognized when teachers or research workers embark upon a project of appraisal, yet it is no less important in any appraisal to indicate all of the significant kinds of behavior which need to be evaluated.

A satisfactory definition of the behavior to be evaluated will also describe each of these significant kinds of reactions more exactly so that those aspects of behavior with which we are primarily concerned in the project will be clearly understood. In the field of literature, for example, we talk a good deal about the importance of developing appreciation. Before we can appraise the degree to which boys and girls are developing literary appreciation, we must describe what we mean by literary appreciation in terms of human reactions. It is particularly difficult to describe objectively the behavior which we call appreciation because our ideas of appreciation come from our own feeling; that is to say, our own recognition of our likes and dislikes led us to speak of an appreciation or a strong liking for something.

With our present ignorance of the objective reactions associated with likes and dislikes the definition of an appreciation usually implies only that others have developed feelings of like or dislike similar to those we ourselves experience.

The definition of literary appreciation or of any other kind of behavior should not only describe the kind of reactions to be expected but should also indicate the range of stimuli which may be expected to bring forth this reaction of appreciation or liking. It is only necessary in the definition to indicate that literary appreciation involves the development of a liking for good literature in contrast to poor literature and then to define good literature from the point of view of the persons whose behavior is to be evaluated. For high-school pupils this means that the definition should include a statement of the kinds of literature which are "good literature" for high-school pupils.

The difficulty in defining literary appreciation, as in defining other kinds of behavior, is due to these two aspects, describing the reactions which are significant and indicating the range of stimuli which may be expected to bring forth these reactions. The definition of literary appreciation is unsatisfactory to the degree that we have only a vague apprehension of the nature of the reactions which we call likes and dislikes and the degree to which we do not indicate the sorts of literature which high-school pupils may be expected to like. If our definition of literary appreciation is vague in either of these respects, our evaluation of the development of literary appreciation among high-school pupils will be correspondingly unsatisfactory.

Fortunately, the problem of characterizing the kind of behavior is not so difficult in the cases of behavior ordinarily apparent in the reactions of other people. Skill in laboratory manipulation, for instance, has made itself evident to us in the reactions of other people as well as ourselves, the habit of cleanliness, the ability to read, the skill in handwriting are all examples of behavior which manifests itself in other people as we come in contact with them. On the other hand, the feeling of inferiority, the satisfactions obtained from seeing good drama, the interest in investigating scientific problems, and sensitiveness to human suffering are all examples of human reactions which have become evident to us largely through our own feelings rather than through our contacts with others. As a result, these types of behavior are difficult to define except in terms of subjective feelings. However, for many purposes they are important. To make no attempt to evaluate such behavior because of the difficulty in defining it is indefensible. In most cases it is possible to define these types of behavior somewhat more accurately than the usual definitions and to make at least a rough appraisal.

The fact that generalization of behavior is less pronounced in some people than in others and the additional fact that a type of behavior which is desirable under some conditions is undesirable under others make it especially important to indicate in the definition the variety of conditions under which the behavior should be expected to appear. For example, we often talk about people developing intellectual curiosity. If we mean by this an interest in making investigations in any field of human endeavor, it is obvious that the evaluation of such behavior involves sampling the reactions of people under a large variety of conditions. If, on the other hand, the teacher of chemistry wishes to discover the degree to which his pupils are developing an interest in investigating chemical problems, then the definition of this behavior should indicate that the interest in investigation is limited to the field of chemistry.

Similarly, an evaluation of effective English expression requires a definition of the behavior "effective English expression" which indicates the limiting conditions under which the behavior may be expected to exist. Generally, such a definition would indicate the types of expression which are significant in the particular case such as social conversation, business letters, scientific reports. The purposes of these types of expressions would also need to be defined, and the audiences for whom the expression is prepared would be suggested. A complete definition of the behavior which is appropriate for a given unit of instruction in English might be one of the following: writing reports of chemical experiments for laymen in chemistry which would make clear to them the nature and the results of the experiments, writing personal letters to high-school friends which would interest the friends in one's experiences, writing business letters to a retail store which would make clear the nature of an error made by the store in connection with a recent purchase. If the behavior to be evaluated is much more general than this, the definition should make clear the generality of the conditions in which the behavior is expected to be expressed.

The critical importance of definition in connection with any evaluation of behavior has not always been recognized. It is one of the chief sources of difficulty in satisfactory measurement. As each task of appraisal is begun, the work is greatly clarified if an understandable definition of the behavior to be evaluated is formulated, a definition which includes all of the more important aspects of behavior related to the problem, which characterizes the types of reactions to be measured and which indicates the limiting conditions under which these reactions are likely to take place.

The second major problem involved in all measurement is to select the situations which give opportunity for the behavior to be expressed and to be recorded for purposes of evaluation. What are the situations in which the ability to understand printed directions may be expressed and in which we may get evidence of the degree to which children possess this ability? What are the situations in which tolerance toward the ideas of other people may be expressed and in which we may get evidence of this tolerance? What are the situations in which the appreciation of good motion pictures may be expressed and in which we may get evidence of this appreciation?

From the standpoint of efficient measurement there are several characteristics to be desired in the situations chosen for evaluation. In the first place, it is necessary that these situations really give opportunity for the expression of the behavior in question or of reactions which are useful indexes of this behavior. Many techniques fail at this point. In the field of written examinations it is common to use, as situations for measuring the pupils' ability to apply principles of a subject, questions which have been completely discussed in class so that they give pupils an opportunity to show their ability to recall what has been discussed in class rather than to apply principles to the solution of problems which are new to them. In literary appreciation it is common to present situations which give pupils an opportunity to indicate the facts they know about good literature rather than their liking for good literature. In the field of drama it is not uncommon to use situations which test the pupils' recall of the teacher's opinion of the quality of certain dramatic productions rather than their own critical evaluation of these dramatic productions. These are common weaknesses of current attempts at appraisal. Situations chosen for purposes of evaluation should meet one of two conditions. Either they should provide an opportunity for persons to express the behavior being measured, or else they should provide an opportunity for persons to react in a way which has been found by actual experiment to be a satisfactory index to the behavior considered.

Another important quality of evaluation is the degree to which extraneous factors are controlled. In written tests the vocabulary of the questions is often an extraneous factor which affects the reactions of pupils and thereby injures the effectiveness of the measurement. The unusual nature of the instruments used in the psychological laboratory may distract the attention of the subjects and thus influence the results. In the observation of children who are carrying on typical play activities the complexity of the situation often introduces extraneous factors which influence the observed behavior. The desire for social approval or the lack of rapport in the use of interest questionnaires may seriously affect the reactions. In connection with every problem of evaluation we ought to consider carefully the methods by which we may control conditions most effectively so that those extraneous factors which seriously affect behavior may be eliminated.

A third quality to seek in the evaluation situation is its practicability from the standpoints of time, effort, and facilities required. There are cases when the observation of children at play will provide situations in which a defined type of behavior may be expressed, but those situations arise so rarely in the typical play of children as to require months of observation before any significant reactions are likely to be observed. This is obviously an impracticable technique for measuring such a type of behavior. A controlled situation in which the opportunity for the defined behavior may be offered at will is obviously much more desirable. The purpose of many testing techniques and of laboratory methods is to control the situation so that the desired reactions will be stimulated at will, and the measurement may be made more quickly than would be the case if we were to depend upon its occasional stimulation in the undirected activities of life. One of the major technical problems in measurement is to control the behavior situation without introducing extraneous factors which seriously affect the reactions taking place in the situation.

The expenditure of effort and facilities is also a real problem in appraisal. If the measurement requires expensive equipment, it is at once beyond the reach of many parents and teachers who are most in need of satisfactory techniques. If the method requires a great deal of additional effort, it is also obvious that it will not be used by a vast majority of people. Too little attention has been paid to the simplification of some of the more effective techniques of evaluation.

A fourth quality to be desired in the situations selected for purposes of evaluation is reliability. It is necessary that these situations so sample the defined behavior that conclusions drawn from the reactions of persons in these situations are dependable. In general, this means sampling the variety of conditions in which the behavior may be expressed and including a large enough number of these situations so that the behavior noted in these situations is typical of the persons whose reactions are measured.

To make a wise selection of situations in which the defined behavior is to be measured requires a thorough canvassing of the possible situations, checking each of the possibilities with reference to the opportunity it provides for expression of the behavior, the degree to which extraneous factors are controlled, its practicability, and its reliability. This means cutting across the usual lines of demarcation separating written examinations, the observation of pupils, the methods of the psychological laboratory, questionnaire methods, personal-interview methods. This elimination of the lines of demarcation is desirable because it is likely to provide a more complete measurement procedure than is possible where one is restricted to a special technique.

The third major problem occurring in every evaluation is that of a record of behavior. The significance of a record is due to the fact that single bits of behavior are far less meaningful and far less capable of objective evaluation than are cumulative records of behavior. No one has emphasized this fact more strongly than Mr. Ben D. Wood who developed the American Council Cumulative Record Form. The experience with this and with other forms of cumulative records clearly indicates the importance of making records in any useful program of evaluation. The possible records which might be made are varied. We may depend upon an individual's memory of the reactions which took place; we may utilize the memories of several observers; we may write a description of the behavior as it takes place, or shortly thereafter; the behavior may itself involve the making of a record as in the case of a written examination or the making of a product such as a dress in a clothing course; we may make motion pictures or sound records. There are, in fact, a wide variety of possible records many of which have rarely been utilized although they merit careful consideration in some situations.

Two characteristics are to be sought in a record of behavior. In the first place, the record should indicate the significant reactions which actually took place rather than a summary interpretation of these reactions. The importance of this quality is due to the fact that the reactions which actually took place are objective data largely free from the subjective interpretation of the individuals making the record, while the summary interpretations involve much more subjectivity for a single bit of behavior recorded. The behavior can be evaluated more objectively and with greater validity as the number of records increases. Most rating scales have failed to take this principle into account with consequent fluctuations in ratings obtained by different observers and an increased difficulty in interpreting the ratings for particular purposes. The recent experimentation with the evaluation of character traits at Rochester Mechanics Institute suggests the value of anecdote records; that is, descriptions of actual behavior taking place in situations noted by the instructor, in contrast with rating scales which provide records only of the summary interpretation of the behavior observed. For some time the faculty at Mechanics Institute had been utilizing rating scales for character traits. They found, however, that the ratings in many cases were almost meaningless for a student might be rated high in a certain trait by half of his intructors and low in the same trait by the other half. The hypothesis was advanced that this was due to the difficulty of determining the meaning of the isolated bits of behavior coming to the attention of any individual instructor at any one time. Accordingly, the anecdote record was devised. This was merely a description made by each instructor of any behavior which he observed which he thought significant. When these anecdote records had been collected from a number of instructors over a period of time, it was found possible by reading these cumulative descriptions of behavior to reach an interpretation which did not fluctuate widely from one competent reader to another. These interpretations are frequently corroborated later.

Judged by the principle that a record should describe accurately all the significant reactions which actually took place, most rating scales, most score cards, many interest questionnaires, and many personal interviews are unsatisfactory. On the other hand, moving-picture records, sound records, many comprehensive observation check lists, many written examinations, and the collection of products resulting from behavior are much more satisfactory. In many cases, it is not difficult to change the record form without changing the situation in which the behavior is expressed. In art, for example, the practice of scoring drawings or objects made by pupils, retaining only the score as a record, may be changed to one in which samples of the objects themselves may be retained for the record, permitting later evaluations at any time.

The second quality desired in a record is practicability. Those requiring a great deal of time, effort, and facilities are obviously handicapped. The ingenuity of technicians can well be directed toward the simplification of records without sacrificing the primary requirement that they give an accurate characterization of the significant reactions which took place. Mr. Tharp's work in the development of oral pronunciation tests in the modern foreign languages is an illustration of a successful attempt to develop a more practicable record of behavior. He experimented with a record sheet in which the student indicated the pronunciation of particular foreign words by selecting the nearest equivalents among English words listed on the sheet. He compared this record with the actual pronunciation which was recorded on a dictaphone and found a close similarity between the two types of records. In our work in botany and zoölogy we have developed a check list of reactions made by students while using the microscope which may be easily checked by an observer and which gives a record closely approximating a motion-picture record of the students' behavior. The value of any comprehensive program of measurement is greatly enhanced by the maintenance of cumulative records of actual behavior which make it possible to interpret more intelligently the development of children and to formulate a more effective educational program in the light of the evidence obtained from these records.

The fourth problem encountered in all attempts at appraisal is the problem of evaluation. Since this has been discussed at some length in a previous article, I shall not repeat the discussion here.[14] The chief difficulties in evaluation are those of determining the standards to use, of obtaining greater objectivity, of determining the scale values for different types of behavior, and of obtaining measurements in units fine enough for purposes of exact appraisal.

Projects involving appraisal, testing, or measurement are all efforts to evaluate human behavior. The kinds of human behavior significant in education are extremely varied and cannot be adequately evaluated by one type of techniques. All evaluation really involves the four major problems already enumerated: defining the behavior to be evaluated, selecting the situations, making a record, evaluating the behavior recorded. By expanding our repertoire of possible techniques of evaluation to include observations, laboratory methods, written examinations, personal interviews, and the collection of products we shall add materially to the potential methods of evaluation in any given case. By selecting the particular techniques to use from this expanded repertoire on the basis of the effectiveness in this given case with which these methods solve the four fundamental problems of evaluation we shall add immeasurably to the adequacy of our evaluations of human behavior.

Notes

1. For a more detailed statement of the objectives see Sampson, Homer C. "Objectives of Elementary Courses in Botany." *Journal of the Michigan Schoolmasters Club* (University of Michigan Official Publication, No. 77, 1931), pp. 54–65.

2. For a detailed description of the microscope test see Tyler, Ralph W. "A Test of Skill in Using a Microscope." *Educational Research Bulletin*, IX (November 19, 1930), pp. 493–96.

3. Tyler, Ralph W. "Measuring the Ability to Infer." *Educational Research Bulletin*, IX (November 19, 1930), pp. 475–80.

4. Tyler, Ralph W. "Ability to Use Scientific Method." *Educational Research Bulletin*, XI (January 6, 1932), pp. 1–9.

5. Ruch, G.M. *The Objective or New Type Examination*. Chicago: Scott Forman and Company, 1929, pp. 149–159.

6. Wood, Ben D. *Measurement in Higher Education*. Yonkers-on-Hudson, NY: World Book Company, 1923, p. 163.

7. Peters, C.C. "The Relation of Standardized Tests to Educational Objectives." *Second Yearbook of the National Society for the Study of Educational Sociology*. New York: Teachers College, Columbia University, 1929, pp. 148–159.

8. Tyler, R.W. "Measuring the Ability to Infer." *Educational Research Bulletin*, IX (November 19, 1930), p. 475.

9. Tyler, R.W. "A Generalized Technique for Constructing Achievement Tests." *Educational Research Bulletin*, X (April 15, 1931), pp. 199–208.

10. The formulation of these objectives and the work on the measurement has largely been done by W.M. Barrows, D.F. Miller, and J.W. Price of the Department of Zoölogy.

11. The construction of the test was suggested by H.C. Sampson of the Department of Botany and was developed through his help and the co-operation of W.M. Barrows of the Department of Zoölogy.

12. Zoölogy is used for illustration because the plan described is being followed in constructing high-school and college tests in botany, chemistry, and zoölogy. This is a part of the work of the Co-operative Test Service of the American Council on Education. Teachers interested in trying out tentative forms of tests in these fields are urged to write to the author.

13. These objectives are discussed at greater length in the following article: Tyler, Ralph W. "Measuring the Ability to Infer." *Educational Research Bulletin*, IX (November 19, 1930), pp. 475–80.

II APPRAISING AND RECORDING STUDENT PROGRESS: THE EIGHT-YEAR STUDY

1 OVERVIEW

Between 1934 and 1942 Ralph Tyler was the Director of Evaluation of the famous Eight-Year Study. *Appraising and Recording Student Progress* is basically a report of the work of the evaluation committee of the Eight-Year Study. It is not an evaluation of the thirty participating schools, since Tyler believed that the responsibility for evaluating a school's program rested with the staff and clientele of the school. He saw the work of his group as that of facilitating the staff in formulating educational objectives and then assisting them in developing assessment techniques to measure them. The reader will notice when reading the excerpts from *Appraising and Recording Student Progress* the influence of his earlier ideas contained in Part I.

Appraising and Recording Student Progress presented us with a number of difficult decisions on what to include and exclude. We decided to make most of our selections from the appraising section of the book. It is this section that contains the best examples of Tyler's work that was later to influence curriculum development, and the teaching of tests and measurements courses. It is the ideas about objectives and evaluation contained in the appraising section of the book that, after Sputnik in 1958, greatly influenced many curriculum development projects in math and science, and later the evaluation of innovative programs funded under Lyndon Johnson's Great Society legislation. It is this section of *Appraising and Recording Student Progress* that had a tremendous influence on the development of different models of program evaluation that began in the 1960s.

The section that dealt with recording student progress is historically interesting. It describes the need to record data at the individual level, the class level, and the school and district levels. It describes ways to record outcomes and report them to students, parents, teachers, colleges, and the general public. Therefore, to give the reader a flavor for this section of the book, we included a short section on reporting results to parents. Most of what follows Part II is from the appraising portion of *Appraising and Recording Student Progress*.

Key Points

- The Eight-Year Study became a training ground for a staff that was comprised of many of the later leaders in testing and evaluation.
- Evaluation is a process by which the values of an enterprise are ascertained, an appraisal of the degree to which the objectives of an institution are being realized. It is an integral part of the educational process.
- Different audiences need different types of information.
- Then, as now, existing commercially available standardized tests did not lend themselves to an appraisal of the unique objectives of a school. Assessment devices must in large part be tailored to fit the desired outcomes of instruction.
- A comprehensive program of evaluation should serve a broad range of purposes: (1) grading students; (2) grouping students; (3) reporting to parents on their student attainment; (4) reporting to school boards on the attainments of students, schools, and classrooms; (5) validating the hypotheses under which an institution operates; (6) guiding students; (7) reinforcing teachers; and (8) providing feedback for public relations.
- In thinking about evaluation, schools should operate under the following eight assumptions: (1) education seeks to change behaviors of students in desirable ways; (2) these behavior changes constitute the educational objectives of a school; (3) evaluation should assess the degree to which these objectives are being obtained; (4) human behavior is too complex to be measured by a single instrument along a single dimension; (5) evaluation must consider how behavior patterns of students are organized; (6) paper-and-pencil examinations are not sufficient to appraise all of the desired outcomes of instruction; (7) the way schools measure outcomes influences

teaching and learning; and (8) the responsibility for evaluation belongs to the school's staff and clientele.

- The general approach to evaluation contains the following seven steps: (1) formulating objectives; (2) classifying the objectives; (3) refining and defining objectives in behavioral terms; (4) identifying situations for assessment of objectives; (5) selecting and trying out promising ways to assess objectives; (6) improving appraisal methods; and (7) interpreting results.
- Evaluation is an ongoing, cyclical process that should lead to a refinement of objectives, learning experiences, and outcomes.
- Teachers and other school personnel need to be oriented and trained in the conduct of evaluations and in the interpretation and use of results. Evaluative feedback provides direction for continued inservice training.
- Selecting educational objectives requires carefully considering a number of factors related to the learners, the school, and the society.
- Objectives that emerged from the Eight-Year Study were classified under the following categories: (1) effective methods of thinking; (2) work habits and study skills; (3) social attitudes; (4) interests; (5) appreciation of music, art, and literature; (6) social sensitivity; (7) personal-social adjustment; (8) information; (9) physical health; and (10) consistent philosophy of life.
- Evaluation roles should be differentiated as follows:

Formulating objectives	— School staff
Classifying objectives	— Evaluation staff
Refinement of objectives	— School and evaluation staffs
Development of assessment devices	— Evaluation staff

- Because the thirty schools in the Eight-Year Study differed so widely from one another, a pervasive objective of the evaluation staff was to develop content-free measures of objectives related to outcomes such as critical thinking, interpreting data, applying principles in new situations, and using proofs in arguments. These measures could be used to assess outcomes related to these higher order thinking skills irrespective of the particular learning experiences used by individuals schools.
- A single traditional number-right score on a test can hide more than it shows. Ways of scoring tests along multidimensions became an important goal of the evaluation staff. Multidimensional scoring could give teachers more useful information about individual and class performance.

2 APPRAISING AND RECORDING STUDENT PROGRESS

This book was originally published by Harper & Brothers as volume III in The Adventure in American Education Series, Written by Eugene R. Smith, Ralph W. Tyler, and the Evaluation Staff. As Chairman of the Series, Eugene R. Smith wrote the Preface.

Preface

When the Directing Committee of the Commission on the Relation of School and College appointed a Committee on Records and Reports, it assigned to this new committee the general task of recommending methods of obtaining and recording information about the pupils. The immediate reason for this assignment was the need of supplying to the colleges data upon which they could decide about the acceptability of candidates who did not present the traditional pattern of subjects for entrance or had not submitted the usual entrance information in terms of marks and examinations.

A second important reason was the desire of schools for help in their guidance programs.

The instructions given this committee specified as its first task the devising of methods of obtaining and recording information about personality. It was necessary, however, from the beginning to try to find ways of testing that would neither determine nor depend upon the content of the courses given in the various schools, yet would be reasonably comparable and objective measures of knowledge and power.

The committee met with some frequency for periods of two or three days at a time. It soon announced to the schools a list of comparable tests that seemed to have value for estimating the degree of mastery attained by pupils in various subject fields. Many of the schools tried these tests, and some added others from quite a wide selection of those of an objective type. It became apparent, however, that even these tests were too much influenced by the content studied to be acceptable to all of the schools. The reason was that the schools were anxious to use the utmost flexibility in meeting the needs of their pupils even when that meant departing markedly from traditional subjects or their content. A period of experimentation followed, during which other work was accomplished. When it was recognized that no matter how valuable existing methods and material for testing might be for various purposes, nevertheless they did not fit the need of the cooperating schools for testing that would measure the *power attained, irrespective of the way in which it had been reached*, the Directing Committee obtained further funds and enlarged the branch responsible for testing, recording, and reporting.

The final organization of this department was headed by an over-all committee called the Committee on Evaluation and Recording. It had responsibility for determining policies, considering reports on work accomplished and giving direction about the next steps to be undertaken. Dr. Ralph W. Tyler was engaged as Research Director for this part of the Eight-Year Study, and was given as his particular assignment charge of the work on evaluation. This assignment included direction of the follow-up study of graduates of the cooperating schools who were attending college, as well as of the study of objectives and of the testing and other evaluation carried on in the schools. Under Dr. Tyler's supervision the Evaluation Staff and a large number of committees assisted in this part of the work. A detailed account is given in Part I of this volume.

Commission on the Relation of School and College

EVALUATION STAFF

Ralph W. Tyler, Research Director

Associate Director	*Associates*	
Oscar K. Buros, 1934–35	Bruno Bettelheim	Louis M. Heil
Louis E. Raths, 1935–38	Paul B. Diederich	George Sheviakov
Maurice L. Hartung, 1938–42	Wilfred Eberhart	Hilda Taba
	Harold Trimble	

Assistants

Herbert J. Abraham	Paul R. Grim	Carleton C. Jones
Dwight L. Arnold	Chester William Harris	W. Harold Lauritsen
Jean Friedberg Block	John H. Herrick	Christine McGuire
Charles L. Boye	Clark W. Horton	Harold G. McMullen
Fred P. Frutchey	Walter Howe	Donald H. McNassor

Secretaries: Cecelia K. Wasserstrom, Kay D. Watson

CURRICULUM ASSOCIATES

H. H. Giles   S. P. McCutchen

A. N. Zechiel

The following served as special curriculum consultants at various times:

Harold B. Alberty	Henry Harap
Paul B. Diederich	Walter V. Kaulfers

John A. Lester

COLLEGE FOLLOW-UP STAFF

John L. Bergstresser	Neal E. Drought
Dean Chamberlin	William E. Scott
Enid Straw Chamberlin	Harold Threlkeld

EDITORIAL COMMITTEE

Harold B. Alberty	Burton P. Fowler
C. L. Cushman	Max McConn

Thomas C. Pollock

THE PARTICIPATING SCHOOLS

School	Head*
Altoona Senior High School, Altoona, Pa.	(Levi Gilbert) Joseph N. Maddocks
Baldwin School, Bryn Mawr, Pa.	(Miss Elizabeth Johnson) Miss Rosamond Cross
Beaver Country Day School, Chestnut Hill, Mass.	Eugene R. Smith
Bronxville High School, Bronxville, N. Y.	Miss Edith M. Penney
Cheltenham Township High School, Elkins Park, Pa.	I. R. Kraybill
Dalton Schools, New York, N. Y.	Miss Helen Parkhurst
Denver Senior and Junior High Schools, Denver, Colo.	(Charles Greene) (G. L. Cushman) John J. Cory
Des Moines Senior and Junior High Schools, Des Moines, Iowa	(**R. C. Cook) J. E. Stonecipher
Eagle Rock High School, Los Angeles, Cal.	Miss Helen Babson
Fieldston School, New York, N. Y.	(Herbert W. Smith) (Derwood Baker) Luther Tate
Francis W. Parker School, Chicago, Ill.	(Miss Flora Cooke) (Raymond Osborne) Herbert W. Smith
Friends' Central School, Overbrook, Pa.	Barclay L. Jones
George School, George School, Pa.	George A. Walton
Germantown Friends School, Germantown, Pa.	(Stanley R. Yarnall) Burton P. Fowler
Horace Mann School, New York, N. Y.	(Rollo G. Reynolds) Will French
John Burroughs School, Clayton, Mo.	(Wilford M. Aikin) Leonard D. Haertter
Lincoln School of Teachers College, New York, N. Y.	(**Jesse H. Newlon) (Lester Dix) Will French
Milton Academy, Milton, Mass.	W. L. W. Field
New Trier Township High School, Winnetka, Ill.	Matthew P. Gaffney
North Shore Country Day School, Winnetka, Ill.	Perry Dunlap Smith
Radnor High School, Wayne, Pa.	Sydney V. Rowland, T. Bayard Beatty

*Many changes in administration occurred in the schools during the period of the Study. Such cases are indicated by names in parentheses given in chronological order of service.

**Deceased.

Purposes and Procedures of the Evaluation Staff*

How the Evaluation Staff Came into Existence

The plan of the Eight-Year Study, as Dr. Smith explained in the Preface, placed upon the cooperating schools the responsibility for reporting in some detail the characteristics and achievements of students who were recommended for admission to college. Furthermore, the Directing Committee of the Study expected the schools not only to record the steps taken to develop new educational programs, but also to appraise the effectiveness of these programs, so that other schools might benefit from their experience.

After the first year it became clear that these tasks were too great for them both to be assumed by the Committee on Records and Reports. The magnitude of the work had become evident when the Committee on Records and Reports reviewed the available tests, examinations, and other devices for appraising student achievement. Most of the achievement tests then on the market measured only the amount of information which students remembered, or some of the more specific subject skills like those in algebra and the foreign languages. The new courses developed in the Thirty Schools attempted to help students achieve several additional qualities, such as more effective study skills, more careful ways of thinking, a wider range of significant interests, social rather than selfish attitudes. Hence, the available achievement tests did not provide measures of many of the more important achievements anticipated from these new courses. Furthermore, the content of most significance in the new courses was frequently different from that which had been included before. Hence, the available tests of information did not really measure the information which students would be obtaining in the new courses. A comprehensive appraisal of the new educational programs could not be carried on unless new means of evaluating achievement were developed.

The Directing Committee obtained a preliminary subsidy from the General Education Board to explore the possibility of constructing devices which could be used in appraising the outcomes of the new work. During the autumn of 1934, the Thirty Schools were visited, inter-school committees were formed, and preliminary steps taken to construct needed instruments of evaluation. By the winter of 1935 it seemed apparent that new instruments could be devised and that a more comprehensive program of

---

*This was originally chapter 1 in *Appraising and Recording Student Progress.*

appraisal could be conducted. Hence, a generous subsidy for the services of an evaluation staff[1] was provided by the General Education Board, and the work was continued until the close of the Study. The Evaluation Staff was primarily concerned with developing means by which the achievement of the students in the schools could be appraised, and the strengths and weaknesses of the school programs could be identified.…

Significance of the Evaluation Project

The term "evaluation" was used to describe the staff and the project rather than the term "measurement," "test," or "examination" because the term "evaluation" implies a process by which the values of an enterprise are ascertained. To help provide means by which the Thirty Schools could ascertain the values of their new programs was the basic purpose of the evaluation project. The project has significance not only for the Thirty Schools but for schools and colleges generally. Adequate appraisal of the educational program of a school or college is rarely made. Yet an appraisal of an educational institution is fundamentally only the process by which we find out how far the objectives of the institution are being realized. This seems a simple and straightforward task, and the efforts at evaluation of certain social institutions are not very complex. For example, in the case of a retail business enterprise the most commonly recognized objectives are two: namely, the distribution of large quantities of goods and the making of profit from the sale of these goods. The methods for determining the quantities of goods sold and the profits are tangible and not very difficult to apply. Hence, the problem of evaluation is not usually considered a perplexing one, and although the business enterprise devotes a portion of its time and energy to appropriate accounting procedures, so as to make a periodical evaluation of its activities, we do not find a high degree of uncertainty about the methods of evaluation.

In education, however, the problem of evaluation is more complex for several reasons. In the first place, since schools generally have not agreed upon their fundamental objectives, there is doubt as to what values schools expect to attain and therefore what results to look for in the process of evaluation. Even when the objectives of a school are agreed upon and stated, they are frequently vague and require clarification in order to be understood. Furthermore, the methods of obtaining evidence about the attainment of some of these educational objectives are more difficult and less direct processes than those used in appraising a business. It is easy to see how to measure the amount of profit in a retail store; it is not so easy to devise ways for measuring the educational changes taking place in students in the school. Finally, the task of summarizing and interpreting the results of an evaluation of the school is complicated. Summaries of educational evaluation are needed for several different groups, that is, for students, teachers, administrators, parents, and patrons. Each of these groups may need somewhat different information, or at least it will be necessary to present the data in different terms. It is easy to see, then, that educational evaluation requires more intensive study than evaluation of many other institutions. The work of the Evaluation Staff should help to demonstrate procedures by which the process of evaluation may be carried on and to provide instruments and devices that may be used in evaluation or that may suggest ideas for the construction of other instruments.

Major Purposes of Evaluation

In perceiving the appropriate place of evaluation in modern education, consideration must be given to the purposes which a program of evaluation may serve. At present the purposes most commonly emphasized in schools and colleges are the grading of students, their grouping and promotion, reports to parents, and financial reports to the board of education or to the board of trustees. A comprehensive program of evaluation should serve a broader range of purposes than these.

One important purpose of evaluation is to make a periodic check on the effectiveness of the educational institution, and thus to indicate the points at which improvements in the program are necessary. In a business enterprise the monthly balance sheet serves to identify those departments in which profits have been low and those products which have not sold well. This serves as a stimulus to a re-examination and a revision of practices in the retail establishment. In a similar fashion, a periodic evaluation of the school or college, if comprehensively undertaken, should reveal points of strength which ought to be continued and points where practices need modification. This is helpful to all schools, not just to schools which are experimenting.

A very important purpose of evaluation which is frequently not recognized is to validate the hypotheses upon which the educational institution operates. A school, whether called "traditional" or "progressive," organizes its curriculum on the basis of a plan which seems to the staff to be satisfactory, but in reality not enough is yet known about curriculum construction to be sure that a given plan will work satisfactorily in a particular community. On that account, the curriculum of every school is based upon hypotheses, that is, the best judgments the staff can make on the basis of available information. In some cases these hypotheses are not valid, and the educational institution may continue for years utilizing a poorly organized curriculum because no careful evaluation has been made to check the validity of its hypotheses. For example, many high schools and colleges have constructed the curriculum on the hypothesis that students would develop writing habits and skills appropriate to all their needs if this responsibility were left entirely to the English classes. Careful appraisal has shown that this hypothesis is rarely, if ever, valid. Similarly, in a program of guidance the effort to care for personal and social maladjustments among students in a large school is sometimes based on the hypothesis that the provision of a well-trained guidance officer for the school will eliminate maladjustments. Systematic evaluation has generally shown that one officer has little effect unless a great deal of supplementary effort is devoted to educating teachers in child development and to revising the curriculum at those points where it promotes maladjustments. In the same way, many of our administrative policies and practices are based upon judgments which in a particular case may not be sound. Every educational institution has the responsibility of testing the major hypotheses upon which it operates and of adding to the fund of tested principles upon which schools may better operate in the future.

A third important purpose of evaluation is to provide information basic to effective guidance of individual students. Only as we appraise the student's achievement and as we get a comprehensive description of his growth and development are we in a position to give him sound guidance. This implies evaluation sufficiently comprehensive to appraise all significant aspects of the student's accomplishments. Merely the judgment that he is doing average work in a particular course is not enough. We need to find out more accurately where he is progressing and where he is having difficulties.

A fourth purpose of evaluation is to provide a certain psychological security to the school staff, to the students, and to the parents. The responsibilities of an educational institution are broad and involve aspects which seem quite intangible to the casual observer. Frequently the staff becomes a bit worried and is in doubt as to whether it is really accomplishing its major objectives. This uncertainty may be a good thing if it leads to a careful appraisal and constructive measures for improvement of the program; but without systematic evaluation the tendency is for the staff to become less secure and sometimes to retreat to activities which give tangible results although they may be less important. Often we seek security through emphasizing procedures which are extraneous and sometimes harmful to the best educational work of the school. Thus, high school teachers may devote an undue amount of energy to coaching for scholarship tests or college entrance examinations because the success of students on these examinations serves as a tangible evidence that something has been accomplished. However, since these examinations may be appropriate for only a portion of the high school student body, concentration of attention upon them may actually hinder the total educational program of the high school. For such teachers a comprehensive evaluation which gives a careful check on all aspects of the program would provide the kind of security that is necessary for their continued growth and self-confidence. This need is particularly acute in the case of teachers who are developing and conducting a new educational program. The uncertainty of their pioneering efforts breeds insecurity. They view with dismay or resentment efforts to appraise their work in terms of devices appropriate only to the older, previously established curriculum. They recognize that the effectiveness of the new work can be fairly appraised only in terms of its objectives, which in certain respects differ from the purposes of the older program. Students and parents are also subject to this feeling of insecurity and in many cases desire some kind of tangible evidence that the educational program is effective. If this is not provided by a comprehensive plan of evaluation, then students and parents are likely to turn to tangible but extraneous factors for their security.

A fifth purpose of evaluation which should be emphasized is to provide a sound basis for public relations. No factor is as important in establishing constructive and cooperative relations with the community as an understanding on the part of the community of the effectiveness of its educational institutions. A careful and comprehensive evaluation should provide evidence that can be widely publicized and used to inform the community about the value of the school or college program. Many of the criticisms expressed by patrons and parents can be met and turned to constructive cooperation if concrete evidence is available regarding the accomplishments of the school.

Evaluation can contribute to these five purposes. It can provide a periodic check which gives direction to the continued improvement of the program of the school; it can help to validate some of the important hypotheses upon which the program operates; it can furnish data about individual students essential to wise guidance; it can give a more satisfactory foundation for the psychological security of the staff, of parents, and of students; and it can supply a sound basis for public relations. These purposes were basic to the Thirty Schools but they are also important to all schools. For these purposes to be achieved, however, they must be kept continually in mind in planning and in developing the program of evaluation. The Evaluation Staff realized that the decision as to what is to be evaluated, the techniques for appraisal, and the summary and interpretation of results should all be worked out in terms of these important purposes.

Basic Assumptions

In developing the program, the Evaluation Staff accepted certain basic assumptions. Eight of them were of particular importance. In the first place, it was assumed that education is a process which seeks to change the behavior paterns of human beings. It is obvious that we expect students to change in some respects as they go through an educational program. An educated man is different from one who has no education, and presumably this difference is due to the educational experience. It is also generally recognized that these changes brought about by education are modifications in the ways in which the educated man reacts, that is, changes in his ways of behaving. Generally, as a result of education we expect students to recall and to use ideas which they did not have before, to develop various skills, as in reading and writing, which they did not previously possess, to improve their ways of thinking, to modify their reactions to esthetic experiences as in the arts, and so on. It seems safe to say on the basis of our present conception of learning, that education, when it is effective, changes the behavior patterns of human beings.

A second basic assumption was that the kinds of changes in behavior patterns in human beings which the school seeks to bring about are its educational objectives. The fundamental purpose of an education is to effect changes in the behavior of the student, that is, in the way he thinks, and feels, and acts. The aims of any educational program cannot well be stated in terms of the content of the program or in terms of the methods and procedures followed by the teachers, for these are only means to other ends. Basically, the goals of education represent these changes in human beings which we hope to bring about through education. The kinds of ideas which we expect students to get and to use, the kinds of skills which we hope they will develop, the techniques of thinking which we hope they will acquire, the ways in which we hope they will learn to react to esthetic experiences — these are illustrations of educational objectives.

A third basic assumption was referred to at the opening of the chapter. An educational program is appraised by finding out how far the objectives of the program are actually being realized. Since the program seeks to bring about certain changes in the behavior of students, and since these are the fundamental educational objectives, then it follows that an evaluation of the educational program is a process for finding out to what degree these changes in the students are actually taking place.

The fourth basic assumption was that human behavior is ordinarily so complex that it cannot be adequately described or measured by a single term or a single dimension. Several aspects or dimensions are usually necessary to describe or measure a particular phase of human behavior. Hence, we did not conceive that a single score, a single category, or a single grade would serve to summarize the evaluation of any phase of the student's achievement. Rather, it was anticipated that multiple scores, categories, or descriptions would need to be developed.

The fifth assumption was a companion to the fourth. It was assumed that the way in which the student organizes his behavior patterns is an important aspect to be appraised. There is always the danger that the identification of these various types of objectives will result in their treatment as isolated bits of behavior. Thus, the recognition that an educational program seeks to change the student's information, skills, ways of thinking, attitudes, and interests, may result in an evaluation program which appraises the development of each of these aspects of behavior separately, and makes no effort to relate them. We must not forget that the human being reacts in a fairly unified fashion; hence, in any given situation information is not usually separated from skills, from ways of thinking, or from attitudes, interests, and appreciations. For example, a student who encounters an important social-civic problem is expected to draw upon his information, to use such skill as he has in locating additional facts, to think through the problem critically, to make choices of courses of action in terms of fundamental values and attitudes, and to be continually interested in better solutions to such problems. This clearly involves the relationship of various behavior patterns and their better integration. The way the student grows in his ability to relate his various reactions is an important aspect of his development and an important part of any evaluation of his educational achievement.

A sixth basic assumption was that the methods of evaluation are not limited to the giving of paper-and-pencil tests; any device which provides valid evidence regarding the progress of students toward educational objectives is appropriate. As a matter of practice, most programs of appraisal have been limited to written examinations or paper-and-pencil tests of some type. Perhaps this has been due to the long tradition associated with written examinations or perhaps to the greater ease with which written examinations may be given and the results summarized. However, a consideration of the kinds of objectives formulated for general education makes clear that written examinations are not likely to provide an adequate appraisal for all of these objectives. A written test may be a valid measure of information recalled and ideas remembered. In many cases, too, the student's skill in writing and in mathematics may be shown by written tests, and it is also true that various techniques of thinking may be evidenced through more novel types of written test materials. On the other hand, evidence regarding the improvement of health practices, personal-social adjustment, interests, and attitudes may require a much wider repertoire of appraisal techniques. This assumption emphasizes the wider range of techniques which may be used in evaluation, such as observational records, anecdotal records, questionnaires, interviews, check lists, records of activities, products made, and the like. The selection of evaluation techniques should be made in terms of the appropriateness of these techniques for the kind of behavior to be appraised.

A seventh basic assumption was that the nature of the appraisal influences teaching and learning. If students are periodically examined on certain content, the tendency will be for them to concentrate their study on this material, even though this content is given little or no emphasis in the course of study. Teachers, too, are frequently influenced by their conception of the achievement tests used. If these tests are thought to emphasize certain points, these points will be emphasized in teaching even though they are not included in the plan of the course. This influence of appraisal upon teaching and learning led the Evaluation Staff to try to develop evaluation instruments and methods in harmony with the new curricula and, as far as possible, of a non-restrictive nature. That is, major attention was given to appraisal devices appropriate to a wide range of curriculum content and to varied organizations of courses. Much less effort was devoted to the development of subject-matter tests since these assumed certain common informational material in the curriculum.

The eighth basic assumption was that the responsibility for evaluating the school program belonged to the staff and clientele of the school. It was not the duty of the Evaluation Staff to appraise the school but rather to help develop the means of appraisal and the methods of interpretation. Hence, this volume does not contain an appraisal of the work of the Thirty Schools or the results obtained by the use of the evaluation instruments in the schools. This volume is a report of the development of techniques for evaluation.

The evaluation program utilized other assumptions but these eight were of particular importance because they guided the general procedure by which the evaluation program was developed. They showed the necessity for basing an evaluation program upon educational objectives, and they indicated that educational objectives for purposes of evaluation must be stated in terms of changes in behavior of students; they emphasized the multiple aspects of behavior and the importance of the relation of these various aspects of bahavior rather than treatment of them in isolation; and they made clear the possibility of a wide range of evaluation techniques.

General Procedures in Developing the Evaluation Program

The general procedure followed in developing the evaluation program involved seven major steps. Since the program was a cooperative one, including both the Schools and the Evaluation Staff, it should be clear that although the report was prepared by the staff, the work was done by a large number of persons. No one of the instruments developed is the product of a single author. All have required the efforts of various members of the school staffs and the Evaluation Staff.

1. Formulating Objectives. As the first step, each school faculty was asked to formulate a statement of its educational objectives. Since the schools were in the process of curriculum revision, several of them had already taken this step. This is not just an evaluation activity, for it is usually considered one of the important steps in curriculum construction. It is not necessary here to point out that the selection of the educational objectives of a school and their validation require studies of several sorts. Valid educational objectives are not arrived at as a compromise among the various whims or preferences of individual faculty members but are reached on the basis of considered judgment utilizing evidence regarding the demands of society, the characteristics of students, the potential contributions which various fields of learning may make, the social and educational philosophy of the school or college, and what we know from the psychology of learning as to the attainability of various types of objectives. Hence, many of the schools spent a great deal of time on this step and arranged to re-examine their objectives periodically.

2. Classification of Objectives. As a second step, these statements of objectives from the Thirty Schools were combined into one comprehensive list and classified into major types. Before classification, the objectives were of various levels of generality and specificity and too numerous for practicable treatment. Furthermore, it was anticipated that the classification would be useful in guiding further curriculum development, because if properly made it would suggest types of learning experiences likely to be useful in helping to attain the objectives. A classification is of particular importance for evaluation because the types of objectives indicate the kinds of evaluation techniques essential to an adequate appraisal. The problem of classification is illustrated by the following partial list of objectives formulated by one school:

1. Acquiring information about various important aspects of nutrition
2. Becoming familiar with dependable sources of information relating to nutrition
3. Developing the ability to deal effectively with nutrition problems arising in later life
4. Acquiring information about major natural resources
5. Becoming familiar with sources of information regarding natural resources
6. Acquiring the ability to utilize and to interpret maps
7. Developing attitudes favoring conservation and better utilization of natural resources
8. Becoming familiar with a range of types of literature
9. Acquiring facility in interpreting literary materials
10. Developing broad and mature reading interests
11. Developing appreciation of literature
12. Acquiring information about important aspects of our scientific world
13. Developing understanding of some of the basic scientific concepts which help to interpret the world of science
14. Improving ability to draw reasonable generalizations from scientific data
15. Improving ability to apply principles of science to problems arising in daily life
16. Developing better personal-social adjustment
17. Constructing a consistent philosophy of life

These sample statements of objectives are of different levels of specificity and might well be grouped together under a smaller number of major headings. Thus, for purposes of evaluation, the several objectives having to do with the acquisition of information in various fields could be classified under one heading, since the methods of appraising the acquisition of information are somewhat similar in the various fields. Similarly, various objectives having to do with techniques of thinking, such as drawing reasonable inferences from data and the application of principles to new problems, could be classified under the general heading of development of effective methods of thinking, because the means of appraisal for these objectives are somewhat similar. Furthermore, the methods of instruction appropriate for these techniques of thinking have similarities even though the content differs widely. Eventually, the following classification was used in general by the Staff:

Major Types of Objectives

1. The development of effective methods of thinking
2. The cultivation of useful work habits and study skills
3. The inculcation of social attitudes
4. The acquisition of a wide range of significant interests
5. The development of increased appreciation of music, art, literature, and other esthetic experiences
6. The development of social sensitivity
7. The development of better personal-social adjustment
8. The acquisition of important information
9. The development of physical health
10. The development of a consistent philosophy of life

This classification is not ideal but it served a useful purpose by focusing attention upon ten areas in which evaluation instruments were needed.[2] It also helped to suggest emphases important in the curricular development of the Eight-Year Study....

3. Defining Objectives in Terms of Behavior. The third step was to define each of these types of objectives in terms of behaviors. This step is always necessary because in any list some objectives are stated in terms so vague and nebulous that the kind of behavior they imply is not clear. Thus, a type of objective such as the development of effective methods of thinking may mean different things to different people. Only as "effective methods of thinking" is defined in terms of the range of reactions expected of students can we be sure what is to be evaluated under this classification. In similar fashion, such a classification as "useful work habits and study skills" needs to be defined by listing the work habits the student is expected to develop and the study skills which he may be expected to acquire.

In defining each of these classes of objectives, committees were formed composed of representatives from the Schools and from the Evaluation Staff. Usually, a committee was formed for each major type of objective. Since each committee included teachers from schools that had emphasized this type of objective, it was possible to clarify the meaning of the objective not in terms of a dictionary definition but rather in terms of descriptions of behavior teachers had in mind when this objective was emphasized. The committee procedure in defining an objective was to shuttle back and forth between general and specific objectives, the general helping to give wider implication to the specific, and the specific helping to clarify the general.

The resulting definitions will be found in subsequent chapters; however, a brief illustration may be appropriate here. The committee on the evaluation of effective methods of thinking identified various kinds of behavior which the Schools were seeking to develop as aspects of effective thinking. Three types of behavior patterns were considered important by all the Schools. These were: (1) the ability to formulate reasonable generalizations from specific data; (2) the ability to apply principles to new situations; and (3) the ability to evaluate material purporting to be argument, that is, to judge the logic of the argument. When the committee proceeded to define the kinds of data which they expected students to use in drawing generalizations, the principles which they expected students to be able to apply, and the kinds of situations in which they expected students to apply such principles, and when they had identified the types of arguments which they expected students to appraise critically, a clear enough definition was available to serve as a guide in the further development of an evaluation program for this class of objectives. This process of definition had to be carried through in connection with each of the types of objectives for which an appraisal program was developed.

4. Suggesting Situations in Which the Achievement of Objectives Will Be Shown.   The next problem was for each committee to identify situations in which students could be expected to display these types of behavior so that we could know where to go to obtain evidence regarding this objective. When each objective has been clearly defined, this fourth step is not difficult. For example, one aspect of thinking defined in the third step was the ability to draw reasonable generalizations from specific data. An opportunity to exhibit such behavior would be provided when typical sets of data were presented to students and they were asked to formulate the generalizations which seemed reasonable to them.

Another aspect of thinking defined in the third step was the ability to apply specified principles, such as principles of nutrition, to specified types of problems, such as those relating to diet. Hence, it seemed obvious that at least two kinds of situations would give evidence of such abilities. One would be a situation in which the student was presented with these problems, for example, dietary problems, and asked to work out solutions utilizing appropriate principles of nutrition. Another kind of situation would be one in which the students were given descriptions of certain nutritional conditions together with a statement regarding the diet of the people involved, and the students were asked to explain how these nutritional conditions could have come about, using appropriate nutritional principles in their explanations.

As a third illustration, the definition of objectives identified as one educational goal the ability to locate dependable information relating to specified types of problems. It seemed obvious that a situation which would give students a chance to show this ability would be one in which they were asked to find information relating to these specified problems.

One value of this fourth step was to suggest a much wider range of situations which might be used in evaluation than have commonly been utilized. By the time the fourth step was completed, there were listed a considerable number of types of situations which gave students a chance to indicate the sort of behavior patterns they had developed. These were potential "test situations."

5. Selecting and Trying Promising Evaluation Methods. The fifth step in the evaluation procedure involved the selection and trial of promising methods for obtaining evidence regarding each type of objective. Before attempting to construct new evaluation instruments, each committee examined tests and other instruments already developed to see whether they would serve as satisfactory means for appraising the objective. Only limited test bibliographies were then available.[3] In addition to examining bibliographies, the committees obtained copies of those instruments which seemed to have some relation to their objectives. In examining an instrument the committee members tried to judge whether the student taking the test could be expected to carry out the kind of behavior indicated in the committee's definition of this objective. Then, too, the situations used in the instruments were compared with those suggested in the fourth step as to their likelihood of evoking the behavior to be measured. The committees recognized that they might be misled by undue optimism in the name or the description of the test, and sought to guard against it. Even though a test was called a general culture test, or a world history test, or a general mathematics test, it was generally found that it measured only one or two of the objectives which teachers of these fields considered important. In order to estimate what the test did measure, it was necessary to examine the test situations to judge what kind of reaction must be made by the student in seeking to answer the questions. It also proved useful to examine any evidence reported which helped to indicate the kind of behavior the test was actually measuring.

At this point most of the committees found that no tests were available to measure certain major aspects of the important objectives. In such cases, it was necessary to construct additional new instruments in order to make a really comprehensive appraisal of the educational program in the Thirty Schools. The nature of the instruments to be built varied with the types of objectives for which no available instruments were found. Every commit-tee, however, found it helpful in constructing these instruments to set up some of the situations suggested in step four and actually to try them out with students to see how far they could be used as test situations. By the time the fifth step had been carried through, certain available tests were selected and tried out and certain new appraisal instruments were con-structed and given tentative trial.

6. Developing and Improving Appraisal Methods. The sixth major step was to select on the basis of this preliminary trial the more promising ap-praisal methods for further development and improvement. This further development and improvement was largely the responsibility of the Evalua-tion Staff. The committees met from time to time to review the work of the Staff, and many teachers were asked to criticize and make suggestions for improvement. Obviously, however, the detailed work had to be done by the Staff.

The basis for selecting devices for further development included the degree to which the appraisal method was found to give results consistent with other evidences regarding the student's attainment of this objective and the extent to which the appraisal method could be practicably used under the conditions prevailing in the Schools. The refinement and improve-ment consisted in working out directions which were unambiguous, modify-ing exercises which were found not to give discriminating results, eliminating exercises which were found to be almost exact duplicates of other exercises in terms of the type of reaction elicited from the student, developing practicable and easily interpretable records of the student's behavior, and making other revisions which gave more clear-cut measures, which provided a more representative and adequate sample of the student's reaction, and which improved the ease with which the instrument could be used.

An important problem in the refinement and improvement of an evalua-tion instrument proved to be the determination of the aspects of student behavior to be summarized and the decision regarding the units or terms in which each aspect was to be summarized. For example, consider a test con-structed to appraise the ability of students to formulate reasonable generalizations from data new to them. An obvious type of test situation would be one in which sets of data new to the student were presented to him and he was asked to examine the data and to formulate generalizations which seemed reasonable to him. When we approach the question of sum-marizing his behavior in some form which provides a measurement or appraisal, we are faced with the problem of identifying aspects, that is, dimensions of the behavior to measure, and of deciding upon units of measurement to use. One aspect which is important in judging the value of the generalization formulated is its relevance. Generalizations which have no relevance to the data are obviously not satisfactory. If this aspect is to be measured, there are several possible units of measurement which might be used. For example, we could set up a subjective scale for degree of relevance and have judges apply this scale to each generalization, rating it at some point on this scale. Another unit of measurement could be used by classifying each generalization as relevant to the data or irrelevant to the data, thus measuring the relevance in terms of the number of the student's generalizations which are classified as relevant. On the other hand, since students may differ markedly in the total number of generalizations formulated, a better unit of measure for the degree of relevance might be the per cent of the student's generalizations which are classified as relevant.

A second aspect which has some importance in appraising generalizations of this type would be the degree to which relevant generalizations are carefully formulated and involve no overgeneralizations, that is, generalizations more sweeping than the data would justify. If this aspect were chosen as part of the appraisal, several possible units could be used in the measurement. One possible unit might be the judgment of the reader of the paper as to the degree to which each generalization was carefully or incautiously formulated. This kind of unit involves a considerable degree of subjective judgment so that many might prefer the simple categorization of each relevant generalization as either going beyond the data or not going beyond the data. In this case, a unit of measurement might be the per cent of relevant generalizations not going beyond the data. Perhaps these illustrations are sufficient to show that it is always necessary in the development of new evaluation instruments or in the use of those which have been developed by others to decide on the aspects of the behavior to be described or measured and the terms or units which will be used in describing or measuring this behavior.

7. Interpreting Results. The seventh and final step in the procedure of evaluation was to devise means for interpreting and using the results of the various instruments of evaluation. The previous steps resulted in the selection or the development of a range of procedures which could be used periodically in appraising the degree to which students were acquiring the objectives considered important in a given school. These instruments provided a series of scores and descriptions which served to measure various aspects of the behavior patterns of the students. As these instruments were used, a great number of scores or verbal summaries became available at each appraisal period. Each of these scores or verbal summaries measured an aspect of behavior considered important and represented a phase of the objectives of the school. The Staff then conducted comparability studies for certain of the instruments so that the scores or verbal summaries could be compared with scores or verbal summaries previously obtained; by this comparison some estimate of the degree of change or growth of students could be made. However, the meaning of these scores became fuller through various additional studies.

One type of study involved the identification of scores typically made by students in similar classes, in similar institutions, or with other similar characteristics. Another helpful study involved a summary and analysis of the typical growth or changes made in these scores from year to year. A third type involved studies of the interrelationship of several scores to identify patterns. These patterns are not only useful when obtained among several scores dealing with the behavior relating to one objective but are also useful in seeing more clearly the relation among the objectives. It was pointed out in the introductory section of this chapter that human behavior is to a large degree unified and that efforts to analyze behavior into different types of objectives are useful but may do some harm if the essential interrelationships of various aspects of behavior are forgotten. It was found important in this seventh step to examine the progress students were making toward each of the several objectives in order to get more clearly the pattern of development of each student and of the group as a whole and also to obtain hypotheses helpful in explaining the types of development taking place. Thus, for example, the evaluation results in one school showed that students were making marked progress in the acquisition of specific information and were also shifting markedly in their attitudes toward specific social issues, but at the same time they showed a high degree of inconsistency among their various social attitudes, and were making little progress in applying the facts and principles learned. These results suggested the hypothesis for further study that the students were being exposed to too large an amount of new material and were not being given adequate opportunity to apply these materials, to interpret them thoroughly, and to build them into their previous ideas and beliefs. A test of this hypothesis was made by modifying the course so as to provide for a smaller amount of new material, the introduction of more opportunities for application, and the emphasis upon thoroughness of interpretation and reorganization. This revision in the course resulted in corresponding improvements in the pattern of student achievement. If this revision had not resulted in corresponding improvements, other hypotheses which might explain the results would have been considered. This procedure illustrates a useful means of interpreting the results of several evaluation instruments. It was found that each school needed methods for interpreting and using the results of appraisal so as to improve the educational program and to guide individual students more wisely.

The usefulness of the evaluation program depends very largely upon the degree to which the results are intelligently interpreted and applied by the teachers and school officers. The Evaluation Staff, however, had some responsibility in developing methods for interpreting the results intelligently and in helping teachers and school officers to use them most helpfully. Hence, in addition to making these studies of the instruments, members of the Evaluation Staff visited a number of the Schools and went over the results with the school staffs, suggesting possible interpretations and indicating methods by which these interpretations could be more adequately verified and used. As a result of these preliminary visits, certain methods of interpretation were developed. At this point members of the school staffs who were participating in summer workshops were asked to try these methods of interpretation and to criticize them. Then, for a period of two years, opportunity was provided for at least one representative from each school to spend a considerable period of time in the staff headquarters to gain further familiarity with the evaluation instruments, with their interpretation, and with their use. These school representatives received the training on the assumption that they would have opportunity for giving leadership to the evaluation program in their respective schools. As a result of this experience, the staff believes that a program of testing or evaluation can reach greater fruition when a systematic attempt is made to provide for the training of teachers and school officers in the interpretation and use of evaluation results.

Division of Labor in the Evaluation Program

The previous description of the development of the evaluation program explained that it involved the cooperation of the school personnel and the Evaluation Staff. This does not imply that teachers, school officers, and Evaluation Staff members were all performing the same functions. Although there was some overlapping of functions, there was also a general plan for division of labor. One major division of labor was based on the principle that the school's duty is to evaluate its program, while the technician's function is to help develop means of evaluation. Furthermore, in following through the steps of evaluation, there was some division of duties. Every faculty member and school officer bore some responsibility for the formulation of the objectives of his school. The classification of objectives into major types of behavior was largely a function of the Evaluation Staff because the primary purpose of this classification was to place in the same group those objectives which involved similar types of student reactions, and which might conceivably involve somewhat similar techniques of appraisal.

The further definition and clarification of each class of objectives was the task of an interschool committee composed of teachers, school officers, and members of the Evaluation Staff. The staff members raised questions and suggested directions for discussion which would help to define or clarify the given type of objective, but most of the defining was done by the representatives of the schools which had emphasized this type of objective.

The interschool committee also suggested situations in which the desired behavior might be shown by students. The school representatives then assumed responsibility for trying out these situations to see if they would serve as means of evaluation. The review of these trials, their criticism, and plans for improving the methods of evaluation were carried on by the entire committee. From this point on, the refining of the evaluation instrument and its development for constructive use was largely the task of members of the Evaluation Staff. However, teachers and school officers gave helpful criticisms and suggestions and eventually determined whether an instrument was worth using and could practicably be used in a given school. Finally, the school staff was expected to assume responsibility for obtaining evidence of growth and studying these results.

This plan has wide applicability. It provides a way in which technicians in testing and evaluation may work constructively with teachers and school officers to develop an evaluation program. It avoids the danger on the one hand of having instruments constructed by technicians who are not clear about the curriculum and guidance program of the school, and on the other hand the formulation of an evaluation program by persons who are relatively unfamiliar with methods of describing and measuring human behavior.

Summary

This brief description of the steps followed in developing the evaluation program should have indicated that the process of evaluation was conceived as an integral part of the educational process. It was not thought of as simply the giving of a few ready-made tests and the tabulations of resulting scores. It was believed to be a recurring process involving the formulation of objectives, their clearer definition, plans to study students' reactions in the light of these objectives, and continued efforts to interpret the results of such appraisals in terms which throw helpful light on the educational program and on the individual student. This sort of procedure goes on as a continuing cycle. Studying the results of evaluation often leads to a reformulation and improvement in the conception of the objectives to be obtained. The results of evaluation and any reformulation of objectives will suggest desirable modifications in teaching and in the educational program itself. Modifications in the objectives and in the educational program will result in corresponding modifications in the program of evaluation. So the cycle goes on.

As the evaluation committees carried on their work, it became clear that an evaluation program is also a potent method of continued teacher education. The recurring demand for the formulation and clarification of objectives, the continuing study of the reactions of students in terms of these objectives, and the persistent attempt to relate the results obtained from various sorts of measurement are all means for focusing the interests and efforts of teachers upon the most vital parts of the educational process. The results in several schools indicate that evaluation provides a means for the continued improvement of the educational program for an ever deepening understanding of students with a consequent increase in the effectiveness of the school.

The subsequent chapters describe in more detail the development of evaluation instruments for certain types of objectives. Space does not permit the description of all the evaluation instruments developed. Tests of effective methods of thinking are described because this objective was of concern to all the schools, and few instruments of this sort had previously been developed. On the other hand, although work habits and study skills were emphasized in most of the schools, the description of the instruments developed is not included in this report. The committee identified the following work habits and study skills for which methods of appraisal were needed:

Range of Work Habits and Study Skills

1.1 Effective Use of Study Time
    1.11 Habit of using large blocks of free time effectively
    1.12 Habit of budgeting his time
    1.13 Habit of sustained application rather than working sporadically
    1.14 Habit of meeting promptly study obligations
    1.15 Habit of carrying work through to completion

1.2   Conditions for Effective Study
      1.21   Knowledge of proper working conditions
      1.22   Habit of providing proper working conditions for himself
      1.23   Habit of working independently, that is, working under his own
             direction and initiative

1.3   Effective Planning of Study
      1.31   Habit of planning in advance
      1.32   Habit of choosing problems for investigation which have
             significance for him
      1.33   Ability to define a problem
      1.34   Habit of analyzing a problem so as to sense its implications
      1.35   Ability to determine data needed in an investigation

1.4   Selection of Sources
      1.41   Awareness of kinds of information which may be obtained
             from various sources
      1.42   Awareness of the limitations of the various sources of data
      1.43   Habit of using appropriate sources of information, including
             printed materials, lectures, interviews, observations, and so
             on

1.5   Effective Use of Various Sources of Data
      1.51   Use of library
             1.511   Knowledge of important library tools
             1.512   Ability to use the card catalogue in a library
      1.52   Use of books
             1.521   Ability to use the dictionary
             1.522   Habit of using the helps (such as the Index) in books
             1.523   Ability to use maps, charts and diagrams
      1.53   Reading
             1.531   Ability to read a variety of materials for a variety of
                     purposes using a variety of reading techniques
             1.532   Power to read with discriminatiion
             1.533   Ability to read rapidly
             1.534   Development of a more effective reading vocabulary
      1.54   Ability to get helpful information from other persons
             1.541   Ability to understand material presented orally
             1.542   Facility in the techniques of discussion, particularly
                     discussions which clarify the issues in controversial
                     questions
             1.543   Ability to obtain information from interviews with
                     people

    1.55 Ability to obtain helpful information from field trips and other excursions

    1.56 Ability to obtain information from laboratory experiments

    1.57 Habit of obtaining needed information from observations

1.6 Determining Relevancy of Data

    1.61 Ability to determine whether the data found are relevant to the particular problem

1.7 Recording and Organizing Data

    1.71 Habit of taking useful notes for various purposes from observations, lectures, interviews, and reading

    1.72 Ability to outline material for various purposes

    1.73 Ability to make an effective organization so that the material may be readily recalled, as in notetaking

    1.74 Ability to make an effective organization for written presentation of a topic

    1.75 Ability to make an effective organization for oral presentation of a topic

    1.76 Ability to write effective summaries

1.8 Presentation of the Results of Study

    1.81 Ability to make an effective written presentation of the results of study

        1.811 Habit of differentiating quoted material from summarized material in writing reports

        1.812 Facility in handwriting or in typing

    1.82 Ability to make an effective oral presentation of the results of study

1.9 Habit of Evaluating Each Step in an Investigation

    1.91 Habit of considering the dependability of the data obtained from various sources

    1.92 Habit of considering the relative improtance of the various ideas obtained from various sources

    1.93 Habit of refraining from generalization until data are adequate

    1.94 Habit of testing his own generalizations

    1.95 Habit of criticizing his own investigations

A number of preliminary instruments were constructed for this extensive list of habits and skills. Most of these have not been sufficiently refined to justify inclusion in this volume.

Aspects of Thinking*

Introduction

The responsibility of secondary schools for training citizens who can think clearly has been so long and so frequently acknowledged that it is now almost taken for granted. The educational objectives classifiable under the generic heading "clear thinking" are numerous and varied as to statement, but there can be little doubt concerning their fundamental importance. Although in recent years there has been increasing recognition of other responsibilities and purposes, there has been little accompanying tendency to demote clear thinking to a minor role as an educational objective. It was therefore not surprising to find considerable emphasis upon this objective in the statements of purposes submitted to the Evaluation Staff by the schools participating in the Eight-Year Study.

The fact that an objective has been stated frequently or with emphasis does not insure that its meaning and implications are sufficiently clear to guide effective teaching or to serve as a basis for the evaluation of achievement. In this respect the "clear thinking" objectives as orginally stated by the schools were no different from other even more "intangible" objectives. An examination of the pertinent educational literature, moreover, revealed that most of the available analyses of these objectives were unsatisfactory for the purpose of evaluation. It therefore proved necessary to devote considerable time to clarification of the objectives and to analysis of the behaviors which would reveal that students were achieving them. In the course of the analysis it was convenient to break up the general objective into a limited number of component parts, and then to analyze each of these in some detail. The aspects of clear or "critical" thinking which were selected dealt with the ability to *interpret data*, with the ability to *apply principles* of science, of the social studies, and of logical reasoning in general, and finally, with certain abilities associated with an understanding of the *nature of proof*. This chapter will be devoted chiefly to the description of each of these aspects as they were eventually analyzed, and to a description of some of the evaluation instruments which were developed to evaluate the associated abilities.

It may be well to note at the outset that the abilities involved in the aspects of thinking listed above are overlapping. Although the abilities call-

---

*Originally chapter 2 in *Recording and Appraising Student Progress*.

ed into action in a successful interpretation of a set of data seem to be primarily inductive, and those utilized in the other aspects are more deductive in nature, it is neither necessary nor desirable to emphasize such distinctions. In connection with any given problem, the process of reflective thinking, as defined by Dewey and others, is likely to call upon a number of the abilities to be described in connection with each major aspect of thinking mentioned above. It should also be noted that other important aspects of thinking — for example, the ability to formulate hypotheses — are only implicitly included in the above list and receive only cursory attention in the following discussion. The separation of clear thinking into these and other aspects is a product of the analysis and is not to be considered as inherent in the process of clear thinking. It was convenient because it facilitated the exploration of the larger objective and the development of practicable means of evaluation. A satisfactory evaluation of the thinking abilities of students involves a synthesis of the data obtained from various instruments.

The four major aspects of clear thinking listed above not only overlap among themselves but they also overlap with other educational objectives. The attitudes and the emotions of students may influence their ability to think clearly in certain situations. This has been explicitly recognized in the analyses of these objectives and in the construction of the evaluation instruments to be described in this chapter. At the moment, it is necessary to mention only that evaluation of the *disposition* to think critically has not been extensively worked upon and is not discussed in the following pages. In the opinion of the Evaluation Staff, the best available means is some sort of observational record, and this method demands only the simplest of techniques supported by alert sensitivity and perseverance on the part of the observer. Evidence of the disposition to think critically collected by this method would, however, be a valuable addition to other evidence relevant to clear thinking of the sort to be described later.

The scope of this phase of the evaluation project made it necessary to omit many details in the discussion of some of the instruments. For purposes of illustration, certain procedures are explained at length in relation to a selected instrument, and are condensed or omitted elsewhere....

I. Interpretation of Data

Analysis of the Objective.   The Committee on the Interpretation of Data, composed of representatives from each school interested in this objective and members of the Evaluation Staff, began with two major questions: What do students do when they interpret data well? What kinds of data should they be able to interpret?

Behaviors Involved in Interpretation of Data.   Some conceived of interpretation as a complex behavior which included the ability to judge the accuracy and relevance of data, to perceive relationships in data, to recognize the limitations of data, and to formulate hypotheses on the basis of data. From the wide range of behaviors which were suggested, the committee selected two which seemed to them to be of paramount importance: (1) the ability to perceive relationships in data, and (2) the ability to recognize the limitations of data.

The first of these involves the ability to make comparisons, to see elements common to several items of the data, and to recognize prevailing tendencies or trends in the data. These behaviors are dependent on the ability to read the given data, to make simple computations, and to understand the symbolism used. It became apparent that these operations vary for different types of data. Thus in the case of graphic presentation the student must be able to locate specific points on the graph, relate these to the base lines, recognize variations in length of bars or slope of graph line, and so on. In many cases, students must understand simple statistical terms (e.g., "average"), the units used, and the conventional methods of presentation of different forms of data.

A second type of behavior which the teachers expect of students is the ability to recognize the limitations of given data even when the items are assumed to be dependable. A student who develops this ability recognizes what other information, in addition to that given, he must have in order to be reasonably sure of certain types of interpretations. He refrains from making judgments relative to implied causes, effects, or purposes until he has necessary facts at hand. He recognizes the error in allowing his emotions to carry him beyond the given facts when he judges conclusions that affect him personally. If he holds rigidly to what is established by the data, the kinds of generalizations that he can make without qualifications are limited. He recognizes that many interpretations must be regarded as almost completely uncertain because the facts given are insufficient to support such interpretations even with appropriately stated qualifications.

These behaviors do not preclude the possibility of making qualified inferences when the situation warrants. This type of interpretation can be made, for example, when the data reveal definite trends. By qualifying the statement with words such as "probably" a student may then *extrapolate*, that is, make interpretations which are somewhat beyond the facts but in agreement with a definitely established trend. Or a student may *interpolate*, in other words, make a qualified inference concerning an omitted point between observed points in a set of data which reveal an established trend. In another case, a student may risk a qualified prediction relative to similar sets of data applying to similar conditions. Even when the inferences are qualified, the student must be careful not to allow his statements to go far beyond the observed facts. These inferences are necessarily confined to a rather narrow range whose extent depends somewhat on the subject to which the data apply. Fundamentally, the objective involves making a distinction between what is established by the data alone, and what is being read into the data by the interpreter.

During the analysis of the objective it was also recognized that the ability to make original interpretations and the ability to judge critically interpretations made by others might not be closely related. When judging a stated interpretation one may derive a clue that directs attention to specific relationships in the data. An original interpretation usually involves the ability to perceive these relationships without the aid of suggestions or directions. In the discussion of this point it was noted, on the one hand, that relatively few individuals have occasion to collect data and make original interpretations, since most of the data encountered in life are already wholly or partially interpreted. Critical judgment of these interpretations is, however, very important. On the other hand, it was noted that some individuals do have frequent need to collect data and formulate original interpretations, and almost everyone has some need of the abilities involved. A decision was made to concentrate primarily upon evaluation of the ability to judge interpretations made by others, and to study the relationship between this and the ability to make original interpretations.

Several other behaviors were recognized as ones which may be considered important in connection with the interpretation of data. One of these is the ability to evaluate the dependability of data; another is the ability to formulate hypotheses. In evaluating the dependability of data, a student might question the competence, bias, or integrity of the person who presents the data; he might attempt to determine the adequacy and appropriateness of the methods, techniques, and controls used in obtaining the data; he might question the adequacy and the appropriateness of the methods of summarizing the data. In formulating hypotheses on the basis of given data, the student might infer probable causes or he might predict probable effects. Information other than that given in the data may be required in order to make a satisfactory evaluation or to formulate a reasonable hypothesis. Thus recall of information might also be regarded as an ability involved in the interpretation of data.

Although the importance of all these aspects of interpretation of data was fully recognized, the teachers selected for more intensive study those behaviors on which they proposed to give the greatest emphasis in their respective schools. Whether a student is making original interpretations or judging interpretations made by others, the teachers expect the student who has achieved the objective to perceive relationships in data and to recognize the limitations of data. These two important behaviors were therefore selected for particular attention in developing evaluation instruments.

Kind of Data. The second major question which had to be answered in analyzing the objective dealt with the kinds of data that students should be able to interpret. The committee recognized several different ways of classifying data. Among these were the following: (1) according to the form of presentation, (2) according to the subjective-matter fields from which the data are drawn, (3) according to problems or areas of living with which the data deal, (4) according to types of relationships inherent in the data, (5) according to the purpose the data are intended to serve, (6) according to various levels of generality, (7) according to the degree to which the possibility of making meaningful interpretations depends upon the knowledge of other facts.

The form of presentation of data may vary. For example, data may be presented in graphical form. Pictures, maps, cartoons, and various types of graphs, such as line or bar graphs, are familiar examples. Data also are often presented in tabular form. Such tables are frequently found in reports of experiments, election returns, scores of baseball games, and so on. Sometimes data are not set off from the prose form of reading matter but are incorporated in the context. This method of presentation is often used in editorials, printed speeches, and news items. Sometimes the same data are presented in several forms; this situation is commonly found in advertisements, for example.

Data may be drawn from various subject fields. Data from the fields of economics and sociology commonly appear in newspapers, magazines, and current books. Data from the fields of physics, chemistry, biology, and other sciences are presented in many publications which are commonly read; advertisements, for example, often incorporate data from these fields.

The classification of data in terms of areas of living or problems would probably make use of categories such as vocation, health, government, transportation, family relationships, and others of similar type. Classification according to types of relationship would emphasize categories such as chronological trends, relationship of parts to a whole, and the like. If data are differentiated in terms of the purposes which they are intended to serve, distinctions may be made, for example, between what purports to be an impartial presentation of facts and a presentation intended to sell a particular idea or defend a special interest. Different levels of generality are illustrated by data showing unemployment in a single city in contrast to data on unemployment in an entire state or country. If the latter are available, often more meaningful interpretations could be made concerning the situation in the single city, and hence this same illustration indicates how additional information may influence the interpretation, and how the amount of such information needed may form a basis of classification.

Although other classifications are possible and were considered, for purposes of evaluation the teachers chose the following criteria for the selection of the data to be presented to students for interpretation: (1) data presented in various forms; (2) data relating to various subject fields; (3) data relating to major problem areas; (4) data including various types of relationships. As is often the case, these criteria are not independent, and a given set of data will satisfy several criteria simultaneously.

In order that the interpretation may not be made from memory, it is necessary that the data be "new" to the student in the sense that this particular organization of the facts has not previously been interpreted for the student by someone else. If he has heard or read an interpretation of this organization of facts, his response may represent recall of an interpretation made by another and not give a measure of his own ability to interpret.

The analysis of the objective thus resulted not only in a description of the behaviors which might be included under the phrase "interpretation of data," but also in a conscious restriction of the scope of the eventual evaluation. This restriction applied to the types of behavior which were to be emphasized, and to the criteria for the selection of data which were to be presented to students.

The Development of Evaluation Instruments. *Preliminary Investigations.* Observations of a student's many overt behaviors in responding to data of various kinds is one way in which evidence of his ability to interpret data may be obtained. This type of evidence can probably be best secured by observational records kept by teachers or other persons trained to observe and record these behaviors. Under certain conditions a student's written materials, such as laboratory notebooks, papers, etc., may be a fruitful source of evidence. However, the time consumed and the possible lack of objectivity of scores present serious difficulties in the use of these techniques. Since these methods usually involved more or less uncontrolled situations, teachers were interested in devising a method that would better stabilize some of the variable factors. The method which was selected makes use of pencil-and-paper tests in which the student reacts in writing to written data. Many methods of obtaining this type of evidence have been experimented with in the Study. A few will be discussed to present some of the approaches used and some of the difficulties the Evaluation Staff has encountered in measuring the abilities involved. One of the most direct methods used was to present the student with sets of written data, ask him to write true statements concerning the data, and to appraise the interpretations which he wrote. However, such a free-response essay-form presents several difficulties in evaluation. It was found that even when the number of interpretations to be made is specified in the directions, individual students tend to use a narrow range of relationships in their responses. Thus, the responses do not adequately sample the types of interpretations which the students are capable of making when their attention is focussed on data relating to their own particular problems or concerns, or when breadth of treatment is encouraged by more specific directions in the test. Moreover, great difficulty is experienced in scoring such a test, for it is often impossible to be reasonably sure what the student means by his written statements. This perplexity may arise from ambiguity or incompleteness of student's statements or from peculiarities in his style. It is possible to attain high objectivity for such a test, but only after elaborate criteria for scoring have been carefully set up. Even with such a device, it is a time-consuming method. In one case, for example, it required approximately 90 hours for each of the trained markers to score 193 papers of ten exercises calling for responses of this type. Because of these difficulties, this method of getting evidence of a student's ability to interpret data is impractical for most teachers.

In order to determine the types of interpretations students should be expected to judge critically and the kinds of errors commonly made in interpreting data, a study was made of interpretations commonly found in editorials, advertisements, news items, reports of scientific experiments, and similar materials. For instance, the conclusions of many reports of experiments were critically studied in relation to the data on which they were based. In this and other such studies it was possible to discover the kinds of relationships involved in the interpretations, the kind of assumptions that were made, the accuracy and adequacy of the inferences made from the data. When students' essay responses were also critically studied in the same way and comparisons made, it became apparent that the interpretations from both these sources were susceptible to virtually the same types of classifications. One classification that could be made was in terms of the kind of relationships involved. For convenience of reference, these types are denoted by various words or phrases, such as "extrapolation," "comparison of points," or "cause." They are as follow:[4]

1. *Reading Points*. This type of statement is usually merely a restatement of the data.

2. *Comparison of Points.* The statement is a comparison of two or more items or "points" in the data.

3. *Cause.* The statement presents a cause of conditions presented in the data.

4. *Effect.* The statement formulates a prediction of a probable effect of the conditions described.

5. *Value Judgment.* The statement presents a recommended course of action suggested by the data, or an opinion of what ought to be or ought not to be.

6. *Recognition of Trend.* The statement describes a prevailing tendency or trend in the data.

7. *Comparison of Trends.* The statement presents a comparison of two or more prevailing tendencies or trends in the data.

8. *Extrapolation.* The statement formulates a prediction of a point or item or fact which is not given in the data and lies beyond points or items or facts which are given in the data.

9. *Interpolation.* The statement formulates a prediction of a point or item or fact of data which lies between points or facts which are given in the data.

10. *Sampling.* The statements concern (a) only a part of the group described in the data, or (b) a larger group containing as a part of itself the group described in the data.

11. *Purpose.* The statement presents a judgment of purpose of the given data.

These types of interpretations may be also arranged into a concise and meaningful classification which emphasizes the difference in degree of accuracy with which they are used by students. Thus, students' responses may include the following:

1. Interpretations which are *accurate.* These interpretations may formulate comparisons, trends, and specific facts which are established by the data as true or false and are correctly stated without qualification. Other interpretations under this classification may be concerned with sampling, extrapolation, or interpolation. They are not fully supported by the given data, but are probably true or probably false on the basis of the trends established in the data, and are stated by the student with sufficient qualification.

2. Interpretations which are overgeneralizations — that is, interpretations containing unqualified or unwarranted statements involving interpolation, extrapolation, and sampling, or statements of cause, purpose, effect which cannot be established by the given data even in qualified form. This

type of error may be referred to as "going beyond the data."

3. Interpretations which are undergeneralizations — that is, which involve unnecessarily qualified statements concerning specific facts, trends, and comparisons which are established in the data. Such departures from accuracy may be referred to as "overcaution."[5]

4. Interpretations which involve "crude errors"; for example, the student errs by misreading the points or trends in the data, by failing to understand meanings of terms, such as "average" and "per cent," or by failing to relate properly the data of a graph to the base lines.

Such analyses provided a basis for construction of a short-answer type of test exercise. This type of test does not present the difficulties in scoring inherent in the essay form and makes it possible for a student to react to many types of data in a limited time. During its development, the short-answer test has passed through several transitional forms. Analysis and statistical study of early forms suggested changes which were incorporated in subsequent forms. For the sake of simplicity of explanation, only the latest form of the interpretation of data test (Form 2.52) will be described in detail.

Structure of Interpretation of Data Test, Form 2.52. The test to be described is intended primarily for the senior high school level. It contains ten sets of data selected to satisfy the criteria set up by the committee interested in the objective. These data are presented in various forms, including tables, prose, charts, and different kinds of graphs. The problems are selected from several fields (such as medicine, home economics, sociology, genetics) and contain data pertinent to such topics as technological unempolyment, heredity, crop rotation, immigration, government expenditures, and health.

Each set of data is followed by 15 statements which purport to be interpretations. The student is asked to indicate his judgment of each of the statements by placing it in one of five categories as indicated by the short code given at the top of the sample exercise. In the sample, the list of responses accepted as correct by a jury of competent persons is given in the margin before each interpretation. A word or phrase describing the main kind of relationship involved follows each interpretation.

A study of the sample exercise in relation to the following summary of the procedure used in constructing the test will indicate how the analyses described previously were utilized. It may also serve as a guide for teachers who wish to construct similar tests suited for use with their own students.

1. The data were selected according to the criteria set up by the committee.

2. Fifteen interpretative statements were made from each set of data. The types of statements included were based on an analysis of types of interpretations which were found in current literature, the judgment of teachers who were concerned with the objective, and the analysis of responses of students who were asked to write original interpretations. This approach was used both to give the students an opportunity to judge statements including typical errors made in interpretations, and to insure the inclusion in the test of types of interpretations which students encounter and are capable of recognizing. These interpretations involve the following types of behaviors: comparisons of points of data, recognition and comparison of trends, judgments of cause, effect, purpose, value, analogy, [6] extrapolation, interpolation, and sampling.

3. The types of relationship involved in the interpretations which the students are asked to judge were distributed among the five response categories as follows:

a. Interpretations adequately supported by the data, and so worded that they are meant to be judged by the students as *true*. These statements require the student to judge interpretations that involve: comparison of points in the data; recognition of trends; and comparison of trends. Ten per cent of the total number of statements in the test are in this category.[7]

b. Interpretations inadequately supported by the data, so worded that they are meant to be judged *probably true*. These statements require the students to judge interpretations that involve a knowledge of the principles of prudent extrapolation, interpolation, and sampling as previously defined. They include inferences that go beyond the data but are suggested by the data and are based on trends or facts in the data. They also include some conclusions that would be popularly interpreted as true. They are intended to contribute information concerning the ability of students to recognize the necessity for qualification in interpretation. About 20 per cent of the total number of statements are in this category.

c. Interpretations inadequately supported by the data, so worded that they are meant to be judged as based upon *insufficient data*. They give opportunity for the student to make judgments concerning statements of analogies relating to the data, concerning statements referring to a cause or an effect of the situation revealed by the data, concerning the purpose the data are supposed to serve, and concerning a recommended course of action supposedly desirable on the basis of the data. Also included are some statements depending upon an injudicious use of interpolation, extrapolation, and sampling. About 40 per cent of the total number of statements are in this category.

d. Interpretations inadequately supported by the data, so worded that they are meant to be judged *probably false*. These include inferences which are suggested by the data but which are contrary to the trends of facts in the data, and conclusions which would be popularly interpreted as false. The same types of interpretations are used here as in *b*. Twenty per cent of the total number of statements are in this category.

e. Interpretations which are contradicted by the data, so worded that they are meant to be judged as *false*. These statements involve the same types of interpretations as are listed in *a* above. Ten per cent of the total number of statements are in this category.

4. Within each test exercise the interpretations were arranged in random order. Directions to the students were formulated. These directions asked students to place each statement in one of the five different categories.

Before the test was considered ready for use, an analysis of student responses was made. In each case where the judgment of a large number of students conflicted with the key, there was an attempt to analyze the student's thinking to see if the conflict in judgment was due to confusion in the test or to an erroneous concept held by the students. Ambiguous statements were revised, and a final key was drawn up. The scores made by students are, therefore, to be considered as a means of comparison of their thinking with the judgments of the jury.

Summarization of Scores. For purposes of exposition, the manner in which the answer sheets from a class are scored may be described as follows. By tabulating a student's response for each item in relation to the jury's key for that item in the proper cell of the following chart, a teacher can describe student's achievement both as to accuracy and as to errors.[8]

As indicated by the chart, student responses can be described in the following terms: *general accuracy, caution, beyond data,* and *crude errors.* This terminology may be defined as follows: *General accuracy* means the extent to which the student agrees with the jury — that is, recognizes true statements as *true*, probably true as *probably true,* etc. The total number of statements which a student judged accurately may be found by counting all of the tally marks in the cells labeled *a, g, m, s,* and *y.* This number may be expressed as a per cent of the maximum possible number of correct responses (150).

Since the judgment of the accuracy of the statements involves different levels of discrimination, depending on whether or not the interpretation needs to be qualified, it was found helpful to derive the following subscores on accuracy: (a) accuracy with *probably true* and *probably false* statements, (b) accuracy with *insufficient data* statements, and (c) accuracy with *true* and *false* statements. They indicate the extent to which the student agrees with the jury in judging these three types of statements taken separately.

The first of these subscores may be computed by counting the tallies in cells *g* and *s*, and expressing this number as a per cent of the maximum possible number of such responses (59 in the case of the test under discussion). The second subscore mentioned above is derived from the number of tallies in cell *m* (expressed as a per cent of 61). The third subscore is derived from the number of tallies in cells *a* and *y* (expressed as a per cent of 30).

The *going beyond the data* score indicates the extent to which the student marks statements keyed probably true as *true*, statements keyed insufficient data as *probably true* or *probably false*, and statements keyed probably false as *false*. The student is then granting the interpretation greater certainty than is warranted by the data.

CHART SHOWING HOW SCORES ARE DERIVED

Jury Key / Student Responses	True	Probably True	Insufficient Data	Probably False	False
True	Accurate a	Beyond Data b	Beyond Data c	Crude Error d	Crude Error e
Probably True	Caution f	Accurate g	Beyond Data h	Crude Error i	Crude Error j
Insufficient Data	Caution k	Caution l	Accurate m	Caution n	Caution o
Probably False	Crude Error p	Crude Error q	Beyond Data r	Accurate s	Caution t
False	Crude Error u	Crude Error v	Beyond Data w	Beyond Data x	Accurate y

In order to determine how frequently a student has "gone beyond the data," one may count the tallies in the cells labeled *b, c, h, r, w, x.* There are 120 opportunities for the student to react in this way, and the per cent of such responses may easily be calculated.

SAMPLE EXERCISE FROM FORM 2.52

(1) are sufficient to make the statement true.

(2) are sufficient to indicate that the statement is probably true.

These   (3) are not sufficient to indicate whether there is any degree of truth or
Data   falsity in the statement.
Alone (4) are sufficient to indicate that the statement is probably false.

(5) are sufficient to make the statement false.

PROBLEM I. This chart shows production, population, and employment on farms in the United States for each fifth year between 1900 and 1925.

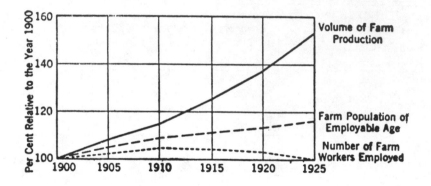

Statements

1. The ratio of agricultural production to the number of farm workers increased every five years between 1900 and 1925.
2. The increase in agricultural production between 1910 and 1925 was due to more widespread use of farm machinery.
3. The average number of farm workers employed during the period 1920 to 1925 was higher than during the period 1915 to 1920.
4. The government should give relief to farm workers who are unemployed.
5. Between 1900 and 1925, the amount of fruit produced on farms in the United States increased about fifty per cent.
6. During the entire period between 1905 and 1925 there was an excess of farm population of employable age over the number of people needed to operate farms.

7. Wages paid farm workers in 1925 were low because there were more laborers than could be employed.
8. More workers were employed on farms in 1925 than in 1900.
9. Since 1900, there has been an increase in production per worker in manufacturing similar to the increase in agriculture.
10. Between 1900 and 1925, the volume of farm production increased over fifty per cent.
11. Farmers increased production after 1910 in order to take advantage of rapidly rising prices.
12. The average amount of farm production was higher in the period 1925 to 1930 than in the period 1920 to 1925.
13. Between 1900 and 1925, there was an increase in the farm population of employable age in the Middle West, the largest farming area in the United States.
14. Farm population of employable age was lower in 1930 than in 1900.
15. The production of wheat, the largest agricultural crop in the United States, was as great in 1915 as in 1925.

The *caution* score indicates the extent to which the student marks statements keyed true as *probably true*, statements keyed probably true as based upon *insufficient data*, statements keyed false as *probably false*, and statements keyed probably false as based upon *insufficient data*. The student is then refusing to attribute to the interpretations as much certainty as the jury was willing to do.

The *crude errors* score indicates the extent to which the student marks true or probably true statements as *false* or *probably false*, or marks false or probably false statements as *true* or *probably true*. This type of error is often due to carelessness in reading the data or interpretations, or to a misunderstanding of some terms involved in the data. Both of the last two scores may be computed in the manner prescribed for previous scores.

Omissions are scored in order to determine the actual number of opportunities the student had to score in other columns.

A form of data sheet on which scores from this test are conveniently summarized is presented on page 57. The scores made by seven students in the twelfth grade were selected for purposes of illustration. At the bottom of the sheet the maximum possible score, the highest score, the lowest score, and the group median and the mean are recorded for each column.

Interpretations of Scores. The achievement of a student as revealed by the test may be analyzed in terms of two related questions. The *first* of these questions is: To what extent does the student recognize the limitations of the data? In general, one may secure some answers to this question chiefly on the basis of the scores on general accuracy (column 1), caution (column 6), and beyond data (column 7).[9] Column 1 gives the per cent of statements in which the student agreed with the jury's key, that is, the student judged as true those statements keyed as true, etc. This is probably the best single summarizing score, although it is of limited value by itself. Columns 6, 7,

SAMPLE DATA SHEET

School ____A____

Grade ____12____

Summary for test   2.52
Interpretation of Data
Date Test Given   6-2-39

Seven Students Selected from a Group of 69

Students	General Accuracy	Accuracy			Omit	Caution	Beyond Data	Crude Errors
		P. T. P. F.	Insufficient Data	True-False				
Students	1	2	3	4	5	6	7	8
1. Peggy	34	20	30	52	0	13	60	32
2. Joseph	71	66	69	71	0	20	23	7
3. William	64	65	54	68	0	7	38	14
4. Homer	51	18	74	52	0	53	22	10
5. Andrew	71	74	60	78	0	6	33	8
6. George	47	11	60	75	0	41	38	8
7. Faye	57	46	53	75	0	21	37	11
Maximum possible	100 per cent in all columns							
Lowest Score	21	11	11	11	0	6	22	5
Highest Score	71	74	74	78	24	53	64	32
Group Median	51	43	45	65	0	22	42	13
Group Mean	50.0	42.2	45.0	60.0	1.3	22.2	43.4	13.9

and 8 reveal the types of judgments that the student made when he failed to be accurate. Thus, column 6 gives the per cent of statements in which the student tended to require more qualifications than the jury. This score gives some measure of the student's tendency to call true statements *probably true*, etc. Column 7 gives the per cent of statements in which the student tended to ascribe more truth or falsity to the interpretation than the data justify. A high score here is usually considered undesirable, since it indicates the tendency of the student to go beyond the limits of the given data, making definite judgments about statements for which the given data yields insufficient information for such judgments. For example, on the sample data sheet it may be seen that Peggy's score on *general accuracy* is low in relation to her class.[10] In those judgments in which she failed to recognize the limitations of the given data and had made no crude errors, she was overcautious less often and went beyond the data more often than was average for her class. In the case of the student called Homer, the pattern of scores indicates that he recognized the limits of the given data with an accuracy about equal to the average for his class. When he failed to judge accurately the limitations of the given data, Homer was overcautious in more judgments and went beyond the data in fewer judgments than was average for his class.

The *second* question that the test scores should answer is: How accurately does the student perceive various types of relationships in the data?

By examining the scores in columns 2, 3, 4, and 8, some tentative answers to this question may be obtained. As stated above, the score in column 1 gives the per cent of accuracy with which the student is able to judge limitations of interpretations dealing with all of the types of relationships in the test. Scores in columns 2, 3, and 4 are subscores of the *general accuracy* score. Each subscore refers to the accuracy with which the student judges certain of the relationships involved in the interpretation. For example, column 2 gives the per cent of accuracy of a student in recognizing those statements which are *probably true* or *probably false*. A high score here indicates that the student persistently applies with success the principles of prudent extrapolation, interpolation, and sampling. Column 3 gives the per cent of accuracy in judging statements which cannot be justified without the use of information from other sources. These statements include relationships such as cause, effect, purpose, analogy, as well as some statements of extrapolation, interpolation, and sampling. Column 4 gives the per cent of accuracy of a student in recognizing those statements which are *true* or *false*. A high score indicates that the student is able to judge accurately statements that involve comparisons of points in the data, and recognition or comparison of trends. The per cent of *crude errors* (column 8) indicates errors in which the student marked interpretations true that the jury considered false or probably false, and vice versa. Such errors may be due to vocabulary or reading difficulties, carelessness, or inability to identify the relationship involved.

The following examples may help to clarify this explanation. Peggy's score in column 2 indicates that she stands low in relation to her group in the ability to make the finer discriminations necessary to judge accurately those extrapolation, interpolation, and sampling statements which are based on trends in the data. She is relatively poor in the accuracy with which she judges statements based on insufficient evidence, cause, effect, or purpose, as well as those extrapolation, interpolation, and sampling items that fall in this category. The score on accuracy with true and false statements (column 4) seems to indicate an ability approaching the average for her class in recognizing trends and comparisons of trends or of points in the data. However, this can be determined only after studying the entire pattern of scores.[11] In view of Peggy's evident tendency to "go beyond the data," the higher score in column 4 may be a result of her tendency to be "gullible" and to mark many statements as true or false.

Homer's scores in columns 2, 3, and 4 seem to indicate a greater accuracy in his judgment of statements based on insufficient data than on the statements classified in the other two categories. However, it is necessary again to consider the entire pattern of scores to make a justifiable inference. Homer's relatively high score on *caution* and low score on *beyond data* imply that he tends to refuse to make judgments of probability and classifies statements that are not well justified by the data as of the *insufficient data* type.

An examination of scores made by Joseph and Andrew shows that, although both boys receive the same score in *general accuracy*, for those judgments in which they fail to be accurate Andrew tends to go beyond the data more often than Joseph.

It is usually inadvisable to interpret scores on this test in terms of national norms, since opportunities to develop these abilities vary markedly from group to group.

II. Application of Principles of Science

Analysis of the Objective. Teachers of science in schools of the Study believed that students should learn to apply knowledge obtained in the science classroom and laboratory to the solution of problems as they arise in daily living. This aspect of critical thinking was frequently mentioned in the list of objectives submitted to the Evaluation Staff. A study of the prevailing curriculum materials for science instruction confirmed the importance of this objective, and therefore a committee was formed for the purpose of clarifying it and of aiding in the development of evaluation instruments for appraising growth in the ability to apply science information. Although this objective had previously been explored to some extent at the college level by Tyler[12] and others, and these explorations had served to show that certain techniques for the measurement of the objective were feasible, it could not be assumed that the available analyses and methods were immediately applicable at the secondary school level. This committee of teachers in the schools therefore aided the Evaluation Staff in clarifying the objective to be appraised and also in finding situations which would give students an opportunity to show the degree to which the objective had been attained. In the present instance, clarifying the objective necessitated an analysis of the behaviors involved in *application* and a selection of the principle to be used.

Behaviors Involved in Application. The analysis of the behaviors involved in *application* separated the process of applying principles into two steps: (1) the student studies a situation and makes a decision about the probable explanation or prediction which is applicable to this situation; (2) he justifies through the use of science principles and sound reasoning the explanation or prediction that he made in the first step. In the first step he acts in the role of an authority who is presented with a problem and asked for a solution. In the second step, he is asked to explain or justify that proposed solution by means of his previous knowledge of what has occurred in similar situations.

The kind of deductive thinking needed for the solution of these problems consists of the search for an explanation of the fact or facts described in the problem situation by means of some *general rule* which asserts a highly probable connection between facts of the kind described in the problem and other facts the student knows to be applicable to similar problems. The question he attempts to answer is: Does the general rule which is suggested by the given facts as an hypothesis for explaining what has happened (or what will happen) actually apply to this specific problem? The answer to this question comes, of course, from experimentation or direct observation. However, if observations have been made in several situations which can be shown to be similar to that one which is described in the test, then without obtaining the empirical evidence one may nevertheless predict with considerable confidence that the same conclusion is also true in this case. It was for the measurement of such behavior that the instruments to be described later were constructed. The teachers felt they needed the most help in evaluating the ability of students to apply principles in *new* situations, and consequently the *remembering* of applications which had been made was not included as a behavior to be directly appraised.

Selection of the Principles.   In the discussions that were held to clarify the meaning of the term *principle* it was found that some teachers were inclined to accept certain statements as representing "principles" whereas others wanted to regard them as statements of "facts." The difficulty was resolved by obtaining an agreement which permitted, for the purpose of testing application, the use of any science information, fact, generalization, understanding, concept, or "law" which proves to be useful (alone or in connection with other information) for predictive or explanatory purposes. Although more inclusive than the definition of principle that is frequently used by science teachers, this agreement seemed satisfactory for the measurement of the objective as this committee conceived it. After the committee had accepted this agreement as to the "principles" which were to be used in the construction of the instruments, teachers were asked to submit statements of those principles which were considered important in their courses and which had received the greatest emphasis in their teaching. These lists included the principles with which their students had had the greatest opportunity to become familiar through reading, discussion, and experimentation.

The original lists from individual teachers included principles from the fields of chemistry, physics, and biology, as well as some that were common to all three fields. After the principles submitted had been classified into subject-matter areas, the complete list was sent to a number of teachers in the Thirty Schools. These teachers were asked to:

1. Select those statements that they would expect their students to apply in making predictions or explanations in new situations.

2. Select those statements that they would expect their students to know in a general way, but not to the extent of being able to use them to make predictions in new situations.

Only those principles which were included in the first category by at least three-fourths of the teachers were considered for use in the tests. Two additional criteria were established to aid in the selection:

3. The principle should have a wide range of applicability to commonly occurring natural phenomena.

4. The principle, with examples of its application to commonly occurring phenomena, should be found in all of the science textbooks commonly used in these schools.

The teachers were also asked to judge the relevance of each principle to the areas of general science, biology, chemistry, or physics, or to all of these areas.

The Development of Evaluation Instruments. During the period of the Eight-Year Study a number of instruments were developed for evaluating the ability to apply principles. Several of these instruments included principles drawn from the subject-matter area of general science; others were restricted to principles drawn from physics, chemistry, or biology. Because the instruments which included principles from general science were used more extensively than the others and because they were the ones experimented with in attempting to arrive at a satisfactory pattern for the test, they will be used to illustrate the construction of tests of application of principles.

Preliminary Investigations. In preparing a test of Application of Principles, the first step after the principles had been selected was to obtain problem situations to which the student might react. Teachers were asked to submit to the committee problem situations which: (1) were new to the students (i.e., they were not ordinarily discussed in the classroom or used in the textbooks); (2) occur rather commonly in actual life; (3) could be explained by the principles which the teachers had selected as important for their students to apply.

Attempts to phrase the problem situations revealed that they might be so described as to demand several different types of response from the student. Four types of response were used; namely, making a prediction, offering an explanation for an observed phenomenon, choosing a course of action, and criticizing a prediction or explanation made by others. An illustrative situation of each type follows:

1. *A farmer grafted a Jonathan apple twig on a small Baldwin apple tree from which he had first removed all the branches. The graft was successful. If a new branch develops from a bud below the point of the graft and produces apples, what kind of apple will it be?* Here the student is asked to make a prediction about a situation in which presumably he has had no actual experience. It is presumed that if he understands certain laws of heredity, he will be able to make a valid *prediction.*

2. *All of the leaves of a growing green plant were observed to be facing in the some direction. Under what conditions of lighting was the plant probably grown?* This example requires that the student offer an *explanation* of an observed phenomenon. Some knowledge of the principles of photosynthesis, growth, and tropistic responses of plants would be required for the solution of this problem.

3. *The rear of an automobile on a wet pavement is skidding toward a ditch. If you were the driver of the car, what would you do to bring the car out of the skid?* The problem requires the student to choose a course of action. A knowledge of the principles of centrifugal force and Newton's laws of motion would enable the student to choose a satisfactory *course of action.*

4. *It was reported in a newspaper that in order to tow down a river a huge oil drum filled with air, the workmen found it necessary to fill the drum with compressed air to increase its buoyancy. Do you believe that this would increase the buoyancy of the oil drum?* This problem asks the student to criticize an explanation which has been given. Knowledge of the fact that air has weight and of the principles of buoyancy are required for a satisfactory solution in this problem.

In none of these problems were the answers expected to be in exact quantitative terms; rather a qualitative understanding of the general outcome was required. It was thought that the kind of activity shown by students in making a prediction of this kind was of more importance for general education than one which required exact substitutions of numerical data in a formula or similar activities frequently used in the laboratory. One often encounters problems in which a principle is used to explain what happens in general when certain factors are varied in the situation, while the need for numerical solutions of problems occurs relatively infrequently for most people. Although the above problem situations are stated in such a way that the student is expected to react somewhat differently in each, it is not likely that he will react intelligently to any of these situations unless he has a knowledge of the principles operating and has recognized their application to the problem. Whether he criticizes a prediction made by someone else or makes the prediction himself, he must base his answer upon the knowledge which he feels is applicable to the situation.

The next step in constructing the test was to determine the reasons which might justify the response to the problem situation, and to find a means of appraising the reasons cited by the student. Science teachers were in rather general agreement that the most valid of all the reasons a student might use for justifying his conclusions would be those that cited established scientific facts, principles, and generalizations. However, in addition to these, it was agreed that the student might cite from his experience, from authoritative materials he had read, or he might use analogous situations familiar to the person to whom he was explaining his decision, provided these experiences, authorities, or analogies were pertinent to the situation he was attempting to explain.

In order to determine whether or not students did use these kinds of reasons, they were asked to write out both their own predictions, choice of action or responses to the situation, and all of the reasons that they believed would support the decision they had made. When these papers were analyzed by the teachers and the Evaluation Staff, the types of acceptable reasons which had been anticipated were found in the students' responses. However, in addition to the reasons which were agreed upon as being acceptable, certain types of errors were also found to occur rather consistently in the written responses of the students. It was found that students frequently used teleological explanations and analogies not closely correspondent to the situation described in the problem. They cited authorities that were questionable, ridiculed positions other than their own, stated as facts certain misconceptions or superstitions, merely restated either the facts given or their own prediction, and made less frequently a variety of other types of errors. They also used, in addition to the principles and facts judged to be acceptable and necessary to the explanation of the problem, other facts and principles that were irrelevant to the solution of the problem. The frequency with which each of these types of reasons was used was not constant, but varied from class to class and from problem to problem. In examinations of sufficient length given to a large number of students, however, these types of errors were found to be most prevalent.

In general, it was possible to infer that the errors were made because:
1. The student did not know the principles.
2. He did not see that a principle he knew applied to the situation.
3. He knew the principle and knew that it applied to the situation, but he was unable to explain adroitly how or why it applied.
4. He used teleology, poor analogy, or poor authority, rather than (or in addition to) correct facts and principles.
5. Although his explanation was correct as far as it was given, he cited facts and principles which were inadequate for a convincing proof for a given selected conclusion or course of action.
6. He confused closely related principles, only one of which was applicable to the problem.
7. He used irrelevant material.
8. He neglected to study the description of the situation carefully enough to note all of the limiting factors in the description.

This list does not include all of the reasons why students made errors but it does help to show why it was difficult to score the written responses.

Construction of Early Short-Answer Forms. The same problems of objectivity of scoring and of adequate sampling that are found in any essay-type test were inherent in these written responses. The teachers found that it was difficult to differentiate among those acceptable uses of generalizations, facts, and principles which were relevant to the problem, and the logical errors, obscured as they sometimes were by illegibility of handwriting and by awkward literary style. It was also difficult to decide when a student had cited enough evidence to support his choice of answer. A second criticism of this form of test was that it limited the number of principles which could be sampled because of the time required by the student to write out the answers. Because of these difficulties, a more objective means of testing this same ability was sought.

Following a study of the responses written out by students, the first of a series of objective test forms in this area was made. The objective form of the test asked the student to select from a list of predictions for each problem situation the one which he thought was most likely to be true, and then to select from a list of reasons those which would be necessary to establish the validity of his choice. The predictions and reasons used in the test paralleled those which had been used frequently by the students when they wrote essay-type responses. When experimental groups were given an examination which required them to *write out* their predictions and reasons for the first half of the testing period, and an examination in which they were required to *select* the correct prediction and the reasons which supported it from a given list during the latter half of the period, it was found that the results on the two types of examinations were quite similar. The coefficient of correlation was in all cases above 0.80.[13] The advantages of more objective scoring and the possibilities for more extensive sampling of problem situations led to the adoption of the objective form.

The procedures used in preparing the early form of objective tests in this area were as follows:

1. The principles to be used in the test were selected in accordance with the criteria formulated by the teachers interested in this objective.

2. Problem situations in which these selected principles would apply were chosen with the following criteria in mind:

2.1 They were to be new in the sense that they had not been used in the classroom or laboratory.

2.2 The situation should approximate a rather commonly occurring life situation.

2.3 The problem should be significant to students in that its solution might help them to solve similar problems which occur in their everyday living.

2.4 The vocabulary used should be at an appropriate level for the students taking the test. They should be able to understand the description of the situation.

3. Several (usually three or more) plausible answers for the problem were formulated. These might be in the form of predictions, courses of action to be taken, causes to be stated, or an evaluation of one of these when it was given. Actually, when possible answers were suggested by listing them in the test, the procedure in every case would be one of evaluation through the selection of what the student thought was the most desirable, whether it was a prediction, course of action or explanation for the phenomena which had been described in the problem.

4. Finally, reasons of the sort used by students were listed, including for each situation those common types of errors which students made when they wrote out their reasons. In addition to correct statements of scientific principles needed for a satisfactory explanation, the following types of statements were formulated:

4.1 *False statements purporting to be facts or principles.* These, if accepted as true, would support one of the alternative conclusions. For example, if the correct principle stated that a direct relationship existed between two phenomena, one might word a false statement in such a way as to indicate that there was no relationship or that the relationship was an inverse one. To remain consistent in his reasoning, the student can use such a statement only to support a conclusion other than the acceptable one.

4.2 *Irrelevant reasons.* These statements are true, but either they have no relationship to the phenomenon described in the problem or they are quite unnecessary in the explanation of the phenomenon.

4.3 *False analogies.* These stated directly or inferred that the phenomenon described in the problem was identical with, or very much like, some other known phenomenon when it actually had little or nothing in common with it; therefore, an explanation for one phenomenon would not be acceptable for explaining the other. Metaphors were sometimes included as an example of a more subtle use of analogy, in that the analogy was implied by the use of words but not definitely expressed.

4.4 *Popular misconceptions.* These included the more common beliefs based upon unreliable evidence or false assumptions. Frequently they were statements of rather common practices based upon accepted but unreliable evidence. Common clichés or superstitions would also be included in this type of statements.

4.5 *The citing of unreliable authorities.* Statements introduced by phrases such as "Science says ...," or "People say ...," or "It is reported in popular magazines that ..." were used. Here a distinction must be made between such very general or unreliable sources and those which might be used with considerable assurance. However, in any case the mere citation of authority did not in any sense explain why a particular point of view was correct; one would need in addition to give the evidence used by this authority to establish his position on the outcome of the problem.

4.6 *Ridicule.* This rather common device of students in their explanations suggested that any position contrary to their own could only be held by someone who did not know the facts.

4.7 *Assuming the conclusion.* These statements assumed what was to be proved. This was most frequently represented in these tests by essentially repeating the conclusion by rewording it without changing its meaning.

4.8 *Teleology.* These statements assume that plants, animals, or inanimate objects are rational or purposive.

An example of the wording of the directions for one of the tests and a sample problem taken from the test follow.

Form 1.3
APPLICATION OF PRINCIPLES
Directions: In each of the following exercises a problem is given. Below each problem are two lists of statements. The first list contains statements which can be used to answer the problem. Place a check mark (✓) in the parentheses after the statement or statements which *answer the problem.* The second list contains statements which can be used to explain the right answers. Place a check mark (✓) in the parentheses after the statement or statements which *give the reasons for the right answers.* Some of the other statements are true but do not explain the right answers; do not check these. In doing these exercises then, you are to place a check mark (✓) in the parentheses after the statements which *answer the problem* and which *give the reasons for the RIGHT answers.*

In warm weather people who do not have refrigerators sometimes wrap a bottle of milk in a wet towel and place it where there is a good circulation of air. *Would a bottle of milk so treated stay sweet as long as a similar bottle of milk without a wet towel?*

A bottle wrapped with the wet towel would stay sweet
        a. longer than without the wet towel ....(   ) a.
        b. not as long as without the wet towel ....(   ) b.
        c. the same length of time — the wet towel
           would make no difference.....................(   ) c.

Check the statements below which give the reason or reasons for your explanation above.

Superstition   d. Thunderstorms hasten the souring of milk ......(   ) d.
Right Principle   e. The souring of milk is the result of the growth
           and life processes of bacteria.................(   ) e.

Wrong	f. Wrapping the bottle prevents bacteria from getting into the milk ....( ) f.
Wrong	g. A wet towel could not interfere with the growth
Wrong	h. Wrapping keeps out the air and hinders bacterial growth ....( ) h.
Right Principle	i. Evaporation is accompanied by an absorption of heat.......................................( ) i.
Authority	j. Milkmen often advise housewives to wrap bottles in wet towels..............................( ) j.
Unacceptable Analogy	k. Just as many foods are wrapped in cellophane to keep in moisture, so is milk kept sweet by wrapping a wet towel around the bottle to keep the moisture in...( ) k.
Right Principle	l. Bacteria do not grow so rapidly when temperatures are kept low ....( ) l.

In formulating statements for these earlier test forms, no consistent pattern was followed. A study of the results obtained by giving Form 1.3 to many science students suggested the desirability of using in each of the testing situations a pattern of reasons which would remain constant throughout the test. It was believed that this would tend to give a greater reliability to the subscores used in interpretation and thus make the interpretations more meaningful. The pattern of reasons to be included was determined through discussions with teachers who had used Form 1.3. They were asked to indicate the types of items in the test which seemed to be most useful in diagnosing students' difficulties. Using their suggestions, tests employing a pattern of responses were constructed by following through these steps: Situations were selected using the criteria described for Form 1.3 but with greater emphasis upon problems of social significance. These situations were worded in a way that would require an explanation, prediction, choice of course of action, or an evaluation of any one of these. Three conclusions were then formulated, one being defensible through the use of science principles as preferable to the other two. In every case the other two conclusions would not be nonsensical, absurd, or preposterous.

The reasons used in the test were arrived at by first supporting the correct conclusion by formulating three statements of facts or principles which support it and by implication eliminate the other two conclusions. Four wrong reasons which, if accepted as true, would support the other conclusions were next formulated. Two of these would tend to support one of the wrong conclusions and two the other. They would all tend by implication to eliminate the right conclusion. One statement was formulated so as to be true but irrelevant to the explanation of the problem. One each of the following kinds of reasons completed the pattern — a teleological statement, ridicule statement, assuming the conclusion, unacceptable analogy, unacceptable authority and unacceptable common practice. Each of these was worded to appear to be consistent with the conclusion keyed as right. Tests following this general procedure were constructed for the areas of chemistry (Form 1.31), physics (Form 1.32), biology (Form 1.33), and general science (Form 1.3a).[14]

A sample problem taken from Form 1.3a is given with the directions and key.

PROBLEM

The water supply for a certain big city is obtained from a large lake, and sewage is disposed of in a river flowing from the lake. This river at one time flowed into the lake, but during the glacial period its direction of flow was reversed. Occasionally, during heavy rains in the spring, water from the river backs up into the lake. What should be done to safeguard effectively and economically the health of the people living in this city?

Directions: Choose the conclusion which you believe is most consistent with the facts given above and most reasonable in the light of whatever knowledge you may have, and mark the appropriate space on the Answer Sheet under Problem —

Conclusions:

   ✓A. During the spring season the amount of chemicals used in purifying the water should be increased. (Supported by 3, 7, 10, 12)

     B. A permanent system of treating the sewage before it is dumped into the river should be provided. (Consistent with 5, 8, 12)

     C. During the spring season water should be taken from the lake at a point some distance from the origin of the river. (Consistent with 12, 14)

Directions: Choose the reasons you would use to explain or support your conclusion and fill in the appropriate spaces on your Answer Sheet. Be sure that your marks are in one column only — the same column in which you marked the conclusion.

Reasons:

False analogy	1. In the light of the fact that bacteria cannot survive in salted meat, we may say that they cannot survive in chlorinated water.
Irrelevant	2. Many bacteria in sewage are not harmful to man.
Right Principle	3. Chlorination of water is one of the least expensive methods of eliminating harmful bacteria from a water supply.
Ridicule	4. An enlightened individual would know that the best way to kill bacteria is to use chlorine.
Wrong Supporting B	5. A sewage treatment system is cheaper than the use of chlorine.
Authority	6. Bacteriologists say that bacteria can be best controlled with chlorine.
Right	7. As the number of micro-organisms increases in a given

amount of water, the quantity of chlorine necessary to kill the organisms must be increased.

Wrong
Supporting B

8. A sewage treatment system is the only means known by which water can be made absolutely safe.

Assuming
Conclusion

9. By increasing the amount of chlorine in the water supply, the health of the people in this city will be protected.

Right

10. Harmful bacteria in water are killed when a small amount of chlorine is placed in the water.

Teleology

11. When bacteria come in contact with chlorine they move out of the chlorinated area in order to survive.

Right
Supporting
A B C

12. Untreated sewage contains vast numbers of bacteria, many of which may cause disease in man.

Practice

13. In most cities it is customary to use chlorine to control harmful bacteria in the water supply.

Wrong
Supporting C

14. Sewage deposited in a lake tends to remain in an area close to the point of entry.

An examination of the complete test would show that the problem situations included in this form of the test deal with personal health, public health, eugenics, conservation, and the like, and many of them involve questions of opinion as well as of the operation of science principles. The desirability of using these types of problem situations was mentioned by many of the science teachers who had used the earlier form of the test; however, after such problems were formulated it was discovered that very little agreement could be secured among these teachers as to the most defensible conclusions for such problems. This difficulty is illustrated by the above problem on water supply. Several science principles might be cited in proposing a solution to the problem of securing for this city a supply of water free from pathogenic bacteria; but whether or not a supply of water free from pathogenic bacteria constitutes an "effective" safeguard of the health of these people and whether or not any proposed method of securing such a supply of water will be "economical" cannot be determined by science principles alone.

In choosing any one of the three conclusions given with this problem, it is necessary for the student to interpret the terms *effectively* and *economically*. If the student regards reasonable safety, such as might be secured by the administration of additional chemicals to the water supply, as an effective safeguard, and if he regards the use of chemicals as an economical practice, then he might defend conclusion A. However, another student might wish to defend conclusion B by pointing out that the use of chemicals assures only a reasonable safety under ordinary conditions and may fail under unusual circumstances, such as the sudden reversal of flow of the river, and that this practice cannot be considered economical in the long run when all the benefits of a sewage disposal system are considered. Still another student might defend conclusion C as representing a more effective safeguard than that of A and a more economical practice than that of B.

The difficulty of keying any of these responses by students as the correct one, unless one knows all of the evidence and values which the student would use to support his point of view, is obvious. Insofar as the student considers the probable effects of these practices upon the people living in the city, upon the people in nearby regions or in towns lying along the river, upon the future as well as the present citizens of this region, and upon the biological life in the waters of this region, he may interpret the terms *effectively* and *economically* so as to justify any of these three conclusions. The pertinent science principles can only aid a person in predicting the effects of each of these practices; they cannot determine whether or not these effects are to be desired. Other students might wish to remain uncertain about which conclusion to choose until further evidence had been obtained about the problem. Such evidence might reveal that it would be better to put into practice all three of the suggested conclusions, i.e., purify the sewage by a permanent system of treatment before it is dumped into the river, take the water from the lake at a greater distance from the shore, and finally add chlorine to the water before it is put into the water mains. It should be clear from this discussion that the effort to construct a test form which involved social values as well as scientific principles led to situations which were well suited for generating a desirable type of thinking, but which at the same time created considerable technical difficulty for the test constructors. In the discussion of the next test in this series a method for solving these difficulties, at least partially, will be discussed.

Structure of Form 1.3b.   In developing Form 1.3b two changes were made: (1) the adoption of a different form of conclusion and the consequent inclusion of reasons to be used if the student were uncertain about the conclusion; (2) addition of acceptable analogy and acceptable authority to the reasons to be used to support or refute the conclusion. A keyed sample problem from Form 1.3b is reprinted here to illustrate these changes:

PROBLEM I
A motorist driving a new car at night at the rate of 30 miles per hour saw a warning sign beside the road indicating a "through highway" intersection 200 feet ahead. He applied his brakes when he was opposite the sign and brought his car to a stop 65 feet beyond the sign. Suppose this motorist had been traveling at the

rate of 60 miles per hour and had applied his brakes exactly as he did before. *He would have been unable to stop his car before reaching the "through highway" intersection.*

Directions:

A. *If you are uncertain about the truth or falsity of the underlined statement, place a mark in the box on the answer sheet under A.*

B. *If you think that the underlined statement is quite likely to be true, place a mark in the box on the answer sheet under B.*

C. *If you disagree with the underlined statement, place a mark in the box on the answer sheet under C.*

Directions for Reasons:

If you placed a mark under A, select from the first ten reasons given below all those which help you to explain thoroughly why you were uncertain and place a mark in Column A opposite each of the reasons you decide to use.

If you placed a mark under B, select from reasons 11 through 24 all those which help you to explain thoroughly why you agreed with the underlined statement and place a mark in Column B opposite each of the reasons you decide to use.

If you placed a mark under C, select from reasons 11 through 24 all those which help you to explain thoroughly why you disagreed with the underlined statement and place a mark in Column C opposite each of the reasons you decide to use.

Reasons to be used if you are uncertain:

Lack of Experience	1. I have never driven an automobile at 60 miles per hour and don't know how far an automobile will travel after the brakes are applied.
Irrelevant "Control"	2. The distance required to bring a car to a stop depends upon the condition of the road surface.
Irrelevant "Control"	3. The reaction time of the driver is an important factor in determining the distance a car will travel before it stops.
Irrelevant "Control"	4. The mechanical efficiency of the brakes will affect the distances required for stopping a car.
Irrelevant "Control"	5. Whether the brakes are of the mechanical or hydraulic type would make a difference in the stopping distance.
Irrelevant "Control"	6. There are too many variable conditions in the situation to enable one to be sure about the stopping distance.
Lack of Knowledge	7. I do not know which mathematical formula to apply in this problem.
Irrelevant "Control"	8. The distance required to bring a car to a stop depends upon the mass of the car as well as the speed.
Irrelevant "Control"	9. Whether he stopped the car or not before entering the intersection would depend upon how good a driver he was.
Irrelevant "Control"	10. The condition of the tires would be a factor to consider in determining the stopping distance for the automobile.

Reasons to be used if you agree or disagree:

Teleology	11. The increasing difficulty of stopping objects at higher speeds

is a part of nature's plan to keep people from driving too fast.

Wrong
Principle

12. The distance required to bring a car to a stop is directly proportional to the speed of the car. (Inconsistent with B)

Acceptable
Practice

13. Many drivers have learned from experience that the distance required to bring a car to a stop is more than doubled when the speed is doubled. (Inconsistent with C)

Unacceptable
Analogy

14. Just as the centrifugal force acting on a car going around a curve is increased four times when the speed is doubled, so will the distance required to stop a car be increased four times when the speed is doubled. (Inconsistent with C)

Right
Principle

15. When brakes are applied with constant pressure there is constant deceleration of the car.

Ridicule

16. Any student of physics ought to know that the distance required to stop a car when it is traveling at 60 miles per hour is more than 200 feet. (Inconsistent with C)

Assuming
Conclusion

17. It would require more than 200 feet for the motorist to bring his car to a stop traveling 60 m.p.h. (Inconsistent with C)

Wrong
Principle

18. As the speed of a car increases, the mechanical efficiency of the brakes decreases considerably. (Inconsistent with B)

Right
Principle

19. When the speed of a car is doubled, the distance required to bring it to rest is increased four times. (Inconsistent with C)

Unacceptable
Authority

20. Automobile mechanics report that cars traveling at 60 miles per hour cannot be brought to a stop within 200 feet. (Inconsistent with C)

Right
Principle

21. The distance moved while coming to rest by an object undergoing constant deceleration is proportional to the square of the velocity. (Inconsistent with C)

Wrong
Principle

22. When the velocity of a car is doubled, the distance required to bring it to a stop may be quickly calculated by multiplying the velocity by four. (Inconsistent with C)

Right
Principle

23. The kinetic energy of a car traveling at 60 miles per hour is four times that of the same car traveling 30 miles an hour. (Inconsistent with C).

Acceptable
Analogy

24. Just as the penetrating distance of a bullet is increased four times when its velocity is doubled, so is the stopping distance of an automobile increased four times when its speed is doubled (Inconsistent with C)

The description of this problem includes an underlined conclusion which the student is asked to judge. The student may agree, disagree, or be uncertain about the conclusion. In the earlier tests he had been asked to select from a list of conclusions the one he thought most appropriately answered the question asked in the description of the science situation. The use of this form of the problem was adopted in order to score the student on his ability to distinguish between problems in which sufficient information was given to enable him to be reasonably sure of his answer, and others about which he should remain uncertain because necessary information was not included in the description of the problem. This form of the problem also enables the teacher to discover those students who have become "over-critical," i.e., who challenge problems by choosing the uncertain response when, in the judgment of the teachers, these problems are so stated that one can either agree or disagree with the conclusion.

An investigation was undertaken to discover what effect the changed form of presenting the conclusion might have upon the results. It was found that it made little difference in which form the conclusion was given....

In the earlier forms of the test all analogy statements were formulated as unacceptable reasons. In this form two analogy statements are used in each problem, one acceptable as a reason for supporting the conclusion, the other unacceptable. The inclusion of acceptable analogy statements makes it possible to score a student on his ability to distinguish between those statements of situations which are closely analogous to the original problem and those which seem to be but actually are not explainable by means of the same underlying principles. The use of authority and practice had also been restricted in earlier test forms to the unacceptable use of such reasons. Because in life students are often forced through exigencies of time and circumstance to use authority, it was thought desirable to include in this test two such statements in each problem, one of which was judged to be acceptable and the other unacceptable. If students then used such statements in justifying their reaction to the conclusion, one would be able to distinguish these students who used authorities discriminatingly from those who either did not cite authorities or who were unable to distinguish between authorities judged acceptable and those judged unacceptable. The inclusion of these statements gives students an opportunity to reveal whether or not they can distinguish between authorities — either persons or institutions — which, because of training, study, experience, etc., should be in a position to give reliable information about the problem, and those which involve the use of false credentials, or transfer of prestige from one field to another, and in reality offer little reliable evidence about the problem.

SAMPLE DATA SHEET

School _Experimental_
Grade ___11___

Summary for
Test ___1.3b___

	Conclusions			Uncertain Knowledge Experience	Reasons			Principles			Controls		Analogies		Authority Practice		Ridicule, Assuming Conclusion, Teleology		Inconsistency	
	Accept-able	Too Uncer-tain	Too Cer-tain		No.	R	%R	No.	R	%R	No.	R	No.	R	No.	R	No.	%	No.	%
Column Numbers	1	2	3	5	7	8	9	11	12	13	15	16	18	19	21	22	24	25	27	28
Student A	8	0	0	1	31	26	84	15	15	100	5	5	6	4	2	2	3	10	0	0
B	7	0	1	0	61	40	66	24	21	88	6	6	12	7	12	7	8	13	0	0
C	7	0	1	0	34	32	94	24	23	96	5	5	5	5	0	0	1	3	1	3
D	4	2	1	5	61	31	51	20	16	80	13	6	8	4	9	5	12	20	14	23
E	2	4	1	10	20	7	35	5	3	60	6	2	1	0	4	2	4	20	0	0
F	4	2	1	4	27	20	74	12	10	83	5	4	6	4	2	2	3	11	7	26
G	3	2	2	4	70	26	37	28	16	57	12	0	10	5	8	5	13	10	14	20
Maximum Possible	8	6	2	20	106	65	100	56	34	100	60	15	16	8	16	9	24	100	97	100
Low Score	1	0	0	0	4	3	22	0	0	0	0	0	0	0	0	0	0	0	0	0
High Score	8	6	2	11	70	33	100	29	24	100	36	13	13	7	9	7	12	30	21	50
Group Median	4	2	1	4	26	14	56	10	8	86	5	2	3	2	3	2	3	13	1	4

Summarization and Interpretation of the Scores on Form 1.3b.   The form of the data sheet on which the several scores are tabulated and summarized is presented on page 152.

The scores made by seven students in the eleventh grade were selected for purposes of illustration. At the bottom of the sheet the maximum possible score, highest score, lowest score, and group median is recorded for each column. These were computed from the class from which these seven students were selected. Some of the scores represent actual number of responses, while others are computed in per cent by using certain of the scores from other columns as bases.

The achievement of the student as revealed by the test may be analyzed in terms of five related questions. The *first* of these questions is: To what extent can the student reach valid conclusions involving the application of selected principles of science, which he presumably knows, to new situations?

Columns[15]   *Column 1* gives the number of conclusions out of a possible eight
1, 2, 3   which the student marked correctly. The eight correct responses were distributed among agreement with the stated conclusion in three problems, disagreement with the stated conclusion in three problems, and uncertainty about the stated conclusion in the remaining two problems. *Column 2* (too uncertain) gives the number of conclusions which the student marked uncertain when the correct response was either "agree" or "disagree." *Column 3* (too certain) gives the number of conclusions which the student marked either agree or disagree when the correct response was "uncertain." When his scores in columns 1, 2, and 3 do not total to eight, either the student marked some conclusions agree which should have been marked disagree, or he marked some conclusions disagree which should have been marked agree, or else he omitted some of the conclusions. If we denote an interchange of the agree and disagree responses by the term "error in fact," the following table may be used to describe the complete scoring of the student's conclusions.

Student \ Key	Agree	Uncertain	Disagree
Agree	Acceptable	Too certain	Error in fact
Uncertain	Too uncertain	Acceptable	Too uncertain
Disagree	Error in fact	Too certain	Acceptable

Thus on the sample data sheet student A marked all eight of the conclusions in agreement with the key. Student D agreed with the key four times, marked two of the conclusions as uncertain when he should either have agreed or disagreed with them according to the key. He also marked one of the conclusions which was keyed as uncertain as agree or disagree. Further he either made an "error in fact" by marking an agree conclusion as disagree or a disagree conclusion as agree, or he omitted one problem. This is shown by the fact that his score on conclusions totals seven rather than eight. One would have to examine his paper to determine whether he had omitted a problem or made an "error in fact," for no score for problems omitted is recorded on the data sheet.

The *second* question is: How does the student explain his uncertainty when he marks the stated conclusion "uncertain"?

Columns Column 5 gives the number of statements which the student used to
5, 15, 16 express either a lack of knowledge about, or experience with, the situation described in the problem. These explain why he marked one or more of the stated conclusions "uncertain." These statements are considered neither "right" nor "wrong" in scoring the test. *Column 15* gives the number of statements which express a desire for control (see the test items themselves to clarify the intended meaning of "Control"). They also are used by the student to explain why he marked one or more of the stated conclusions "uncertain." In two of the eight problems there is actually a need for further clarification or control of certain factors involved in the problem, *Column 16* gives the number of statements, used by the student in these two uncertain problems, describing "controls" which are considered to be essential additional information necessary for the solution of the problems. and hence are valid reasons for marking the conclusion uncertain. In the remaining six problems, the controls are considered to be unnecessary for the solution of the problem. The difference between the scores in columns 15 and 16 gives the number of unnecessary controls marked by the student. It should be borne in mind that a student has an opportunity to score in columns 5 and 15 when he marks a conclusion "uncertain," but has an opportunity to score in column 16 only when he marks the conclusion "uncertain" in one of the two problems where the uncertain response is regarded as the correct one.

Student D, as shown in column 5, used five statements which expressed either a lack of knowledge about, or experience with, those problems which he marked as uncertain. Generally speaking, a high score in column 5 will be associated with a low score in column 1. The correlation between column 1 and column 5 is — .34. The fact that he has a score of one in column 3 indicates that he marked one of the problems which was keyed as uncertain in agreement with the key, while the score of six in column 16 indicates that he must have judged correctly the other uncertain problem. His score of two in column 2 would account for the seven unacceptable control statements which were used (difference between columns 15 and 16) for in these two problems he was attempting to justify an uncertainty through the use of "control" statements when according to the key he should have either agreed or disagreed with the conclusion. In summary, student D marked four of the conclusions in agreement with the key. He was too uncertain in two of the problems and too certain in one. He either omitted one problem or made an "error in fact" by marking an agree conclusion disagree or a disagree conclusion as agree. He used five statements to indicate that he did not understand some of the problems where he was uncertain about the conclusion, and thirteen statements of "controls," six of which were considered to be acceptable.

The *third* question is: To what extent can the student justify logically his agreement with, his uncertainty about, or his disagreement with the stated conclusions?

Columns 7, 8, 9, 27, 28 *Column 7* give the total number of reasons used by the student to explain his decisions about the stated conclusions (excepting those which express a lack of knowledge about, or experience with, the situation described in the problem scored in column 5). Students vary a great deal in their comprehensiveness, that is, in the extent to which they use a large number of reasons to explain their decisions about the stated conclusions. The meanings of every subscore on reasons for a chosen student must be interpreted in the light of the score which he received in column 7. *Column 8* gives the number of correct or acceptable reasons used by the student. *Column 9* gives the per cent accuracy of the student in supporting his decisions about the stated conclusions with acceptable reasons. Thus the score in column 9 is computed by dividing the score in column 8 by the score in column 7 and expressing the result in per cent. This score helps to "smooth out" differences due to one student's using more reasons than another.

Column 27 gives the number of reasons selected by the student which were *inconsistent* with his decisions about the stated conclusions. This means that these reasons actually supported responses to the stated conclusions which were contradictory to the responses which the student made. *Column 28* gives the per cent of the student's reasons which were inconsistent with his decisions about the stated conclusions. Thus the score in column 28 is computed by dividing the score in column 27 by the score in column 7, and expressing the result in per cent.

Student B used 61 reasons to explain the eight conclusions which he marked, while student G used 74 (column 7 plus column 5). Both of these students used a great many more reasons than the average for their class. Of the 61 reasons used by student B, 40, or 66 per cent, were keyed as acceptable; while for student G only 26, or 37 per cent, of the 70 reasons he used were keyed as acceptable. (The scores in column 5 are considered as neither right nor wrong, and are not used in this computation — they are only used to make a judgment about how aware the student was of his lack of knowledge.) Student B used only reasons which were consistent with the conclusions he had chosen. However, 14, or 20 per cent, of the 70 reasons used by student G were contradictory to the conclusions he had chosen. This shows that student G was not as discriminating in his choice of supporting reasons as was student B.

The *fourth* question is: What kinds of reasons does the student select to explain his decisions about the stated conclusions?

Columns The total number of reasons selected by the student to explain the
11, 15, conclusion he has selected (*column 7*) is broken down into the number
18, 21, of science principles (*column 11*), the number of controls (*column 15*),
24, 25 the number of analogies (*column 18*), the number of appeals to
authority or common practice (*column 21*), and the number of times
ridicule, teleology, assuming the conclusion were used (*column 24*).
The score in column 15 has been discussed above in connection with
the second question. From one point of view it may be desirable to rely
entirely upon the use of science principles to explain one's agreements
or disagreements with the stated conclusions. However, in this test, the
test directions permit the discriminating use of "sound" analogies,
"good" authorities, and "dependable" common practices in explaining agreement or disagreement with the conclusions. The use of
ridicule, assuming the conclusion, or teleology is unacceptable. *Column 25* gives the per cent of the student's responses which could be
classified as calling upon ridicule, assuming the conclusion, or
teleology to explain his agreement or disagreement with the stated conclusions. Thus the score in column 25 is computed by dividing the score
in column 24 by the score in column 7 and expressing the result in per
cent.

The *fifth* question is: To what extent does the student discriminate between acceptable and unacceptable reasons in the various categories?

Columns Column 12 gives the number of correct statements of science principles
12, 13, which the student used to explain his responses to the stated con-
16, 19, clusions. The difference between the scores in columns 11 and 12 gives
22 the number of incorrect or technically false statements of science prin-

ciples used by the student. *Column 13* gives the per cent accuracy of the student in his use of science principles. Thus the score in column 13 is computed by dividing the score in column 12 by the score in column 11 and expressing the result in per cent. The scores in column 16 were discussed above in connection with the second question. *Column 19* gives the number of "sound" analogies used by the student. The difference between the scores in columns 19 and 18 gives the number of unacceptable or false analogies selected by the student. *Column 22* gives the number of acceptable appeals to authority or common practice which the student used in explaining his decisions about the stated conclusions. The difference between the scores in columns 22 and 21 gives the number of unacceptable appeals to authority or common practice selected by the student.

Student C used a total of 34 reasons to justify the eight conclusions he selected. Twenty-four of these were restricted to principles, of which 23, or 96 per cent, were keyed as acceptable. He also used five acceptable analogies, and only one statement which was classified as unacceptable because it was a ridicule, teleological, or assuming the conclusion type of reason. He did not use authority or common practice to explain his choice of conclusions.

In making interpretations of a student's scores, all of his scores on reasons should be judged in relation to his score in column 7. Per cent scores should be judged in relation to the number of items on which the per cent is based. That is, one out of two may have quite a different meaning than 10 out of 20. Reference to the "maximum possible," the "lowest score" and "highest score," and the group median (all given at the bottom of the summary sheet) will provide a frame of reference for judging the student with respect to the members of his own class. . . .

If students have been placed in situations in the classroom and laboratory where resourcefulness, adaptability, and selective thinking have been essential for the solution of problems, and if the emphasis given to teaching science principles has been upon their applications to the solution of problems involving commonly occurring natural phenomena rather than on the mastery of science information as an end in itself, then students should have little difficulty in behaving in the manner anticipated by this test. Such students would have had many opportunities to apply the principles of science as they learned them to a number of situations in the laboratory and classroom, and would have been encouraged to be alert for similar opportunities for application as they occur outside the classroom.

Experience of teachers with this objective seems to indicate that the objective is not attained through any one particular teaching unit. Rather it is the outcome of the way in which emphasis has been given to the objective with all the science materials taught in the classroom and laboratory. Consequently, teachers may wish to use from time to time during the semester or year classroom exercises which can be used for checking on these abilities and giving a tentative appraisal of progress. A considerable number of such exercises, much simpler in form than the tests of Application of Principles, have been constructed by classroom teachers in summer workshops.

III. Application of Principles of Logical Reasoning

The following discussion deals with the evaluation of the ability to judge the logical structure of arguments presented in written form. This ability will have much in common with the ability to judge the logical structure of arguments presented verbally, pictorially, or otherwise. Some students will have occasion in later life to write essays, prepare speeches, and the like. For these students an emphasis upon the producer aspect of applying logical principles is easily justified. Almost all students, however, will read editorials and advertisements, listen to political speeches, and the like. Hence this consumer aspect of applying logical principles (for example, taking note of the need for definition of terms) may be considered an objective of general education.

The Development of Evaluation Instruments. *Preliminary Investigations.*   The first step toward the construction of a test for this objective was the preparation of a list of logical principles which secondary school students might be expected to apply. A few principles were found explicitly stated in secondary school textbooks (particularly of geometry) and the list was extended by reference to books on logic. From this list the four principles were selected. Teachers of mathematics were particularly concerned with the objective, and their interests largely determined the choice which was made. The principles stated relative to definitions, indirect (or *reductio ad absurdum*) argument, and "if-then" reasoning play an important role in the teaching of geometry. The fallacy of *argumentum ad hominem* was included because the claim has so frequently been made that the study of geometry, which as usually taught offers little opportunity for this sort of error, provides a standard of comparison for reasoning in other situations. Consequently if the acquaintance with this standard is functional, it should enable the student to recognize the fallacy.

The second step toward the construction of a test consisted of a search of current newspapers, magazines, and legal casebooks for suitable reasoning situations. These sources were chosen because of the emphasis being given in several of the schools upon reasoning in life situations. The legal cases which formed the basis of several test problems were typical of those reported almost daily by the press, but were believed to be of greater interest to students. . . .

Structure of the Application of Principles of Logical Reasoning Test, Form 5.12. A study of the following explanation of the structure of the test problems in comparison with the sample test problem presented below will serve to clarify the objective further and to indicate the extent to which it is measured by the test. A list of the responses accepted as correct by a jury of competent persons (i.e., a test key) is given in the margin.

Problem IV
In January, 1940, Commissioner K.M. Landis submitted a plan to give financial aid to minor league baseball teams to restore fair competition by preventing certain major league teams from controlling the supply of players. Several leaders in the baseball world objected to this plan; some declared that Landis should enforce the rules governing the operation of baseball teams, but should not make interpretations which would change the intended meaning of the rules set up by the proper committees.

Larry MacPhail, president of the Brooklyn Dodgers, speaking at a dinner in Boston, expressed grave concern over the situation. The following statements are quoted from his remarks: "In the matter of Landis versus the present system, he sits as prosecutor, judge, and jury, and there is no appeal. If baseball is to be dominated by any selfish group, it won't be long before professional football or some other sport will replace baseball as the great national game, and none of us want that."

Directions: Examine the conclusions given below. If by "us" Mr. MacPhail means all persons at the dinner, and if they accept his remarks as true, which one of the conclusions do you think is justified?
Conclusions
   A. Logical persons at the dinner will conclude that they do *not* want baseball to be dominated by a selfish group.
   B. Logical persons at the dinner will conclude that, if the domination of baseball by a selfish group is prevented, baseball will not be replaced as the great national game.
   C. It is impossible to say what a logical person at the dinner will conclude.
                    A: *Statements which explain why your conclusion is logical.*
Mark in column B: *Statements which do not explain why your conclusion is logical.*
                    C: *Statements about which you are unable to decide.*
Statements
A 1. Since we assumed that Mr. MacPhail referred to all persons present at the

dinner when he said "none of us," and that those present accepted his
statements as true, the conclusion which we reached follows logically.

B   2. Logical persons at the dinner may agree or disagree with Mr. MacPhail.

B   3. Without knowing the assumptions of logical persons, we cannot predict
their conclusions.

A   4. If no person at the dinner wants professional football or some other game
to replace baseball as the great national game, then the logical ones cannot
want baseball to be dominated by a selfish group.

A   5. If we accept the assumptions on which an argument is based, then, to be
logical, we must accept the conclusions which follow from them.

B   6. Sometimes the meaning of a word or phrase used in an argument must be
carefully defined before any logical conclusion can be reached.

B   7. A changed definition may lead to a changed conclusion even though the
argument from each definition is logical.

B   8. If the domination of baseball by a selfish group results in some other sport
replacing baseball, then, if such selfish domination is prevented, baseball
will not be replaced.

B   9. Mr. MacPhail considered every possibility — either baseball will or will
not be replaced as the great national game — and thus made a sound indirect argument.

A 10. If a conclusion follows logically from certain assumptions, then one must
accept the conclusion or reject the assumptions.

B 11. If one removes the fundamental cause for other games replacing baseball,
baseball will not be replaced as the great national game.

B 12. The soundness of an indirect argument depends upon whether all of the
possibilities have been considered.

In each problem the student is given a paragraph, three conclusions, and
twelve statements. He is directed to read the paragraph carefully and to
choose the one of the three conclusions which he thinks is justified by the
paragraph. In the test as a whole the student judges the logical appropriateness of the conclusions drawn in eight different situations. In two
of these the definition principle operates; in two others the indirect argument principle operates; in two others the *argumentum ad hominem* principle operates; and in the remaining two the if-then principle operates. It
should be noted that the number of possible correct conclusions is small,
especially if considered with respect to the opportunity to use the correct
principles separately. Consequently the major emphasis is placed upon the
students' reactions to the statements which follow the conclusions in each
test problem.

The statements offered to the students are of several kinds, including: (a)
General or abstract statements of the logical principle involved in that particular test situation; (b) Specific statements of the logical principle involved

in the particular test situation; (c) General or specific statements of logical principles not pertinent to the particular test situation, statements which appeal to authority, statements of personal opinion, or statements which are otherwise irrelevant.

The student is directed to mark each statement in one of three ways according as it is: (a) Relevant for explaining why his conclusion is logical; (b) Irrelevant for explaining why his conclusion is logical; (c) Not sufficiently meaningful to him to permit a decision.

In the test as a whole the student judges the relevance of 96 statements, and is given the opportunity to reveal his lack of understanding of any of these statements. The variety of the statements including specific and general statements of the principles, statements of authority, personal opinion, prejudice and the like provides an opportunity to make many of the common logical errors. The sample of statements in the test includes 36 relevant and 60 irrelevant statements. Of the 36 relevant statements, 16 are specific and 20 are general. Of the 60 irrelevant statements, 20 are general statements of the four principles of the test, 19 are specific statements of these principles, and 21 are specific statements of the other kinds mentioned above.

Summarization and Interpretation of the Scores on Form 5.12. During the experimental stages of Form 5.12, the test results for a sample population of 351 students were studied intensively in an attempt to discover the most convenient and most meaningful form for reporting the results. An item analysis or record of the responses of all students to each item on the test was prepared. The individual student papers were scored by entering the number of responses of each separate kind on a tentative data sheet. Fourteen scores were summarized for each student, and more than eight additional scores were considered during the study. Certain important scores were selected and studied with reference to the item analysis in an effort to see more clearly the relationships between each of these scores and the responses of students to individual test items.

The 351 students comprised 12 separate classes in four public schools. Certain facts about the backgrounds of these different classes were known. The responses of each class to the individual test items (taken from the item analysis), and the median scores of each class (taken from the data sheets), were studied in an attempt to discover the degree of agreement or disagreement of these results with the known facts about the various classes of students. The results of this study indicated that the students who secured good total scores were also the students who did well with the individual test items. Moreover, it was found that the classes which had had most contact

Certain correlation coefficients between the scores which had been summarized were computed. It was found possible to reduce the number of scores on the data sheet to 11 without an appreciable loss of information. It was again found that separating the responses to specific statements of principles from the responses to general statements of principles did not yield results of practical significance....

Scores on this test may be interpreted in terms of the answers to the following three questions:

1. To what extent can the pupil reach logical conclusions in situations which may involve his attitudes and prejudices?
2. To what extent can the pupil justify his conclusions in terms of certain principles of logical reasoning?
3. How well can the pupil apply each of the four principles of logical reasoning?

By study of the various scores reported on the data sheet, the teacher may obtain evidence relative to each of these questions. Different patterns of behavior analogous to those described for the test on Interpretation of Data are identifiable in terms of the relation of the separate scores to the group averages....

A Related Instrument.   A group of objectives which are closely related to those discussed in connection with the discussion of Logical Reasoning... relate to what is popularly known as "propaganda analysis." During the Eight-Year Study some attention was given to evaluation with respect to these objectives. This section will give a brief account of this project.

The definition of propaganda which was adopted is as follows: Propaganda represents any use of the spoken or written word, or other forms of symbolization (pictures, movies, plays) designed to convince people to hold certain opinions, to give allegiance to particular group or cause, or to pursue some kind of social action predetermined by the source of the propaganda. As used in this sense, propaganda has no unpleasant or "bad" overtones. Our concern with it is to better understand which groups are selling what kind of propaganda; the possible social consequences and implications of this; the symbol appeals which are used and their relation to behavior dynamics of individuals; the relation of susceptibility to propaganda to social conditions; etc.

Propaganda also is used to characterize forms of argument which are untenable in terms of certain intellectual or logical criteria such as: documenting evidence, presenting several sides of a problem, drawing conclusions which follow logically from the data, minimizing the use of slogans and "emotional" terms, etc. Used in this sense propaganda does have unpleasant overtones and our problem is to teach pupils to react critically to it by applying criteria of good argument. The scope of this report takes both of these definitions into consideration.

Among the behaviors which were listed as important objectives of education related to propaganda analysis were the following:

  a. Recognition of the purposes of authors of propaganda — that is, ability to make more discriminating judgments as to the points of view which it is intended the consumer should accept or reject. (In the broad sense, this refers to the generally accepted concept of "reading comprehension.")
  b. Identification of the forms of argument used in selected statments of propaganda. (This refers to reading comprehension in a different sense.)
  c. Recognition of forms of argument which are considered intellectually acceptable and which are not employed in certain statements.
  d. Critical reaction to the forms of argument which represent typical devices employed in propaganda.
  e. Ability to analyze argument in terms of principles of the nature of proof.
  f. Recognition of the relation of propaganda to the social forces which breed it.
  g. Knowledge of the psychological mechanisms involved in the susceptibility of people to certain language symbols.

The evaluation instrument entitled Analysis of Controversial Writing (Form 5.31) was developed to obtain evidence concerning the achievement of the first four behaviors listed above.... The test contains ten samples of writing on controversial issues selected from magazines and newspapers. The choices were made on the basis of the following criteria: (1) the selection should focus upon a controversial issue; (2) liberal and conservative sources were represented on each issue; (3) the group of selections should make use of a variety of propaganda devices; (4) the issues involved should represent areas of tension for pupils.

In each problem the pupils were first directed to read the quotation carefully, and then in Part I to mark them so as to indicate statements where there is:

  A. evidence that the author of the quotation wants you to *agree with or accept* the idea in the statement.
  B. evidence that the author wants you to *disagree with or reject* the idea in the statement.
  C. *no evidence* as to whether the author wants you to agree or disagree with the idea in the statement.

Twelve statements follow these directions. The examples below are taken from Problem I, based on a selection whose tenor may be judged from the closing sentence in one paragraph: "The American system of private industry and business has distributed more income to more people than any other system in the history of the world."

1. The present purchasing power of workers is possible only under a system of private ownership of industry.
2. Workers should receive higher wages than they receive at present.
3. The present system of private ownership is superior to any other way of organizing industry.
4. Industry still has far to go in distributing wealth more evenly between the workers and the owners.
5. The profits of corporations should be turned over to the workers rather than to stockholders.

In Part II, the student was to decide:[16] first, which of the following statements represent forms of arguments used by the author in this situation, and second, which ones represent desirable forms of argument whether used by the author or not.

1. Assumes that the point of view expressed in the article is that which is held by the majority of Americans.
2. Gives facts in such a way that the reader can check their source to see whether they have been reported accurately.
3. Uses statistics for industries in which wages are among the highest to illustrate the rise in wages.
4. Presents some of the major advantages and disadvantages of our system of private ownership of industry.
5. Indicates that there will be undesirable consequences to industry if our present industrial system is changed.
6. Tries to make us feel sympathetic toward industrial owners.

Ten statements of this general sort were used in Part II of each Problem. In both parts the various statements were so chosen that a student responding according to the directions could reveal evidence of his status with respect to the first four behaviors listed above.

The scores of the pupils in Part I are tabulated in the following descriptive categories:

General Objectivity. Scores in this category represent the per cent of total correct responses and show the relative objectivity with which the pupil interprets highly biased material.

Non-Recognition of conflicting points of view. Pupils who have difficulty in recognizing ideas which are contradicted by the author's data can be identified through scores in this category.

Misconception of author's purposes. Scores in this category indicate a pupil's tendency to attribute conservative ideas to liberal articles and liberal ideas to conservative articles. Such scores indicate a kind of gross error in judgment and, if relatively large, suggest inability of the pupil to comprehend the general ideas which the authors are trying to sell to the reader.

Suggestibility. Scores in this category indicate the extent to which the pupil indiscriminately attributes conservative ideas to conservative articles and liberal ideas to the liberal articles. (A score of this kind means that the pupil says that the author wants him to "accept" an idea which is keyed "insufficient evidence." The items keyed "insufficient evidence" reflect the general point of view in the articles.)

Except for the category "general objectivity," the scores in Part I categories are separated into "liberal" and "conservative." Thus in the "suggestibility" category each pupil has two scores, one showing his suggestibility in interpreting the conservative articles and one showing suggestibility toward the liberal articles.

The scores on Part II are tabulated according to the following categories:

Identification of propaganda techniques used in the articles. This category indicates the degree to which the pupil can recognize the use of the forms of argument keyed as "propaganda techniques."

Confusion of propaganda techniques used and not used. This category shows the extent to which the pupil indicates that the techniques keyed as "not used" were used in the articles.

Uncritical toward the use of propaganda techniques. The tendency of the pupil to approve the use of propaganda techniques is indicated under this heading.

Recognition of acceptable nature of certain forms of argument. Recorded in this category are scores showing whether the pupil approves of the use of the acceptable forms of argument.

Gullibility. Scores in gullibility show the tendency of the pupil to indicate that the acceptable forms of argument keyed as "not used" are used in the articles. Due to the nature of the test items, gullibility means attributing "fairness," "impartiality," "open mindedness" to the authors of the articles.

In constructing Part I of the test, the basic hypothesis was that pupils whose attitudes toward the five social issues included in the test were strongly liberal would tend to be more "suggestible" toward the conservative articles than toward the liberal articles. This was based on the notion that the liberal pupil would more willingly exaggerate the ideas of conservative authors than those of liberal authors. Similarly it was believed that the scores of such pupils in the other columns of Part I would tend to differ as between the sub-categories "liberal" and "conservative." To check this hypothesis an attitude scale consisting of items used in the test was given to approximately one hundred pupils....

Conclusion. The two principal uses for these types of instruments are: (1) the diagnosis and description of the strengths and weaknesses of individual students and of groups of students in relation to the objectives as they have been operationally defined in the tests; (2) the measurement of growth in the abilities required for successful achievement. The scores on the data sheets will yield significant descriptions of students with respect to the objectives. The interpreter must, however, clearly understand the structure of the test problems and the relationship of this structure to the problem-solving process. For certain students the interpreter may desire even more detailed evidence from the test results than that which appears on the data sheet. An examination of the responses of a particular student to certain items on a test may yield such evidence. More often the suggestions raised by an examination of the data sheet will lead the teacher to seek evidence from other sources to confirm or deny these suggestions. For example, a student may reveal a tendency to use many reasons on the nature of proof test but fail to discriminate between relevant and irrelevant reasons. This tendency may or may not be confirmed by the teacher's experience with the student in daily classroom activities.

The uses of these instruments are not fundamentally different from those of many other types of tests. Thus after studying the test results the teacher may wish to provide curriculum experiences designed to overcome obvious weaknesses of a group as a whole, or of individuals within the group. This may lead to a special unit of work for the whole class; special assignments undertaken by a particular student with the advice of the teacher; special attention by the teacher to certain details of the written work handed in by one or more of the students; and the like. In other cases, growth toward this objective might be one of the desired outcomes of the work of a class over a longer period of time. For example, every activity of a class over a period of a year might be designed to make some contribution to the students' concept of proof.

In this connection it will be useful to measure the growth of individuals and of classes toward the objective. Although the students may remember the general nature of these tests for several months, they can scarcely be expected to remember the answers to specific items on the test. Hence the practice effect of taking the tests once will probably not be a serious factor influencing the scores on a second administration of a test several months later. If such studies of growth are desired, it is especially important, of course, that the specific exercises in the tests should not be "taken up in class." It is also important to keep in mind the effect of the total testing situation upon the test results. This total situation involves more than a careful explanation of the test directions to students, and the provision of adequate time for the completion of the test. In the case of many tests, and particularly those which have been described, it involves also the "readiness" of the class for the tests, their attitude toward the tests as a diagnostic instrument rather than as a marking device, and the like. Ideally, the class should look upon these test as an opportunity to demonstrate their ability to do clear thinking rather than as a burden and a threat.

The chief feature of all of these tests is the extent to which they make possible a description of a student's thinking ability in terms of at least tentative answers to a series of questions which are quite general and comprehensive. Successful performance depends relatively little, compared with the usual achievement test, upon knowledge of particular bodies of subject-matter content, and relatively much upon broad principles of science and of scientific thinking. The objectives demanded tests to probe among the higher mental processes applied not to materials of the sort commonly used in psychological investigations, but rather to those commonly found in reading of newspapers and magazines, or elsewhere in daily life. This approach is fundamentally different from one which seeks to synthesize a description of a student's thinking abilities from data on many simpler but more readily controllable psychological reactions. The experience of the Evaluation Staff has been that this endeavor has led to increasing complexity in the test instruments in spite of the demands of practicality for greater simplicity. This increasing complexity was tolerated in order to maintain close correspondence between the stated objectives and the behavior demanded of the student, and in the hope that the instruments of this sort may eventually be simplified.

Evaluation of Social Sensitivity*

Introduction

Origin and Scope of the Objectives Related to the Development of Social Sensitivity. In any social situation, an individual is aware of, and responds to, certain factors and lets others go unnoticed. Thus, on observing an old man selling apples on the street corner, one individual may be aware only of the convenience of having apples easily available to him, or be annoyed at having the man clutter up the street corner. The awareness and attendant feelings in this case are self-centered; there is little consideration for the apple man. Another person may "see" primarily an old man trying to make

---

*Originally chapter 3 in *Appraising and Recording Student Progress*.

a living. He may in addition feel sympathy for a man who has to make a living in such a precarious way, or feel that this way of earning a living is the man's just due, determined by his ability. Attention in this case is centered on the apple man as a human being. To a third person this experience may suggest the problem of security in old age. He may wonder why there is not a more satisfactory provision for old people to make their living. Awareness and sympathy in this case center not only on the apple man. He becomes a symbol for a whole group of people, or for an issue, and sympathy for him is likely to evoke concern for the problem or issue which he symbolizes. Depending on the type of response, various impulses to action may also suggest themselves. Annoyance with the apple man may suggest activity leading to his removal. Sympathy toward him may lead to consideration of ways of helping him. Concern about injustices in the social order tends to suggest the need for correcting them.

Several different behaviors are involved in these responses. Personal sympathies and aversions largely determine the pattern of initial awareness. The knowledge one possesses, and the attitudes and viewpoints one has, determine how one interprets the experience. One's ability and inclination to relate and reorganize ideas gained from previous experiences and to apply them to the new situation add insight. The inclination and ability to relate the feelings evoked and positions taken in specific situations to more general and abstract ideas add to both the coherence and the depth of one's insights in a given case. All of these behaviors, although capable of analytic distinction, are related to each other in any given experience.

The term "social sensitivity" has been used to refer to this complex of responses. In the common usage of the term the emotional factors — such as the feelings of sympathy or aversion, attitudes of approval or dis- approval — have been emphasized. However, this term can also be used to connote the intellectual responses — such as the range and quality of the elements perceived in a given experience or the significance of the ideas associated with it.

In the first statements of objectives submitted by the schools in the Eight-Year Study the term "social" was used in connection with many types of behavior somewhat similar to the ones described above. Frequent among the statements were terms such as social consciousness, social awareness, social concern, social attitudes, social integration, sense of social respon- sibility, social understanding, social intelligence. Thus many schools seemed interested in promoting a greater awareness of social aspects of the im- mediate scene as well as of the issues underlying current social problems. At the same time concern was expressed that unless students achieve clarification of their personal patterns of social values and beliefs, intelligent social thinking would remain an elusive object of educational effort. The apparent blocking of rational thought by personal prejudices and biases, by a warped sense of values, or by the tendency to react in terms of social stereotypes, was recognized, and many statements of objectives emphasized the importance of a clearer, more consistent, and more objective pattern of social values and beliefs. A good deal of attention was also devoted to the problem of helping students apply the values, loyalties, and beliefs they developed to an increasing range of life problems. The term "social sensitivity" was adopted to serve as a consolidating focus for this apparently heterogeneous yet highly related complex of objectives.

In order to see more clearly what was implied in these statements of objectives from the schools, two committees were established. These committees undertook to make a coherent analysis of social sensitivity as a total objective and to clarify and specify some of the more crucial aspects of it sufficiently to lay a foundation for the development of evaluation instruments. Some of the significant aspects of social sensitivity which were emphasized in the course of the analysis are described in the following section.

Significant Aspects of Social Sensitivity.   The first exploratory meetings of the committees revealed a diversity of concepts regarding social sensitivity. In the course of the discussion sensitivity was defined, by implication, as awareness, ways of thinking, interest, attitude, and knowledge. A whole range of problems representing significant areas of social sensitivity was also mentioned. These ranged from such "immediate" social patterns as relations with other people to such general social issues as unemployment, effective democracy, and social justice.

To get a clearer and a more concrete picture of the specific behavior involved in this objective, the committee undertook to collect anecdotal recordings of behavior incidents illustrating any aspect of social sensitivity which teachers in the Thirty Schools thought important. This material was carefully analyzed and the various types of specific behavior were listed. Altogether, 74 types of behavior were indicated or implied by the anecdotes submitted by committee members and other teachers. The list below gives a few illustrations:

1. The student frequently expresses concern about social problems, issues, and events in conversation, free writing, creative expression, class discussion.

2. The student is fairly well informed on social topics; he has a reasonable background and perspective, and would not often be misled by misstatements.

3. When facing a new situation, problem or idea, he is eager for more information, seeks to identify significant factors in the situation, carries thought beyond the immediate data.

4. He is critical about expressed attitudes and opinions and does not accept them unquestioningly; distinguishes statements of fact from opinion or rumors, discerns motives and prejudices.

5. He is able to discern relevant issues and relationships in problems, ideas, and data. He relates ideas widely and significantly and discriminates among issues.

6. He judges problems and issues in terms of situations, issues, purposes, and consequences involved rather than in terms of fixed, dogmatic precepts, or emotionally wishful thinking.

7. He reads newspapers, magazines, and books on social topics.

8. He is able to formulate a personal point of view; he applies it to an increasingly broader range of issues and problems.

9. He is increasingly consistent in his point of view.

10. He participates effectively in groups concerned with social action.

A classification of these behaviors resulted in the following list of major aspects of social sensitivity of concern to teachers in the Thirty Schools:

1. Social thinking; e.g., the ability (a) to get significant meaning from social facts, (b) to apply social facts and generalizations to new problems, (c) to respond critically and discriminatingly to ideas and arguments. (Statements 4 and 5 above, for example, would fall into this classification.)

2. Social attitudes, beliefs, and values; e.g., the basic personal positions, feelings, and concerns toward social phenomena, institutions, and issues. (Statements 8 and 9.)

3. Social awareness; that is, the range and quality of factors or elements perceived in a situation. (Statements 1 and 6.)

4. Social interests as revealed by liking to engage in socially significant activities. (Statements 3, 7, and 10.)

5. Social information; that is, familiarity with facts and generalizations relevant to significant social problems. (Statements 2 and 3.)

6. Skill in social action, involving familiarity with the techniques of social action as well as ability to use them. (Statement 10.)

The committee on social sensitivity took the responsibility for developing instruments for evaluating three of these aspects; namely, the ability to apply social generalizations and facts to social problems, social attitudes, and social awareness. The present chapter is chiefly devoted to a description of the instruments pertaining to these aspects. Instruments dealing with other phases of social thinking — such as the interpretation of social data, and critical reactions to arguments and propaganda — have been discussed in the chapter on Aspects of Thinking. The appraisal of social interests is discussed in the chapter on Interests. No new instruments were developed to evaluate the acquisition of social information, primarily because published tests were already available and because teachers felt relatively little need of assistance in this task. As far as securing evidence of skill in social action is concerned, observational records seemed to be the most effective method. These are discussed briefly in the following section.

Informal Methods of Getting Evidence on Social Sensitivity

An objective which involves as diverse types of behavior as those described in the preceding section obviously necessitates the use of several approaches and several techniques for its appraisal. These will include paper-and-pencil tests as well as observational techniques, each being employed according to its appropriateness to the behavior that is being evaluated. Thus the ability to think through social problems can be adequately appraised by using paper-and-pencil tests. For the evaluation of some other aspects of social sensitivity, such as the identification of social beliefs, paper-and-pencil tests are recommended chiefly because they are economical and because these behaviors are rather difficult to observe directly and objectively. Still other types of behavior, such as the disposition to act on one's beliefs, or the degree of participation in social action and in discussion of social problems, require direct observation of overt behavior. Many of these observational and informal techniques involve only a more effective use of procedures employed and materials secured in the course of normal teaching procedures.

Anecdotal records are an effective way of securing concrete descriptions of significant behavior of individuals or groups. Since they are a way of recording direct observations, anecdotal records are appropriate for securing evidence on all types of overt behavior. However, since such a descriptive record is highly time-consuming, the function of anecdotal records in a comprehensive evaluation program is usually supplementary: to give vivid, intimate, concrete material to help make more meaningful other more systematic but less colorful types of evidence. The nature and role of anecdotes and the criteria for selecting and writing them have been described elsewhere.[17] Here it may suffice to give a few illustrations of anecdotes pertaining to social sensitivity.

A disposition on the part of a group to consider the effects of one's actions upon the welfare of others, and to apply ethical principles in making decisions, is illustrated by the following incident:

The school newspaper had been supported by the income from advertising solicited from small neighborhood stores which the students did not patronize. A student questioned the ethics of such a procedure in the student government assembly. Others in charge of the business management of the paper defended the method on the grounds that it was a general practice with school papers and there was no other way of supporting a printed publication. Another group proposed other ways of earning money, involving more work on the part of the student body. The latter suggestion was accepted.

Class discussion often reveals the degree to which students are capable of using present events to speculate about their consequences.

In connection with a report of a demonstration by members of the League for Industrial Democracy protesting against the "Rex" sailing with munitions for abroad, speculation was aroused regarding the consequences of an embargo. How effective would government control of the sale of munitions be? What devious ways, such as selling to a neutral country, would be devised? (This discussion occurred during the Italian conquest of Ethiopia.)

Personal attitudes toward social issues are often reflected in the daily incidents in the school, as in the following:

Gene came into my room, explaining that she had had an argument with some members of her group over their attitudes during trips they had made to Harlem and the East Side of New York. Jane had told her that she could not see how anybody could like slumming. Gene had objected to such an attitude, since the purpose of the trip was to study the living conditions of people in an unfortunate situation. To her, she said, those trips, together with the study of housing and income, had been one of the most meaningful experiences. She wants to write on that problem.[18]

Students' writing presents other opportunities for securing evidence on social sensitivity. Much writing contains some expression of social attitudes and of social values held by the author, provided its content is analyzed from that standpoint. Often only a listing of the topics chosen for creative writing over a period of time or for free choice "research" reveals trends in social sensitivity. Thus, frequent choice of social problems to write about or frequent emphasis on social context and social implications is an indication of real interest in social matters. Free choice writing, however, provides only sporadic evidence, and not necessarily on the particular aspects of behavior a teacher may wish to explore. To secure more systematic evidence, controlled assignments in which all students respond to the same general problem, issue, or experience, are often employed. Below is a sample of written responses to the following paragraph assigned as a topic to the whole class: "Nothing can be done about poverty. There have been and always will be poor people, incapable people, unambitious people, dirty work to do, survival of the fittest...."

Roy: I think something could be done about poverty. They could be taught many things they have no chance to learn today. They should be housed in a healthy environment. I think there will always be poor people, unambitious people, incapable people, and dirty work to do, but I do not think that a very great percentage of the poor today are poor because of these reasons. They don't have a chance. I don't think that 42 per cent of the Americans today fall into that lazy and unambitious class, yet 42 per cent of Americans are poor. There must be something wrong with our system today.

John: I can find little pity for white and colored trash who have never amounted to anything.... I think that the smarter man should make more money and that it would wreck any advancement of civilization so to restrict initiative as to pay the man who carries twice the load as much as the mass below him gets.

Mary: Very few people would at any time...be willing to *give* their money away. Of course, they can be made to give it to the government, but it seems to me to be a shame if people are taxed so heavy to aid all the poor. Surely I agree something could be done, but I can imagine my own feelings if the majority of the voters, who are middle class and poor, should vote for a tax that would take away a large part of the money and savings I had worked for and made.

Even this limited sampling reveals the possibilities of this method of learning about the social viewpoints of the students. These excerpts reveal an interesting variety of views regarding causes and cure of poverty and unemployment. Different positions are taken toward taxation. Personal sympathy for people in different economic circumstances or lack of it is shown. One can even gain some idea of the nature and degree of awareness of social conditions in each student.

Records of free choice activities of all sorts often yield surprisingly useful information. Thus records of free reading may give clues regarding students' social interests, level of social awareness, and maturity and direction of social outlook. Records of activities of all sorts, in-school and out-of-school, such as participation in school government, vacation activities, attendance at motion pictures, lectures, and concerts, and other leisure-time activities are also useful, particularly when the nature of the activity is recorded in addition to its frequency.[19] Although these records serve primarily as evidence of interests, analysis of their content also serves for evidence of social sensitivity.

Free response tests employing a form akin to projective techniques are also useful devices for getting at personal responses to social issues. Their advantage lies in their indirection. The individual is not asked directly to reveal his social values. He is provided an apparently innocent object of attention to which he can respond freely and personally. The object of attention is so chosen as to draw out revelations of his pattern of social sensitivity. In a completely free response test, only a brief statement is given, and students are asked to list all of the thoughts that occur to them in connection with that subject.

> *Problem.* The following quotation from a local produce market appeared in a daily paper:
> > "Cooking onions — 30 cents per bu."
> *Directions:* List all of your thoughts about this quotation which might be of social importance. Number your ideas 1, 2, 3, 4, etc.[20]

Certain ideas about students' understanding of, and attitudes evoked by, the problem can be gained from mere examination of each student's responses. However, clearer descriptions of each student, as well as of groups of students, are possible when the responses are summarized in terms of certain general criteria. Thus, the responses to the exercise above could be summarized in terms of the frequency of purely personal association (such as, "I don't like onions"); in terms of frequency of responses showing awareness of the implications of this situation to immediate personal-social values, like the family budget or diet (such as, "If onions are so cheap, they could be used more frequently in family menus"); or, finally, in terms of how frequently the wider social implications are mentioned (such as, "If onions are so cheap, what about the income and the standard of living of those who work in onion fields"). A summary could also be made in terms of how frequently each student mentioned important considerations and how relevant his remarks are to the problem.

More controlled forms of essay tests were used by the evaluation committee in explorations preliminary to the drafting of objective test forms. Students were given a problem situation, with several courses of action listed, and were asked to choose the course of action they thought most desirable. They were then asked to indicate the reasons they would use in supporting their choice. All such free exercises are, of course, fraught with certain difficulties. To score the responses objectively is a time-consuming process. The fact that each student expresses his thoughts in a somewhat personal way interferes with the possibility of assigning his responses a precise and fully objective meaning. However, when teachers are able to develop valid exercises of this sort and take the care and the time necessary for a diagnostic analysis of the responses, tests of this sort have a real role to play, particularly since they can be made more readily an integral part of teaching than is the case with more formal tests.

Aspects of Appreciation*

Introduction

All of the lists of objectives submitted by schools in the Eight-Year Study mentioned the development of a wide range, an increasing depth, and a personal selection of interests and appreciations. Accordingly, an interschool Committee on the Evaluation of Interests and Appreciations was formed early in the Study and met frequently to analyze this area of objectives. One of its first conclusions was that, although interests and appreciations are so closely related that it is often impossible to distinguish them in specific instances, techniques for evaluating them would be sufficiently different to justify a division of labor. The committee was therefore divided into subgroups after arriving at a common understanding of the objectives to be considered. Many subtle distinctions were drawn between interests and appreciations, but their common purport seemed to be that interests emphasize "liking" an activity, while appreciations include "liking" but emphasize "insight" into the activity: understanding it, realizing its true values, distinguishing the better from the worse, and the like. The sub-committees on appreciations developed instruments chiefly in the fields of literature and the arts, which are reported in this chapter.

Appreciation of Literature

Since there are somewhat different points of view as to what is meant by the objective "Appreciation of Literature,"[21] it is important to recognize at the outset that the analysis which will be described here is restricted to an analysis of certain types of students' reactions to reading. This restriction should not be taken to imply that other behaviors might not be included under the heading "Appreciation of Literature"; a number of articles and studies might be cited to illustrate the range of behaviors which have, at various times, been identified with appreciation. Carroll,[22] for example, mentions information, sensitivity to style, understanding of "deeper meanings," and emotional response, as included in appreciation. In developing his tests of prose appreciation Carroll chose to measure students' ability to differentiate the good from the less good and the less good from the very bad.[23] This ability has been regarded by many as an important element in, or index of, appreciation. Logasa and Wright, to cite a second example,

---

*Originally chapter 4 in *Appraising and Recording Student Progress*.

have made a rather extensive analysis of appreciation[24] and have published tests of the following behaviors: discovery of theme, reader participation, reaction to sensory images, discrimination between good and poor comparisons, recognition of rhythm, and appreciation of fresh expressions as opposed to triteness. Instead, the restriction mentioned above merely implies a selection, on the part of the committee, of behaviors which (1) were regarded by them as important aspects of appreciation, and (2) were not being adequately appraised by the available instruments. A major question which the committee wished to be able to answer is: "How do students react to their reading?" For convenience, certain of these reactions to reading have been designated as "Aspects of Appreciation."

The Committee's Analysis of Students' Reactions to Reading.   The Committee on the Evaluation of Reading was organized in the fall of 1935. In selecting members for this committee the schools recognized that teachers other than teachers of literature are often responsible for guiding the reading of students and hence should participate in the evaluation of reading outcomes. For this reason, in addition to the field of English, other areas, such as social studies, the core program, the school library, and school administration, were represented by various members of the committee....

The Committee on the Evaluation of Reading undertook, as its first task in developing instruments for appraising students' reactions to their reading, to clarify what was meant by "reactions to reading." A preliminary analysis of students' reactions to reading was made, at the request of the committee, by Carleton Jones of the Evaluation Staff and was submitted to them for revision. After some discussion, the committee selected from the preliminary analysis seven behaviors or reactions to reading which seemed to them to be of considerable importance. These are:

1. *Satisfaction in the thing appreciated.* Appreciation manifests itself in a feeling, on the part of the individual, of keen satisfaction in and enthusiasm for the thing appreciated. The person who appreciates a given piece of literature finds in it an immediate, persistent, and easily-renewable enjoyment of extraordinary intensity.

2. *Desire for more of the thing appreciated.* Appreciation manifests itself in an active desire on the part of the individual for more of the thing appreciated. The person who appreciates a given piece of literature is desirous of prolonging, extending, supplementing, renewing his first favorable response toward it.

3. *Desire to know more about the thing appreciated.* Appreciation manifests itself in an active desire on the part of the individual to know more about the thing appreciated. The person who appreciates a given piece

of literature is desirous of understanding as fully as possible the significant meanings which it aims to express and of knowing something about its genesis, its history, its locale, its sociological background, its author, etc.

4. *Desire to express one's self creatively.* Appreciation manifests itself in an active desire on the part of an individual to go beyond the thing appreciated: to give creative expression to ideas and feelings of his own which the thing appreciated has chiefly engendered. The person who appreciates a given piece of literature is desirous of doing for himself, either in the same or in a different medium, something of what the author has done in the medium of literature.

5. *Identification of one's self with the thing appreciated.* Appreciation manifests itself in the individual's active identification of himself with the thing appreciated. The person who appreciates a given piece of literature responds to it very much *as if* he were actually participating in the life situations which it represents.

6. *Desire to clarify one's own thinking with regard to the life problems raised by the thing appreciated.* Appreciation manifests itself in an active desire on the part of the individual to clarify his own thinking with regard to specific life problems raised by the thing appreciated. The person who appreciates a given piece of literature is stimulated by it to re-think his own point of view toward certain of the life problems with which it deals and perhaps subsequently to modify his own practical behavior in meeting those problems.

7. *Desire to evaluate the thing appreciated.* Appreciation manifests itself in a conscious effort on the part of the individual to evaluate the thing appreciated in terms of such standards of merit as he himself, at the moment, tends to subscribe to. The person who appreciates a given piece of literature is desirous of discovering and describing for himself the particular values which it seems to hold for him.

An example may aid in clarifying each of these seven behaviors. Let us suppose that a student has read a particular novel, such as Dickens' *Tale of Two Cities*, and that during the reading of this book he has read attentively and with absorption (1). Let us also suppose that he has derived such satisfaction from the book that he plans to read it again and to read other novels by Dickens (2). Perhaps his curiosity about Dickens as an author, about the literary currents of the middle nineteenth century, about the historical novel as a type, or about the French Revolution has been aroused by his reading (3). He might want to sketch Carton riding to the guillotine or try to conceive in words some scene or character which grows out of his reading (4). While reading he might "lose himself" in the events of the book, he might, like Booth Tarkington's Willie Baxter, become one with

Carton and feel that "It is a far, far better thing that I do..." (5). Many problems might be suggested or raised again for him by his reading; he might want to think through what friendship or love implies, what the proper ends of life are, what terror and force effect in the world (6). Finally, he might want to compare this novel with others by Dickens and others of its type, compare his judgments of it with those of other persons, seek out its values and its limitations (7).

This statement of important reactions to reading is a selective one and should be regarded as such. A number of other reactions or responses to reading might be identified and judged to be of importance by other teachers or test makers....

Instruments Which Were Developed to Appraise Students' Reactions to Their Reading. A number of instruments were developed for the evaluation of students' reactions to their reading. Three of these instruments make use of a questionnaire technique which consists essentially of asking students to observe themselves, in retrospect, and to record these observations. This technique was arrived at in the following manner. The committee first discussed ways in which the seven types of reaction to reading might be manifested in readily observable student behavior and prepared a list of overt acts and verbal responses which, they judged, would in certain situations reveal the presence or absence of each of these seven types of behavior. A few of the overt acts and verbal responses which were included in this list are:

1. *Satisfaction in the thing appreciated*
   1.1 He reads aloud to others, or simply to himself, passages which he finds unusually interesting.
   1.2 He reads straight through without stopping, or with a minimum of interruption.
   1.3 He reads for considerable periods of time.
2. *Desire for more of the thing appreciated*
   2.1 He asks other people to recommend reading which is more or less similar to the thing appreciated.
   2.2 He commences this reading of similar things as soon after reading the first as possible.
   2.3 He reads subsequently several books, plays, or poems by the same author.
3. *Desire to know more about the thing appreciated*
   3.1 He asks other people for information or sources of information about what he has read.

3.2 He reads supplementary materials, such as biography, history, criticism, etc.

3.3 He attends literary meetings devoted to reviews, criticisms, discussions, etc.

4. *Desire to express one's self creatively*

4.1 He produces, or at least undertakes to produce, a creative product more or less after the manner of the thing appreciated.

4.2 He writes critical appreciations.

4.3 He illustrates what he has read in some one of the graphic, spatial, musical, or dramatic arts.

5. *Identification of one's self with the thing appreciated*

5.1 He accepts, at least while he is reading, the persons, places, situations, events, etc., as real.

5.2 He dramatizes, formally or informally, various passages.

5.3 He imitates, consciously and unconsciously, the speech and actions of various characters in the story.

6. *Desire to clarify one's own thinking with regard to the life problems raised by the thing appreciated*

6.1 He attempts to state, either orally or in writing, his own ideas, feelings, or information concerning the life problems with which his reading deals.

6.2 He examines other sources for more information about these problems.

6.3 He reads other works dealing with similar problems.

7. *Desire to evaluate the thing appreciated*

7.1 He points out, both orally and in writing, the elements which in his opinion make it good literature.

7.2 He explains how certain unacceptable elements (if any) could be improved.

7.3 He consults published criticisms.

The committee next suggested that one method of securing evidence of these seven types of response in secondary schools would be to ask students to report on these behaviors themselves. The advantage of asking students to observe themselves and to record these observations, as compared with the collection of anecdotal records or the use of interviews, is primarily one of practicability. The committee also recognized that the use of a questionnaire technique demands that certain assumptions be fulfilled if the method is to give valid evidence. Most important among these assumptions are: (1) that the overt behaviors and their accompanying situations specified in the items are significant evidence of the seven types of behavior; (2) that the students are capable of observing these overt behaviors, of remembering them, and of recording them; (3) that the students are honest in their responses to each item. The extent to which these assumptions actually are fulfilled will depend upon both the characteristics of the questionnaire itself and the situation in which the student is asked to respond to the questionnaire. First, let us review the construction of one of these three questionnaires, pointing out the criteria in its construction which were made necessary by these assumptions; later we shall consider the administration of such an instrument and the conditions under which its use is most apt to give valid evidence.

Questionnaire on Voluntary Reading.   Of the three appreciation questionnaires — The Novel Questionnaire, The Drama Questionnaire, and The Questionnaire on Voluntary Reading — which were developed during the period of the Eight-Year Study, The Questionnaire on Voluntary Reading was used and studied most extensively; for this reason it will be chosen to illustrate the construction of an instrument to measure students' responses to their reading. This questionnaire was designed to measure the extent to which students exhibit the seven types of response to their "free" or voluntary reading of books. The directions to the student on the questionnaire read in part as follows:

QUESTIONNAIRE ON VOLUNTARY READING

Directions to the Student

The purpose of this questionnaire is to discover what you really think about the reading which you do in your leisure time. Altogether there are one hundred questions. Consider each question carefully and answer it as honestly and as frankly as you possibly can. *There are no "right" answers as such.* It is not expected that your own thoughts or feelings or activities relating to books should be like those of anyone else.

The numbers on your Answer Sheet correspond to the numbers of the questions on the questionnaire. There are three ways to mark the Answer Sheet:

A — means that your answer to the question is *Yes*.
U — means that your answer to the question is *Uncertain*.
D — means that your answer to the question is *No*.

If it is at all possible, answer the questions by *Yes* or *No*. You should mark a question *Uncertain* only if you are unable to answer either *Yes* or *No*.

Please answer *every* question

One hundred questions which the student is asked to answer make up the items of the questionnaire. An illustrative set of items, grouped under the seven types of response,[25] follows:

"Derives satisfaction from reading"
1. Is it unusual for you, of your own accord, to spend a whole afternoon or evening reading a book?
2. Do you ever read plays, apart from school requirements?

"Wants to read more"
1. Do you have in mind one or two books which you would like to read sometime soon?
2. Do you wish that you had more time to devote to reading?

"Identifies himself with his reading"
1. Have you ever tried to become in some respects like a character whom you have read about and admired?
2. Is it very unusual for you to become sad or depressed over the fate of a character?

"Becomes curious about his reading"
1. Do you read the book review sections of magazines or newspapers fairly regularly?
2. Do you ever read, apart from school requirements, books or articles about English or American literature?

"Expresses himself creatively"
1. Have you ever wanted to act out a scene from a book which you have read?
2. Has your reading of books ever stimulated you to attempt any original writing of your own?

"Evaluates his reading"
1. Do you ordinarily read a book without giving much thought to the quality of its style?
2. Do you ever consult published criticisms of any of the books which you read?

"Relates his reading to life"
1. Has your attitude toward war or patriotism been changed by books which you have read?
2. Is it very unusual for you to gain from your reading of books a better understanding of some of the problems which people face in their everyday living?

It will be observed that this statement of the seven types of behavior differs somewhat from that given on pages 178 and 179. The major purpose of this rewording was to place the emphasis, for several of these types of behavior, on what students actually do rather than on what they desire to do.

The first criterion that the items included in the questionnaire had to satisfy was that they must deal with behaviors which were judged by teachers who prepared and used the questionnaire to be significant evidence of the seven types of response to reading. In a sense, then, the items constitute a definition, in terms of what students do and say, of what these teachers meant by "Derives satisfaction from reading," "Wants to read more," etc. In order to insure that this criterion was satisfied, the items were drawn originally from the list of overt acts and verbal responses which the committee judged to be significant evidences of the seven types of response. Then, as use of the questionnaire in a number of schools gave opportunity to secure from teachers additional judgments of the significance of these items, the questions were revised.

In selecting and phrasing items it was necessary to consider several additional criteria. The assumption that students are capable of observing these overt behaviors in themselves, of remembering, and of recording them demands first of all that each item deal only with those behaviors which secondary school students are apt to exhibit and only with situations in which students are apt to find themselves. This is almost an obvious criterion, for if we expect the student to report on his behavior we must ask him questions about things he actually has an opportunity to do. The committee, in preparing the list of overt acts and verbal responses, and teachers, in judging the significance of items included in the early forms of the questionnaire, were asked to consider whether or not each of the specific acts or verbal responses is something which secondary school students are apt to do or say. It was possible later, by studying the responses of students to each item on the questionnaire, to check these judgments of teachers to some extent. Second, this assumption demands that each item deal with behavior and situations which the student is apt to remember. This criterion immediately rules out certain types of questions. In general, we would not expect students to remember, for example, exactly how many books they had read during the summer; yet we might expect them to remember whether or not they had read a book during the preceding week. In general, we would not expect them to remember the details of an argument with a friend about the merits of a particular book; yet we might expect them to remember having tried to defend their judgment of a book. Third, this assumption demands that any judgments or generalizations which the student is asked to formulate be relatively simple ones. An item which calls for an extensive introspection, for the rating of one's self on an abstract and undefined quality, for making fine distinctions between causes or effects, etc., thus would be ruled out. Fourth, this assumption demands that each question be so phrased that it is readily understood by the student and can be answered with a minimum of writing. That the question must be understood if he is to answer it intelligently is obvious. That his ability to express himself in writing may become a factor which, for this test, may inappropriately condition the evidence and the judgments made from the evidence, was also recognized. The selection of *Yes, No,* and *Uncertain* as the particular pattern of "controlled response" for the questionnaires eliminated the necessity of the student's writing out his answers, but made it necessary that each question be so phrased that it could be answered with one of the three responses provided.

The assumption that students are honest in their responses also suggests criteria which each item must meet. Certain activities and certain situations may have such a "prestige" value that questions dealing with them would tempt the student to say that he took part in them, whether he actually did or not. Questions dealing with any activity which is ordinarily participated in because of its "social" value thus were ruled out, as were all questions dealing with activities in which participation might be dependent primarily upon an economic factor. Likewise, items which deal with activities or situations, the disclosure of which might threaten the student's sense of security, may tempt him to disavow actual participation in these activities or situations. Questions which asked students to admit the reading of certain kinds of materials which are commonly frowned upon, such as comic magazines, or to disclose any of his more intimate feelings or relationships with other persons also were ruled out. The final criterion for the selection of the items, then, is that they deal only with overt acts and verbal responses which the student might be expected to report honestly.

[*Section on Summarizing and Scoring the Questionnaire on Voluntary Reading Omitted — Eds.*]

Interpretation and Uses of Evaluation Data*

The preceding chapters have explained the development of evaluation instruments in several major areas of objectives. References to methods of interpretation and uses of these instruments were confined to single instruments or pairs of instruments. Other problems of interpretation and uses were encountered when a whole program of evaluation was developing. The present chapter is devoted to these problems.

---

*Originally chapter 7 in *Appraising and Recording Student Progress.*

[Editors' Note: A large section of "Interpretation and Uses of Evaluation Data" has been omitted. The excluded material deals largely with the method of interpreting test information in guiding individual students. It includes a long and detailed illustrative case study of one student. The key points in the excluded section are:
• Methods of interpretation and uses of evaluation data should be based on: (1) the function which interpretation is to serve; and (2) the data and assumptions on which they are based.
• The functions of interpretation are: (1) a translation of scores or other data into meaningful information; (2) suggesting hypotheses about the possible causes of identified strengths and weaknesses; and (3) suggesting hypotheses about needed remediation.
• Evaluation is analytic and requires the interpreter to break the data up according to different configurations of objectives. Evaluation is also synthetic and requires the interpreter to interpret any single aspect of behavior in terms of a total pattern of behavior.
The part concerning interpretation of evaluation data for purposes of program evaluation is reprinted next. We begin within the section entitled For Checking the Effectiveness of Curriculum in Achieving Major Objectives.]

In the Eight-Year Study it was recognized that as long as there were important differences in objectives and curriculum practices among schools, it would be inappropriate to measure progress by the same standards, particularly if these standards represented nothing more than an average of the performance of different groups under varying circumstances. The pattern of interests in a school for foreign students in New York City could not necessarily be considered appropriate as a "norm" or desirable pattern of interests for a suburban school in the Middle West, and the average of the two patterns might not be desirable for either school. Similarly, one would not expect students in a school which was barely beginning to explore the methods of developing critical thinking to be judged by the same criteria as were students who have had long and careful training.

Difficulties were also encountered because of the methods of using norms to which teachers had been accustomed. The national average had been invested with almost magical significance, so that many teachers were too easily satisfied if their groups came up to it, even when they might have greatly exceeded it, and too easily discouraged if their groups fell below it, even though their progress was all that could be expected. For this reason, only tables of medians of comparable groups in other schools were made available to the evaluation representatives of schools in the Eight-Year

Study, who were trained to interpret them. These gave a rough and admittedly cumbersome method of estimating the relative progress of comparable groups, but it was hoped that by this very fact a more thoughtful use of norms would be stimulated.

A third possible method of interpreting scores to indicate the success of a program in reaching its objectives was a comparison of the level of ability revealed by the tests with the level of ability required in life situations. Thus, if the use of the correct scientific principles in life problems were the objective of the school, and the tests revealed that students accepted a variety of popular misconceptions as scientific principles, then the school had not done enough in this direction, even though all other schools showed a similar weakness.

This sort of interpretation, however, had always to be made cautiously, because the level of accomplishment demanded by life situations was often a matter of vague conjecture. It was thus easy to expect too much or too little of students. The present level of achieving these newer intangible objectives may be too much determined by inadequate methods of helping students achieve them. Nevertheless, some comparison of pupils' performance with life demands was inescapable if we were not always to rest content with what other schools were doing. Perhaps none of them was doing enough.

For Checking Hypotheses Underlying the Program

An important purpose of evaluation was to check the hypotheses underlying the school program. Often new practices were introduced in the hope of producing certain desirable changes in students. These changes might not come about, or they might be accompanied by other changes which were less desirable. One public school introduced a core program with several purposes in mind, one of which was to develop better social attitudes. A comprehensive testing program revealed that while the social attitudes developed were clearer, more consistent, and more liberal than in most schools in the Study, the students had serious difficulties with techniques of precise thinking. In drawing inferences from data, they exhibited little caution and showed a tendency to go beyond the data. In applying facts and principles they failed to discriminate those which were valid and relevant from their opposites. Apparently in emphasizing social values the school relied too much on generalizations and too little upon the careful analysis of factual data.

In another school the evaluation of reading revealed that one group specializing in science and mathematics showed a more limited appreciation than all others, including those in other grades specializing in the same field. They found little enjoyment in reading; they did not identify themselves with their reading or relate their reading to life problems. Since this was a marked deviation from the type of responses prevailing in the school, the problem was considered by the faculty. It developed that a special course in literature was offered to this group. On the hypothesis that science students are interested in scientists, this course concentrated on biographies of scientists and mathematicians. Since it was not the intention of the staff to narrow the reading interests of these students, a broader program was agreed upon.

Still another school had hoped to develop democratic attitudes by means of a program of extra-curricular activities organized by the student council, while conducting its academic curriculum in the usual manner. The results of the test on Beliefs about School Life revealed that a large majority of these students preferred authoritarian methods of classroom management, approved of social distinction of all sorts, and in general had tendencies toward undemocratic attitudes. These results called into question the efficacy of this program of student activities for the purpose of democratizing school life. In the course of an investigation by a group of students and faculty members, it was discovered that the student council was run by an inner clique. Many of the student activities tended to be exclusive and to have other undemocratic characteristics. The active participation was limited largely to students in the upper grades. In the light of the facts brought out by this study, a reorganization of student activities was undertaken, involving a closer relationship between curricular and extracurricular activities.

Such instances indicated that special care had to be exercised when changes were introduced into the program to find out not only whether the intended results were produced but also whether undesirable features did not accompany them. Even if no major changes had been made, the hypotheses on which the school had always operated might be faulty. Hence, evaluation data needed to be examined with special reference to the *issues* underlying the program.

Possibility of Interpretation

The foregoing discussion may have left the impression that interpretation of evaluation data required very unusual insight and patience, and too extensive knowledge of evaluation for the classroom teacher to master. There is no getting around the fact that a thoughtful interpretation of the evidence of students' progress and the effectiveness of curriculum practices is complex, and that it can be learned only by long practice supplemented by careful explanation. Yet there is no reason to believe that further progress in getting a more adequate picture of pupil growth will ever return to the primitive simplicity of school marks. Reducing the amount of data secured is no solution, for a few scattered data can only raise questions, not answer them. A rich and full program of evaluation can suggest answers to a great many questions, but only by thoughtful interpretation and not by chance. Teachers must learn to get meaning from the extensive and well-integrated sets of data now available. Unless somebody knows what the scores mean and takes them into account in his teaching, it is obvious that there is no point in getting them.

On the other hand, the process of interpretation is not so difficult for busy teachers in a large public school as the foregoing may suggest. When teachers know the pupils concerned, hypotheses to account for their test scores readily occur to them. Then, too, if evaluation is carried on continuously, the evidence accumulates gradually, and only a few data need be interpreted at any one time, and fitted into what one already knows about students. Also, the processes which appear elaborate, when written down and explained verbally, easily become part and parcel of the common sense thinking of thoughtful teachers. Finally, when evaluation is undertaken as a common task for the school, with the whole faculty cooperating in interpreting the results, the task for any one individual is reduced.

Philosophy and Objectives*

The Foreword and the Preface explain the relation of this work to the general undertaking, including the original organization of this department and the way in which it later became a part of the work carried on under the direction of the Committee on Evaluation and Recording. In addition to the Committee on Behavior Description, there were organized working committees for the preparation of progress forms in each of several subject fields, forms for use in transfer from school to college, and forms to be used in reporting to the home. Because the American Council on Education had a cumulative record card that was soon to be revised, no committee was appointed to work on this type of form, although it was needed to complete

---

*Originally chapter 9 in *Appraising and Recording Student Progress: Part II, Recording for Guidance and Transfer.*

the set. The revision has now been made and the new form is described in this report.

Of special significance in consideration of the material in this book is the community of interest and acceptance of common philosophic bases for work that characterized the different groups that are responsible for it. As a matter of fact, there was throughout the study a considerable amount of overlapping membership, so that not only members of the staff but other individuals worked on committees for evaluation and ones for recording, or on committees devising record forms for two different, although related, purposes. This common membership helped the effort that was made to avoid unnecessary duplication or conflict between those responsible for evaluation and those working on recording. Some problems were, of necessity, attacked from both angles, but with advantage rather than waste of time. Various groups, for example, studied the objectives of teachers and schools, but always in relation to particular problems, and always with the results obtained by other groups available for comparison and use. The list of objectives prepared by the Evaluation Staff was particularly helpful to all the committees on recording and reporting.

All record forms that can do so provide space for information of the kinds obtained by the Evaluation Staff, so that this can be related to the other data and so can help to make a more complete description of the pupil.

Although it will be said again in relation to various forms and their use, it must be emphasized here that no single result of evaluation procedures or of observations recorded on the forms is considered to be independent of other information about a pupil. All the information obtained, as would be true if he were studied by a psychologist or psycho-analyst, contributes to the more complete understanding of him that becomes the basis for the school's dealing with him.

Philosophy and Objectives

The original Committee on Reports and Records considered with great care former methods of recording facts about personal characteristics or traits, and the words used in describing and reporting about them.

Out of this study and the discussion of the problems facing the committee came the philosophy and objectives that governed the later work. The list of objectives in explicit or implicit form was reexamined by the other committees, and was generally accepted as a guide, though it was realized that some of it applied most completely to the study of personal characteristics.

General Purposes and Philosophy of Recording

1. (a) The purpose of recording is not primarily that of bookkeeping. Instead the fundamental reason for records is their value as a basis for more intelligent dealing with human beings.

The first purpose of records is therefore that of forming a basis for *understanding individuals* so that effective guidance can be given.

(b) Since the educational process is a continuous one that should not be set back at certain transfer points, it becomes necessary that guidance shall continue across such points in such a way as to increase the probability of continuity in dealing with the person.

An extended purpose of records hence becomes that of furnishing *transferable information* for guidance.

(c) Because of the need of cooperative and consistent dealing with a boy or girl by home and school, as well as the right of the home to information as complete and reliable as possible about progress and development, records should furnish the material on which reports can be founded, and reports should be considered an essential and consistent part of the recording system.

A third purpose of record keeping is therefore to provide the information needed for *reports to the home*, and to add effective ways of giving such information.

(d) Information is needed at all stages of education, and particularly at points of transfer from one institution to another, or from an institution to employment, in order that qualifications of the individual for the new experience can be fairly judged.

A fourth purpose of record keeping is therefore to provide information, and methods of transferring it to others, that will give evidence regarding a pupil's *readiness* for succeeding experiences. This would apply to fitness for a particular college or other institution.

2. What might be considered an indirect but nevertheless important purpose of records is that of stimulating teachers to consider and decide upon their objectives, judge something of the relative importance of their aims, and estimate their own work and the progress of their pupils in relation to the objectives chosen.

Many teachers think almost entirely in terms of the most obvious objectives concerned with the learning of subject matter and evaluate their results only in terms of such aims. They give little or no consideration to the changes in their pupils that should come about as a result of the experiences undergone, and so they fail to bring about the development that is possible. Through well planned records they can be helped to a wider vision and a more constructive influence.

It is evident that the most valuable and complete record that could be made by observation of an individual would consist of a record of his behavior throughout life, or that portion of it under observation. It is believed that any observational technique that has value must consist in using the parts of such a record that can be collected and arranged in the time at a teacher's disposal. This can be done by recording significant incidents of behavior and interpretations of them (the "anecdotal" method), by characterizing in one way or another the kinds of behavior observed (sometimes called "behavior description"), or by a combination of characterization and of supplementary analysis in paragraph form.

Where a teacher deals with a small number of pupils, or carries a light schedule, the recording of extensive anecdotal material seems possible and highly valuable. Some institutions and teachers use such a method even when the written material cannot be extensive. The more the demands on the teacher through appointments or pupil load, the less is it possible to write voluminously, and the more does it seem necessary for each instructor to digest his observations into quickly recorded (but not too quickly arrived at) judgments about the typical behavior of the pupils. No "checking" system, however, can fit all of the significant differences among people, no matter how well it is devised, so such a system must allow for supplementary notes that modify or add completeness to a description.

As this committee was trying to devise a method and blanks for recording facts about a pupil in abbreviated form, it was necessary to agree upon working objectives for producing the kind of forms that would serve the purposes desired. The following objectives were used.

Working Objectives for Records and Reports

1. Any form devised should be based on the objectives of teachers and schools so that a continuing study of a pupil by its use will throw light on his successive stages of development in powers or characteristics believed to be important.

2. The forms dealing with personal characteristics should be descriptive rather than of the nature of a scale. Therefore "marks" of any kind, or placement, as on a straight line representing a scale from highest to lowest, should not be used.

3. Every effort should be made to reach agreement about the meaning of trait names used, and to make their significance in terms of the behavior of a pupil understood by those reading the record.

4. Wherever possible a characterization of a person should be by

description of typical behavior rather than by a word or phrase that could have widely different meanings to different people.

5. The forms should be flexible enough to allow choice of headings under which studies of pupils can be made, thus allowing a school, department, or teacher to use the objectives considered important in the particular situation, or for the particular pupil.

6. Characteristics studied should be such that teachers will be likely to have opportunities to observe behavior that gives evidence about them. It is not expected, however, that all teachers will have evidence about all characteristics.

7. Forms should be so devised and related that any school will be likely to be able to use them without an overwhelming addition to the work of teachers or secretaries.

8. Characteristics studied should be regarded not as independent entities but rather as facets of behavior shown by a living human being in his relations with his environment.

This last objective is a fundamental one. It has been observed in the work on both evaluation and recording, and must be kept in mind in considering whatever has been produced. The one great danger in the use of any forms that offer opportunity for recording facts about people is that those who use them may revert to the idea of "marking," using the material on the forms as a scale for rating, instead of as an abbreviated basis for description of the person's behavior in some area or under some conditions. The various record forms too should be considered as supplementing each other so as to give a more complete description of the individual than a single form could present....

Teachers' Reports and Reports to the Home*

During the Study various schools wrote to the chairman of the Committee on Evaluation and Recording asking about tendencies in reports to parents and expressing dissatisfaction with existing forms. A sub-committee[26] was therefore appointed to investigate the practices of schools, to analyze tendencies in reporting, and to make recommendations of forms for teachers' use and for sending reports to the home. This committee's first step was to collect report forms from schools of various kinds, and to ask the schools

---

*Originally chapter 11 in *Appraising and Recording Student Progress*.

to say how and why present practices were unsatisfactory and to comment on what reports should be. The report cards obtained were carefully studied, and the criticisms and suggestions sent in by the schools were analyzed. Quite a number of schools, however, sent no forms, saying that they had nothing that would be of any help in the undertaking. It became clear at once that the most general demand was for something that would replace numerical or letter marks, and would give more usable information about a pupil's strengths and weaknesses.

Many schools were convinced that the single mark in a subject hid the facts instead of showing them clearly. The mark was, in effect, an average of judgments about various elements in a pupil's progress that lost their meaning and their value when thus combined. The schools believed that the value of a judgment concerning the work done by a pupil in any school course or activity depended on the degree to which that judgment was expressed in a form that showed his strengths and his weaknesses and therefore presented an analyzed picture of his achievement that would be a safe basis for guidance.

There was also a feeling that marks had become competitive to a degree that was harmful to both the less able and the more able, and that they were increasingly directing the attention of pupils, parents, and even teachers, away from the real purposes of education toward the symbols that represented success but did not emphasize its elements or its meaning.

The commonest method of replacing marks proved to be that of writing paragraphs analyzing a pupil's growth as seen by each teacher. This method is an excellent one, since good descriptions by a number of teachers combine to give a reasonably complete picture of development in relation to the objectives discussed. On the other hand, a report in this form is very time-consuming for teachers and office, as well as difficult to summarize in form for use in transfer and guidance. The committee decided on a compromise that would make place for giving definite information about important objectives in an abbreviated form and would allow for supplementing this with written material needed to modify or complete the information.

To find the objectives, the list collected by the Evaluation Staff and the forms worked out by the committees for the various subject fields...were studied. It was discovered that there were five objectives that were common to all fields and experiences, and about which knowledge would be particularly valuable to parents as well as to pupils. These five objectives were therefore chosen as headings to be reported on by all teachers and to be used in reports to the home. The wording adopted for them is not, however, identical with the wordings on the forms used in subject fields. The reason is that this committee had to draw from the large amount of information asked for on the subject forms that which could be condensed into simple phrases that would have meaning and importance on a report to the home. The headings follow:

Success in Achieving the Specific Purposes of the Course
Progress in Learning How to Think
Effectiveness in Communicating Ideas:
  Oral
  Written
Active Concern for the Welfare of the Group
General Habits of Work

The question of classifications to indicate degrees of success or growth in relation to these objectives proved a difficult one. After much discussion and experimentation it was decided to take as a point of departure the usual expectation for one of the age group and the background of the pupil in question. Two classifications above and two below are used. They are defined as follows:

IS OUTSTANDING: The pupil has reached an *outstanding* stage of development in the characteristic and field indicated: that is, a stage distinctly above that usual for pupils of the same age and similar opportunities.

IS ABOVE USUAL: The pupil has reached a stage of development somewhat *higher* than usual, perhaps with promise of eventually reaching a superior level.

IS AT USUAL STAGE: The pupil is at approximately the *usual* stage of development for age and opportunity.

IS BELOW USUAL: The pupil is sufficiently *below* the usual stage in this field to need particular help from the home and school or greater effort on the part of the pupil.

IS SERIOUSLY BELOW: The pupil is *seriously below* an acceptable standard in the field indicated.

In this particular these forms depart somewhat from the descriptive method that is emphasized in the work of all the committees, though taken as a whole these blanks are still highly descriptive. This departure, however, should not be thought of as too inconsistent, since the purpose of these forms affected to some extent the method to be used. It seems likely that the time will come when each pupil is judged primarily in accordance with his ability and his opportunities, rather than in comparison with others. There is still demand, however, for information that will tell parents with some definiteness where their children are showing strengths or weaknesses as judged by normal expectations. These forms try to meet that demand and at the same time to describe the pupil's progress in a way analytical enough to give helpful guidance.

In addition to the section that tells the degree of success a pupil is achieving in the five objectives listed, there are three other sections of the report. The first gives opportunity for the teachers to point out weaknesses a pupil should particularly try to eradicate. There are eight of these listed, and the subjects in which the weaknesses are evident are shown on the home report:

Accuracy in following directions
Efficient use of time and energy
Neatness and orderliness
Self-reliance
Persistence in completing work
Thoughtful participation in discussion
Conscientiousness of effort
Reading

There is also opportunity for the teachers to report on the pupils' likelihood of success in continuing to work in their fields, both in later years in school and in advanced institutions.

A section for "General Comment" appears on the teacher's report, and on the report to the home. Some schools copy the most valuable of the teachers' comments upon the home report form. Others summarize criticisms and suggestions in this space. Occasionally so much of value should be sent that an attached sheet must be used, but in general the space for comment seems to be sufficient.

In all the details that have been mentioned the teachers' report and the home report are identical, although they differ in arrangement, since the home report is designed to combine the reports of all the teachers into a single form that can be read easily.

There are two forms of the report to the home. They include the same material but differ in arrangement in a way that produces somewhat different emphases. Form A tends to emphasize the objectives in which a pupil is strong or weak, while Form B goes further in showing a pupil's degree of success in individual subjects. A school can choose either form or can do as a school represented on the committee has done. This school liked the completeness of the teachers' reports so well that it decided to send copies of all of them to the parents instead of using the combined report form.

While one of the greatest values of these forms is the way in which they provide for guidance by analyzing a student's progress instead of trying to express several factors in one "mark," the form has other advantages.

An important one is the degree to which it directs the minds of pupils, parents, and teachers away from marks toward the fundamental objectives with which pupils should be concerned. Incidentally, in this procedure it is not easy to compare two reports in a way to make the less able pupil feel inferior or the more able one become smug, for in such an analysis even the poorest student is likely to find some appreciation, while the best student is likely to discover some weaknesses to be corrected.

It hardly seems necessary to point out the fact that this form, like the "Behavior Description," attempts to describe somewhat fully a phase of the behavior of a person. In this case, it is principally the pupil as one who is learning and developing mental power that is observed. As in the other form, the pupil is studied by a number of teachers, and the mode and distribution of response in different environments is recorded. The comment appearing on the form sent to the parents becomes an analysis of what is shown under the various headings, and a recommendation of ways in which the pupil can be helped to overcome his weaknesses and use his ability more effectively.

A word of warning about the introduction of such report forms may not be amiss. Pupils and parents should receive some explanation of the meaning of the information given so that they will not be confused by the very completeness of what is said and will not be antagonized by the unfamiliar material.

Notes

1. During the exploratory period, Oscar K. Buros of Rutgers University served as Associate Director. After helping to get the plan outlined, Mr. Buros resigned as Associate Director of the Evaluation Staff and returned to Rutgers University. From July 1935 until September 1938, Mr. Louis E. Raths served as Associate Director. The staff was then housed at The Ohio State University. When Mr. Tyler, the Director, moved to the University of Chicago in September 1938, Mr. Maurice L. Hartung was made Associate Director. Others who served as members of the staff at least part time for one or more years were: Herbert J. Abraham, Dwight L. Arnold, Bruno Bettelheim, Jean Friedberg Block, Charles L. Boye, Paul B. Diederich, Wilfred Eberhart, Fred P. Frutchey, Paul R. Grim, Chester William Harris, Louis M. Heil, John H. Herrick, Clark W. Horton, Walter Hower, Carleton C. Jones, W. Harold Lauritsen, Christine McGuire, Harold G. McMullen, Donald H. McNassor, George V. Sheviakov, Hilda Taba, Harold Trimble, Cecelia K. Wasserstrom, Kay D. Watson, Leah Weisman.

Throughout the years these persons have worked together as a unified staff. Although authorship of chapters is indicated [elsewhere]..., in a very real sense this report is a staff document, the product of all members of the staff. Each chapter was criticized and revised several times by all those who were members of the staff at the time the report was written.

2. The appraisal of the development of physical health, requiring, as it does, technical medical training, was not worked upon by the Evaluation Staff.

3. Now, any group working on an evaluation program will find useful a more complete bibliography of evaluation instruments, such as the Buros *Mental Measurements Yearbook*. This bibliography not only lists tests and other appraisal instruments which are commercially available but also includes several critical reviews of these tests written by teachers, curriculum constructors, and test makers. These reviews help in selecting from available instruments those which might be worth a trial.

4. For examples of statements of these types, see the sample problem on page 130.

5. Overcaution is not considered an error by everyone. Some consider it evidence of a tendency to suspend judgment until further evidence is available.

6. Although in this Study analogy was not found to be used to any great extent in student-written interpretations of data, this type of interpretation is encountered extensively in advertising, newspaper articles, etc. It was also the thought of the Evaluation Staff that analogy is one aspect of scientific thinking which they desired to measure in several different contexts. It appears also in the Application of Principles of Science tests.

7. This distribution was based upon studies of reliabilities of early forms.

8. In practice, the scoring may be done on the electric scoring machine, or if one is not available, by use of punched key stencils.

9. The column numbers used in the following paragraphs refer to the data sheet...on which scores are recorded.

10. This discussion of interpretations of test scores is quite informal. For a more rigorous interpretation of a "relatively" high or low score, the standard error of measurement of each category for the particular population under consideration is useful....

11. Intercorrelations have been computed to investigate the extent to which scores described above are statistically independent.... Although positive correlation exists between each of the subscores on general accuracy, the intercorrelation is not sufficiently high to permit the prediction of one score from another. However, a high negative correlation exists between the score on *beyond data* and *insufficient data*, and between *general accuracy* and *crude errors*. From a statistical standpoint it is possible in both these cases to predict one of these scores from the other without appreciable loss of information about the student, but teachers find it less difficult

to interpret the individual scores when all these scores are retained.

12. Tyler, Ralph W. *Constructing Achievement Tests*. Bureau of Educational Research, The Ohio State University.

13. Tyler, Ralph W. *Constructing Achievement Tests*. Bureau of Educational Research, The Ohio State University.

Frutchey, Fred P. "Evaluating Chemistry Instruction." *Educational Research Bulletin*, XVI (January 13, 1937).

Raths, Louis E. "Techniques of Test Construction." *Educational Research Bulletin*, XVII (April 13, 1938).

Heil, Louis M. "Evaluation of Student Achievement in the Physical Sciences — The Application of Laws and Principles." *The American Physics Teacher*, VI (April, 1938).

14. A junior high school test, Form 1.3j, which uses a somewhat different and less complex technique, was also constructed.

15. The column numbers used in the following paragraphs refer to the summary sheet...on which the scores are recorded.

16. The following quotation is an excerpt from the directions.

17. The Commission on Secondary School Curriculum. *The Social Studies in General Education*. New York: Appleton-Century Company, 1940, pp. 347-50.

Jarvie, L.L., and Ellingson, Mark. *A Handbook on the Anecdotal Behavior Journal*. Chicago: University of Chicago Press, 1940.

Traxler, Arthur E. *The Nature and Use of Anecdotal Records*. New York: Educational Records Bureau, 1939. (Mimeo)

18. It is possible to interpret the incidents given above in several different ways. A single incident does not necessarily prove anything about the behavior of an individual, and a number of anecdotes covering a period of time must be collected before any generalization is attempted.

19. For further discussion of the use of reading records and activities records, see *The Social Studies in General Education*, pp. 345-46.

20. This exercise was used in Ohio and Michigan at the time when there were strikes in onion fields, and reports of them appeared in the daily newspapers.

21. Cf. Broom, M.E. "Literature and Aesthetics." *The High School Teacher*, VIII (October, 1932), pp. 293-94.

22. Carroll, Herbert. "A Method of Measuring Prose Appreciations." *English Journal*, XXII (March, 1933), p. 184.

23. *Op. cit.*, p. 185.

24. See "Tests for Measuring Appreciation." *School Review*, XXXIII (September, 1925), pp. 491-92.

25. In the questionnaire itself, the items are ungrouped; they are, how-

ever, readily classified by use of the scoring key.

26. The members of the committee were: Helen M. Atkinson; Derwood Baker; Genevieve Coy; Rosamond Cross; Burton P. Fowler; I.R. Kraybill; Elvina Lucke; Eugene R. Smith, Chairman; John W.M. Rothney, Research Assistant.

III TYLER'S RATIONALE FOR CURRICULUM DEVELOPMENT

1 OVERVIEW

Tyler always saw evaluation as an integral part of the curriculum development process. While his rationale for evaluation was articulated first because of his work on the Service Studies and the Eight-Year Study, in 1936 he developed a rationale for curriculum development. In the 1950s he used his curriculum rationale with students at the University of Chicago. In 1950 he published a monograph entitled *Basic Principles of Curriculum and Instruction* (University of Chicago Press). *Basic Principles of Curriculum and Instruction* has become a classic in education. It has been reprinted numerous times, and currently is widely used in curriculum and evaluation courses. We strongly recommend this excellent monograph to any student of education.

Since this work is readily available, we have not included excerpts from it. However, it is such a key work of Tyler's we felt it would be valuable to include a 1966 reprint of a *Kappan* article where Tyler gives his reflections on *Basic Principles of Curriculum and Instruction*. Tyler gives the background of the monograph and then goes on to describe his thoughts about it.

Basic Principles of Curriculum and Instruction, like his views on evaluation, are grounded in the belief that educators must clarify and validate

199

their objectives. Educators must then go on to develop learning experiences to help students attain those objectives. Finally, educators must continually evaluate students' progress in their attaining the objectives. The Tyler rationale was widely used in many of the large-scale curriculum development projects of the 1960s. It remains a widely respected and widely used process to develop, review, and revise curricula at all levels of education.

Key Points

- Tyler's rationale grew out of the Eight-Year Study and the lack of a generalized approach to curriculum development that educators could use to review and revise their curricula.
- The rationale is keyed to four points: (1) clarification of purpose; (2) selection of learning experiences; (3) the organization of these experiences; and (4) the assessment of progress toward the attainment of the school's objectives.
- A program's objectives should be clarified through: (1) studies of the learner and (2) studies of contemporary life. Objectives should then be screened through (1) the school's philosophy of education; (2) theories of learning; and (3) suggestions from subject matter specialists.
- Learners should be treated as active, purposeful human beings and given a role in controlling the learning situation.
- Objectives should be written at the level of general principles, using specific learning outcomes as illustrations or translations of the objective's intent.
- Learning experiences at a minimum should: (1) provide opportunities to practice the behaviors the program is trying to develop; (2) be satisfying; (3) be feasible; (4) be varied in terms of the methods employed; (5) provide students with models of the behavior to be emulated; and (5) provide continuous evaluative feedback to the teacher and learner.

2 NEW DIMENSIONS IN CURRICULUM DEVELOPMENT

I have been asked to comment on my 1960 monograph titled *Basic Principles of Curriculum and Instruction*, indicating how this formulation came to be and to what extent I have "rethought, changed, updated, clarified my position." This is an assignment which I have found interesting, although it is provincial in focusing attention on one person's work.

The stimulus for me to construct a comprehensive outline of the questions to be answered and the steps to be taken in developing a curriculum, including the program of instruction, arose from my work with the staff of the Eight-Year Study, which officially occupied the period 1934–42. This was a monumental curriculum project for that time, since it involved 30 secondary school systems ranging across the continent from Boston to Los Angeles. This study grew out of the problems of the depression, the great increase in the proportion of youth attending high school (many of whom would have preferred to go to work but were unable to find employment), and the comparative rigidity of the high school curriculum, particularly for those students who wished to keep open the option of college attendance.

Reprinted from *Phi Delta Kappan*, Vol. 48, September 1966, pp. 25–28.

As the project began, the schools encountered great difficulty in identifying the problems to be attacked and in organizing and assigning task forces to work on these curriculum problems. There seemed to be little in common among the schools in their use of terms, in the emphasis being given to the subject fields, to student needs, and to social demands, and there was no clear-cut way in which the educational philosophies of the schools and theories of learning were considered. There were also varied views about the means of education. I was asked to devise a rationale to guide the efforts of the schools in their development of new curricula.

The rationale developed in 1936 was also employed in the Cooperative Study in General Education, a curriculum project of 22 colleges carried on in the period 1939–46. The modification which resulted from its use at the college level were incorporated in 1950 in the syllabus written for a course I taught at the University of Chicago entitled "Basic Principles of Curriculum and Instruction."

So much for the background of the monograph. The other matter I have been asked to comment on concerns changes that have take place in "my position" since 1950. It is hard for one introspectively to chart the course of this thinking over 15 years in an area that has been as active as the field of curriculum, development. Hence what I have to say is likely to be incomplete and, at points, in error. I still find adequate and highly useful the original statement of the four divisions of curriculum inquiry, namely:
1. What educational purposes should the school seek to attain?
2. What educational experiences can be provided that are likely to attain these purposes?
3. How can these educational experiences be effectively organized?
4. How can we determine whether these purposes are being attained?

I also find still useful the three recommended sources for getting information helpful in deciding on objectives, these being: (1) studies of the learner, (2) studies of contemporary life, and (3) suggestions from subject specialists, along with employment of a philosophy of education and a theory of learning primarily as screens for selection and elimination among possible objectives obtained from the three sources. In working with different individuals and groups, I make clear that these sources can be used in any order, not necessarily the one presented in the syllabus, and that philosophy and psychology formulations may also be used to indicate areas for inclusion and exclusion prior to systematic studies of these sources of objectives.

In connection with investigations of curriculum objectives, the greatest change in my thinking relates to the conceptions of the learner and of knowledge and to the problem of the level of generality appropriate for an objective. The use of programmed materials in schools has involved me in observations and discussions that bring into sharp contrast the differing formulations of objectives and theories of learning, as between those who perceive the learner as being "conditioned" by the learning situation so as to respond in the way specified by the teacher or the designer of the program, and those who perceive the learner as an active agent exploring learning situations so as to learn to manipulate them for his purposes. It is somewhat like the difference implied by the cartoon showing one rat saying to another, "We've got this psychologist under control. He gives us food whenever we press the lever."

John Dewey commented more than 30 years ago on the truly educative environment as one in which there is a balance between factors under the learner's control and those that he could not influence. A learning situation in which the learner can exercise no control in terms of his purposes teaches him to conform or to rebel, but not to master. A learning situation in which all the factors are under the learner's control leads to whimsical or undisciplined behavior. Desirable learning results from the learner recognizing factors in the situation to which he must adapt and the others that he can manipulate in terms of his purposes.

I now think it is important in curriculum development to examine the concept of the learner as an active, purposeful human being. This appears to be an important psycho-philosophic factor to consider at an early stage in work on objectives.

The use of programmed material has also raised for explicit consideration in formulating objectives the question of the learner's role in developing and using knowledge. Is knowledge something outside of man that he has discovered and can now make available to learners, or is knowledge man's effort to explain phenomena with which he comes in contact, so that the learner can produce knowledge? The idea of learning by discovery, or Whitehead's comment that "knowledge is like fish, it must be caught fresh each day," takes on more meaning to curriculum workers when they treat knowledge as a growing product of man's effort to understand.

A related issue is the question of the structure of a discipline. Some programmed materials operate on the assumption that the knowledge to be learned is not primarily an organized system, such that stochastic learning processes are appropriate. However, learners can understand the structure of the discipline, that is, the question it deals with, the kind of answers it seeks, the concepts it uses to analyze the field, the methods it uses to obtain data, and the way it organizes its inquiries and findings. When they gain this understanding of the structure, they learn more effectively and efficiently the content involved in it. Hence I now seek to explore the nature of the knowledge and structure of an area before deriving and formulating objectives involved in that area.

The level of generality appropriate for an objective is perhaps the most puzzling question about objectives currently faced by curriculum workers. This problem is briefly discussed in the 1950 monograph in connection with the use of a psychology of learning, and is the third area of greatest change in my thinking relating to the formulation of objectives. In the 1950 discussion, a contrast was drawn between the highly specific objectives that are formulated when learning is viewed as building up connections between specific stimuli and specific responses as compared to objectives when learning is viewed as the development of generalizations, such as generalized ways of attacking problems, generalized modes of reaction to generalized types of situations, and generalizations which subsume many specific items. When empirical investigations are made of children's ability to generalize where no special instruction has been provided, the majority of children show a low level of accurate generalization. This, like the earlier studies of Thorndike, is often interpreted to mean that objectives should be quite specific on the ground that children are unable to learn more generalized kinds of behavior.

However, when carefully controlled studies are made with a defined level of generalization as a goal, such as generalizing the process of the addition of one-digit numbers from 20 specific illustrations, most of the 7-year-old subjects succeed. I think this is a question to be treated experimentally, aiming at as high a level of generalization as the experiments show to be successful. The purpose is to help the student perceive and use a generalized mode of behavior, as shown by his ability to deal appropriately with the specifics subsumed under the generalization. In short, he should be able to move easily from the general to the specific, and vice versa, recognizing specific illustrations of the general and recognizing the general principle that covers a number of specifics. The level of generality of the objective should then be stated in the curriculum plan, with specifics used as illustrations, rather than treating the specifics as ends in themselves.

One of the confusing aspects of this problem of level of generality has been the use of factor analysis and other methods for indicating relations among data as though they were indicators of inherent relations, inherent in the neural mechanisms, and thus subject to little, if any, change through learning. Only by recognizing that the interrelationships of responses students make to tests and other stimuli are indications that reflect not only inherent factors but also ways in which the student perceives the situation, and the connections that he has learned or not learned, have we been led to work experimentally on helping students to build new patterns of reaction representing different interrelationships among the data.

My thoughts about planning of learning experiences have been elaborated considerably since 1950. In the monograph, mention is made of five general principles that are helpful, namely:

1. The student must have experiences that give him an opportunity to practice the kind of behavior implied by the objective.

2. The learning experiences must be such that the student obtains satisfactions from carrying on the kind of behavior implied by the objective.

3. The reactions required by the learning experiences are within the range of possibility for the students involved.

4. There are many particular experiences that can be used to attain the same educational objectives.

5. The same learning experience will usually bring about several outcomes.

These five, although useful, are not adequate to give us much guidance in devising learning experiences as can be provided when use is made of experimental work both in learning and in curriculum evaluation. Hence, during recent years, I have modified the earlier five and added several others to give additional help on this task. These are now stated as 10 conditions for effective learning. The first two are the same as the first two principles given above. The other eight are:

3. The motivation of the learner, that is, the impelling force for his own active involvement, is an important condition.

4. Another condition is that the learner finds his previous ways of reacting unsatisfactory, so that he is stimulated to try new ways.

5. The learner should have some guidance in trying to carry on the new behavior he is to learn.

6. The learner should have ample and appropriate materials on which to work.

7. The learner should have time to carry on the behavior, to practice it until it has become part of his repertoire.

8. The learner should have opportunity for a good deal of sequential practice. Here repetition is inadequate and quickly becomes ineffective.

9. Another condition is for each learner to set standards for himself that require him to go beyond his performance, but standards that are attainable.

10. The tenth condition, related to the ninth, is that to continue learning beyond the time when a teacher is available, the learner must have means of judging his performance to be able to tell how well he is doing. Without these means, his standards are of no utility.

In actual use, each of these ten conditions is elaborated much more fully. They have served to focus attention on some of the places where learning experiences are likely to be inadequate.

In connection with the problem of guiding the learner in carrying on the desired behavior, I have found that students commonly observe the teacher's behavior as a model to direct their own. This is a useful guide if the teacher does frequently demonstrate the behavior the student is expected to acquire, but some teachers do not furnish an observable model of the desired learning. The teacher who lectures to a class may only be demonstrating ways of giving out information rather than showing the student how he goes about solving problems. Often when students cannot gain a clear picture of what they are to do by observing the teacher they depend upon other students to show them or tell them. This frequently results in misunderstanding of what the student is to do. In general, clear observable models are useful ways of guiding the desired behavior.

In trying to practice something new, the student needs to attend to those significant features of his behavior that serve to control it appropriately. In the case of a skill like handwriting, he needs to attend to the form of the letters he is making rather than to the gross movement of his hand and arm. In the case of a skill like swimming, he may best control his efforts by attending to critical movements of arms, legs, and body, rather than to the distance he moves through the water. In the case of problem solving, he usually needs help in noting what factors to observe and what previous knowledge to use in order to attack the problem successfully. Hence, guidance of the learning of the student includes helping him to focus his attention on those aspects of the total situation that enable him to control it and carry it on successfully.

I have also added to my own thinking about the total curriculum and the instructional program recognition of the influences upon learning of the school environment, the peer group values and practices, and the types of personality identification available in the school. We have learned a great deal from Pace and Stern about the "press" of the college environment. Using the College Characteristics Index, they have shown the variety of "presses" among the different colleges. Each type of "press" influences students somewhat differently in terms of what goals to seek, what values are acceptable, what kinds and amounts of study are approved. There is some evidence to indicate similar variations among schools. Hence the "press" of school or college is a significant matter to consider and, if necessary, to change, in order to attain desired objectives more effectively.

Within the same school or college, peer groups exert a powerful influence on the things that are learned, the efforts made, and the satisfaction obtained. Some peer groups enhance the work of teachers, some insulate the student from the influence of the faculty, and others partially counteract the efforts of teachers. In planning and developing the instructional program, peer groups should be considered and steps taken to utilize their influences constructively toward the attainment of significant educational objectives.

As children and young people grow up, they often find persons who seem particularly attractive and seek to emulate them. The young child may begin this process of identification with his mother, following her around the house and attempting to imitate her behavior. During the years of development, other persons in turn are objects of identification. This process is one of the ways in which young people learn, and with a variety of constructive personalities available, the outcomes are positive and include the acquisition of attitudes, values, and interests, as well as skills and practices. In some schools and colleges, however, the range of constructive personalities that are close enough to the students to permit attraction and emulation is too narrow, so that many children and youth find no one on the faculty enough like them to be drawn into identification. This is another consideration for instructional planning that should seek to use all important resources for learning that can be provided.

Nothing has been said thus far about changes in my thinking regarding the organization of learning experiences and evaluation. Recently, I have been giving considerable attention to the problem of organization and to the elaboration of a more helpful rationale for this area. As you know, I am also nearly over my head in a new evaluation project called "Assessing the Progress of Education." This is furnishing grist for a rather thorough reexamination of the process of evaluation. I hope later to report on these developments.

IV NATIONAL TESTING PROGRAMS

1 Overview

Dr. Tyler was a leading figure in the development of two major national testing programs: the United States Armed Forces Institute (USAFI) Testing program and the National Assessment of Educational Progress (NAEP). Both of these testing programs reflect Tyler's philosophy of testing and evaluation. Throughout his career he has believed (1) that tests should be designed, constructed, and used to assess progress against valued and carefully defined objectives; and (2) that tests should provide feedback to help those in education and the larger society to recognize and reward meritorious achievement.

The USAFI program helped America serve the educational needs of young people who had left school to defend their country during World War II. Part of the USAFI testing program would later evolve into the General Educational Development Tests (GED). Since 1942, the GED program has continued to assess the progress of adults who had dropped out of school before attaining their high school diploma. The GED program provided a gateway to opportunity for countless adults over the years.

NAEP has provided longitudinal data on how well students of various ages are attaining educational objectives valued in the United States. Data from NAEP have informed many recent reform proposals. These same data

211

have led to the recent recognition of the need to concentrate on the development of higher order thinking skills.

NAEP is currently expanding to state level efforts. When NAEP was originally proposed there was fear that it would lead to a national testing program and to invidious state comparisons. Now there are moves by some state officials to use NAEP assessments precisely for inter- and intrastate comparisons. Another benefit of NAEP has been recent new technical developments relative to scaling and reporting that may make the NAEP results more useful.

We chose a short description by Tyler of the USAFI program and two of his earliest writings on NAEP where he gives his rationale and hopes for NAEP.

Key Points

- Through testing people can earn credit for their out-of-school learning. Credentialing tests that open doors to students can stimulate independent study and continuing education. Such tests can help place those returning to formal educational programs.
- A key to the success of such national testing programs was the extensive efforts to involve diverse groups from U.S. society in the development and oversight of the programs.
- In the USAFI program three distinct types of tests were developed: (1) end-of-course exams; (2) subject matter specific tests; and (3) a test of general educational development.
- The USAFI tests earned the endorsement of major accrediting agencies which formally approved of the program.
- To maintain the reputation of the program, USAFI put a major effort into maintaining test security.
- NAEP involves sampling items across samples of students. Through this approach a wide range of objectives could be measured without unduly burdening any individual examinee. This method also assuaged fears associated with reporting individual, classroom, school, district, and state level results.
- NAEP data are useful in informing public policy. These data cannot be used to appraise individual students, teachers, curriculum materials, or organizational arrangements.
- There are important differences between testing for purposes of sorting and grading and testing for improving instruction.
- Setting objectives affords opportunities to involve parents and lay people in the educational process.

- Appraisal techniques can be developed to gather information about all children, not just the so-called "average" child.
- A variety of appraisal techniques is possible. Appraisal of student learning should not be limited to paper-and-pencil tests. Appraisal techniques should be used with the entire range of students in a school.
- If appraisal techniques are to aid teachers in their work, they need to include placement tests, diagnostic tests, mastery tests, and tests of generalization.

2 APPRAISAL OF EDUCATIONAL ACHIEVEMENT GAINED IN THE ARMED FORCES

Many men and women in the armed forces are making substantial additions to their educational development as a result of their military experience. They find three types of opportunity for educational growth while in the Army or Navy. In the first place, the armed services provide a vast program of technical training. It is estimated that 63 per cent of all the men and women in the Army and a larger percentage of the naval personnel are given some type of technical training, which includes not only the better known fields of mathematics and science but many others such as accounting, foreign languages, military law, and the like. The technical courses vary in length from a few weeks to more than a year. Undoubtedly, millions of

Originally published in *Educational and Psychological Measurement*, Vol. III, Summer 1943, pp. 97–104.

the members of the armed services will increase their technical skills and knowledge as a result of these specialized training programs.

A second source of educational development available to the armed forces is the program of off-duty education. All branches of the service participate in the work of the United States Armed Forces Institute, formerly called the Army Institute, which has its headquarters at Madison, Wisconsin. The Armed Forces Institute provides correspondence instruction under two plans. One plan enables a member of the armed forces to enroll in correspondence courses offered by 80 recognized colleges and universities. Under this arrangement the student pays only a part of the tuition while the balance of the cost is borne by the Institute. The instruction, however, is handled in the usual manner by the college or university offering the course. Under the second plan, courses, most of which are at the high school level, are offered directly by the United States Armed Forces Institute. Some of these courses involve the use of the self-teaching materials, while in others the lesson-service is provided through contract by the University of Wisconsin. More than 500 courses are available by correspondence instruction through the Armed Forces Institute. The enrollment is about evenly divided between men and women overseas and those in the continental United States. Registrations are increasing at a rapid rate, the new enrollments in February having been more than double those in January.

The off-duty educational program of the Army and Navy includes opportunities for class instruction as well as correspondence courses. Wherever teachers, most of whom work on a voluntary basis, can be found, classes are organized to meet the demands of the members of the armed forces. The nature of these courses varies widely. In the Panama Canal Zone the popular courses in the Navy include courses in Spanish and geography. Mathematics is popular among both Army and Navy groups. At some of the camps, studio work in art has developed to a surprising point. In some places discussion groups on contemporary issues have been formed. These off-duty educational opportunities have been greatly facilitated by the recent development of excellent libraries. The armed forces have the largest library program in the world. The library facilities in the more permanent camps are better than in many of the civilian communities of the country.

Judging from the experience in the last war the greatest demand for educational work in the armed forces will come during the period after the armistice is signed and before demobilization takes place. Men and women in the armed services are then looking forward to their induction into civilian life. Many of them are concerned with improving their occupational chances and with completing their education. Undoubtedly, the period immediately following the armistice will find a tremendous number actively participating in the educational programs of both Army and Navy.

The third type of educational opportunity is informal. For many members of the armed forces the informal experiences of military life will contribute in greater or less degree to their education. Some, no doubt, will increase their knowledge of geography through wide travels. Others will get some conceptions of anthropology as they come in contact with cultures markedly different from their own. Some in the medical corps will undoubtedly learn something of anatomy, physiology and elementary chemistry. Although these informal experiences may be minor in their effects on educational development for the majority, there is no doubt that they will influence the educational maturity of many men and women.

When members of the armed forces return to civilian life a considerable number will want to continue their education. Many others will want some symbol as evidence of their educational attainment because of the value of such a credential in job placement and for social prestige. During the last war many educational institutions granted blanket credit for military service. This proved unsatisfactory for the student as well as for the educational institution and the public. Many students were given as much as a year of advanced standing without evidence of competence. A considerable number failed out in school or college when they attempted to go on at this advanced level. The schools and colleges found it difficult if not impossible to provide satisfactory instruction for men so obviously misplaced. Employers did not know how to evaluate diplomas or other school records based on military service but backed by no evidence of educational attainment.

Recognizing the need for a more rational plan (1) for placing members of the armed forces on their return to educational institutions, (2) for granting appropriate credit for educational attainment while in military service, and (3) for motivating the educational work of the soldier and sailor, a special committee of educators recommended to the Armed Forces Institute that a procedure be provided which would enable members of the armed forces to demonstrate their educational attainments so that educational institutions might give proper recognition and fair credit. The committee pointed out that the educational work in the Army and Navy could not be satisfactorily evaluated in terms of textbooks used, academic training of the staff, hours spent in study, and other similar features sometimes used in accreditation of civilian institutions. The educational work in the armed forces goes on under widely varying conditions with vastly different motivation and under the direction of instructors with widely variable abilities. The committee saw that the only fair way to appraise the educational attainments of men in the armed services was through a plan which involved the demonstration of the competence of the soldier or sailor through examinations. If satisfactory examinations could be constructed, it would then be possible for a member of the armed forces to demonstrate his educational attainments no matter how they may have been gained, whether through military training, the educational program, informal experiences, or some combination of these. Acting on the recommendation of this committee the War Department contracted with the University of Chicago Board of Examinations to prepare tests and examinations for this purpose. As University Examiner, I serve as the director of what is now known as the Examinations Staff for the United States Armed Forces Institute. The staff includes not only experienced examiners from the University of Chicago Board of Examinations but a number of other examiners drawn from other institutions. In general, an examiner working in a particular field is one who has had his own graduate training in that field, has taught in that field, and has had further training in examination construction. Thus, the examiner for the physical sciences is a man with a Ph.D. in physics, who has been a teacher of the physical sciences for a number of years, and had a year of post-doctoral training in test construction.

The examination staff has been directed to construct four types of examinations, only two of which are primarily to serve as a basis for placement and credit. The first type includes the tests given students at the completion of courses taken in the Institute. These are end-of-course tests and are used primarily to determine whether the student has mastered the work of the course and as a basis for awarding him a certificate for this completion of the course. Because of the conditions under which course work must go on with men overseas many of the courses are short and are not equivalent to a semester or year course in high school or college. For example, the usual high-school physics course covers three of the Institute courses. Hence the end-of-course tests are not generally to be used as a basis for placement or credit in school or college.

The second type includes subject examinations. Tests of this type are built to measure the man's competence to deal with the material commonly provided in high-school or college courses or subjects. For example, the subject examination in high-school physics covers the content commonly included in high-school physics and attempts to measure the degree to which the objectives commonly emphasized in high-school physics courses have been attained. On the basis of this examination it should be possible for a high school to know how well the student has mastered the major elements of physics as this subject is commonly outlined in American high schools. As another example, the subject examination in accounting covers the content commonly included in accounting courses and attempts to measure the student's competence in terms of the objectives commonly emphasized in accounting courses. The report on these subject examinations should be of particular value to the school or college in placing a member of the armed forces when he returns to school or college and in granting him a fair amount of credit for his educational attainments.

The steps followed in constructing a subject examination are those which are commonly recommended in examination construction. The examiners meet with teachers in this field to identify the educational objectives which students are expected to attain in this field. These objectives are defined as clearly as possible in terms of behavior; that is, in terms of definite things which the student should be able to do which indicate that he has attained this objective. On the basis of this definition of each objective it is possible to specify the kinds of exercises needed to test the student's attainment of the objective. Following these specifications a large number of test exercises are collected for each of the objectives. A sufficient number of exercises is obtained to provide for two or more forms of the test. These exercises are then tried out with groups of students in school or college and, where possible, with special adult groups. On the basis of this preliminary try-out some exercises are eliminated because they are not discriminating or are ambiguous.

The resulting revised examination is submitted to one or more critics nominated by a professional organization in that field. For example, the physics test is submitted to persons nominated by the American Association of Physics Teachers, the college mathematics tests to critics nominated by the American Mathematical Society. These critics are asked to check the examinations for comprehensiveness of coverage both in content and objectives, for accuracy of material, and for validity of exercise, that is, whether each exercise is a fairly valid measure of the objective it is supposed to test. On the basis of these criticisms the examination is revised once more and where possible is given another try-out with school or college groups. It is then available for use by the Armed Forces Institute.

It should be noted that the Institute does not propose to dictate to the educational institution regarding the amount of credit to be granted. The Institute submits to the educational institution a record of the examination results. It is possible for the educational institution to interpret these results in several ways. The examinations have been constructed to yield part-scores so that it is possible to report, for example, that the soldier can solve simple linear equations, knows the important technical terms in algebra but cannot solve simultaneous linear equations. This descriptive method is often useful in deciding whether the soldier is ready to go on with intermediate algebra and can be given credit for having completed first semester algebra.

In many cases it will be possible to report the results in comparative terms, that is, in terms of the percentile rank for students who are completing this course in school or college. This may help an individual school or college to decide whether to allow credit and how much. Finally, it is possible for the school or college to obtain copies of one of the alternate forms of the test and by giving the tests to its own students to determine whether the score made by the soldier is comparable to scores made by the students in the local school or college. By means of one or more of these three methods it should be possible for a school or college to use the results of the subject examinations effectively.

The third type of test constructed by the examination staff includes the tests of general educational development. The direction of the construction of these tests is in the hands of Professor E.F. Lindquist of the State University of Iowa. Two batteries have been developed, one for the high-school level and the other for the college level. They have been prepared for immediate use in the placement of casualties returning to educational institutions. The tests include the kinds of exercises in the several subject fields which have proved to be good predictors of further success in these fields. The items in science, social science and literature are in the form of reading and interpretation exercises. The reading material has been so chosen and the exercises so constructed that they require a good deal of basic knowledge and vocabulary in the subject field as well as ability to analyze and synthesize the reading matter presented in order for the student successfully to answer the questions. The items in English composition include not only some relating to mechanics but also some that require the student to make choices involving clarity, organization, and taste in language. This placement battery should prove particularly useful for members of the armed forces who have been out of school for some time but who have had a good many educational experiences since leaving school. When it is recalled that the members of this Army on the average have a much better education than the soldiers in the last war, tenth-grade median as compared with a sixth-grade median, when it is remembered that a larger porportion of the soldiers in this Army are high-school graduates than had graduated from the eighth grade in the last war, it is clear that there will be need for finding a basis for appropriate placement of many persons at advanced high-school and college levels.

These tests of educational development are now being standardized on a very carefully selected sample of educational institutions, chosen so as to be highly representative of the country at large. The almost universal cooperation of every institution asked to participate in the standardization program will assure the most adequate set of norms ever developed. Hence, the results of the battery of tests of educational development should be easy to interpret by both high schools and colleges, particularly since the norms will be available by geographical regions and by types of institutions.

The fourth type of test will be of use only in certain individual cases. These are tests constructed specifically to measure the soldier's competence in certain highly technical fields of special military importance, such as ultra-high frequency electronics. These tests are given to the men and women who complete the training courses in these fields and wish to use the examination results as evidence of competence when candidates for com missions. Some colleges and universities are also using the results of these examinations in the case of former students who are candidates for degrees. The results serve as evidence of attainment in the student's major field or as an elective course.

This brief description of the work of the examinations staff for the United States Armed Forces Institute should suggest the possible values of this program in facilitating smooth transition from military to civilian life. Not only may the examination results be of value to employers who want to know about the soldier's competence in some field like auto mechanics, accounting, or mathematics, but they should be helpful in educational guidance. They should be useful in determining the appropriate placement of the student in school or college. They should assist the school or college to arrive at a fair estimate of advanced credit to be allowed for educational achievement while in military service. A large proportion of our youth have had their education interrupted in order to serve their country. The success of this country as a democracy largely depends upon the educational level of its citizens. If we can develop a plan which will encourage men and women in the armed forces to continue their education when they return from the war, a plan which gives them fair credit and places them at a point where they do not duplicate previous learning nor find themselves floundering in new and too difficult work, a large part of this group whose education has been interrupted may have a chance to complete it. This is an important contribution to our national life.

3 THE OBJECTIVES AND PLANS FOR A NATIONAL ASSESSMENT OF EDUCATIONAL PROGRESS

The current debate regarding this project is confused because of the failure to distinguish among the various kinds of educational appraisal. Hence, it may be helpful in beginning this description to relate assessment to the other more common types of evaluation. The most frequent use of evaluation is to appraise the achievement of individual students. This is usually done with several purposes in mind. It may furnish a further incentive for students to study because they know they will be tested. It may be used as one of the factors in their promotion. It provides information that can be used by the student and counselor in planning for further education, and it often serves as one of the bases for awarding scholarships.

A second use of evaluation is to diagnose the learning difficulties of an individual student or an entire class to provide information helpful in planning subsequent teaching. A third use of evaluation is to appraise the

This paper... [was] presented at a joint AERA-NCME symposium held in Chicago, Illinois, in February 1966. It was originally published in the *Journal of Educational Measurement*, Vol. 3, No. 1, Spring 1966.

educational effectiveness of a curriculum or part of a curriculum, of instructional materials and procedures, and of administrative and organizational arrangements.

Each of these kinds of evaluation is an essential part of the processes of teaching or administration. Teachers and administrators are using evaluation of one sort or another as one of their normal procedures. The information gained from these appraisals is focused upon individual student's efforts, class performance, or the effectiveness of the plans, materials, and procedures used by the teacher, the school or the school system.

There is a fourth use of evaluation which is to assess the educational progress of larger populations in order to provide the public with dependable information to help in the understanding of educational problems and needs and to guide in efforts to develop sound public policy regarding education. This type of assessment is not focused upon individual students, classrooms, schools, or school systems, but furnishes over-all information about the educational attainments of large numbers of people.

The distinction may be illuminated somewhat by comparing the situation in education and in the field of health. The public has information about the incidence of heart diseases, cancer, and other diseases for different age and occupational groups, and for different geographic regions. This information is useful in developing public understanding of the progress and problems in the field of health where greatest effort and support may be needed. At the same time, physicians have evaluative procedures to diagnose diseases, to appraise the progress patients are making and to evaluate the effectiveness of treatments. The physician's evaluative techniques are devised to serve his purposes and the public health assessments are designed to provide the public with helpful information. One type does not take the place of the other.

This is a rough parallel to the difference in education between the tools needed and used by teachers and administrators and those needed to gain information helpful for the guidance of responsible citizens. Heretofore, little attention has been given in education to the assessment problem because the need for wide public understanding of educational progress and problems was not widely recognized. Now it is.

Because education has become the servant of all our purposes, its effectiveness is of general public concern. The educational tasks now faced require many more resources than have thus far been available, and they must be wisely used to produce maximum results. To make these decisions, dependable information about the progress of education is essential, otherwise we scatter our efforts too widely and fail to achieve our goals. Yet we do not now have the necessary comprehensive and dependable data.

We have reports on numbers of schools, buildings, teachers, and pupils, and about the moneys expended, but we do not have sound and adequate information on educational results. Because dependable data are not available, personal views, distorted reports, and journalistic impressions are the sources of public opinion and the schools are frequently attacked and frequently defended without having necessary evidence to support either claim. This situation will be corrected only by a careful, consistent effort to obtain valid data to provide sound evidence about the progress of American education.

In recognition of this need, Carnegie Corporation of New York, a private foundation, in 1964 appointed an Exploratory Committee on Assessing the Progress of Education. I was asked to serve as Chairman. The Committee's assignment is to confer with teachers, administrators, school board members, and others concerned with education to get advice on the way in which such a project may be constructively helpful to the schools and avoid possible injuries. The Committee is also charged with the development and try-out of instruments and procedures for assessing the progress of education. The Committee has been working on these assignments for nearly two years.

Jack Merwin is reporting on the progress that has thus far been made on these assignments. It is anticipated that the national assessment would be in charge of a commission of highly respected citizens. They and the commission staff would prepare reports of the findings of the assessment, much as we now obtain reports of the findings every ten years of the decennial census. These reports would be available to all people interested in education, providing them in this way with significant and helpful information on what has been learned by each of the 192 populations to be incorporated in the assessment. In subsequent years, the progress made by each of these populations since the preceding assessment would also be reported.

A good deal of public confusion has been encountered. The project is being confused with a nation-wide, individual testing program, and several common fears are expressed by those who make this confusion. They note that tests used in a school influence the direction and amount of effort of pupils and teachers. In this way, if national tests do not reflect the local educational objectives, pupils and teachers are deflected from their work. This criticism does not apply to the assessment project because no individual student or teacher can make a showing. No student will take more than a small fraction of the exercises. No scores will be obtained on his performance. He will not be assessed at any later time and can gain no desired end, like admission to college or a scholarship.

A second fear is that such an assessment enables the Federal government to control the curriculum. This is also a misunderstanding. The objectives to be assessed are those which are accepted by teachers and curriculum specialists as goals toward which they work. They have been reviewed by lay leaders throughout the country so as to include only aims deemed important by public-spirited citizens. This project will report on the extent to which children, youth, and adults are learning things considered important by both professional school people and the informed public.

A third fear is sometimes raised that this project would stultify the curriculum by not allowing changes over the years in instructional methods and educational goals. It should be made clear that the project will assess what children, youth, and adults have learned, not how they have learned it. Hence, the assessment is not dependent upon any particular instructional methods. For example, we shall report the percentage of 13-year olds who can comprehend the plain sense of a typical newspaper paragraph. We will not be reporting the methods of reading instruction that are used in various schools. Or, as another illustration, we shall report on the percentage of adults who participate regularly in civic affairs but not on the methods used in teaching high school civics.

The matter of changing educational goals is a relevant question because the objectives determine what will be assessed. Our plan calls for a review one year in advance of each assessment of the objectives of each field in order to identify changes and to include the new objectives in the next assessment.

Through the various conferences with school people and interested laymen, the Committee has been able to identify concerns and problems that such an assessment must deal with. As the plans are shaping up, it appears to be possible to conduct the project in a way that will not injure our schools but will provide greatly needed information.

The need for data on progress has been recognized in other spheres of American life. During the depression, the lack of dependable information about the progress of the economy was a serious handicap in focusing efforts and in assessing them. Out of this need grew an index of production, the Gross National Product, which has been of great value in guiding economic development. Correspondingly, the Consumer Price Index was constructed as a useful measure of the changes in cost of living and inflation. Mortality and morbidity indices are important bases for indicating needed public health measures. Facing the need for massive efforts to extend and improve education, the demand for valid information to support the requests and to guide the allocation of resources must be met. The assessment of the progress of education should make an important and constructive contribution to this purpose.

4 NATIONAL ASSESSMENT — SOME VALUABLE BY-PRODUCTS FOR SCHOOLS

A major purpose of the national assessment program is to provide the lay public with census-like data on the educational achievements of our children, youth, and adults — data which will furnish a dependable background of information about our educational attainments, the progress we are making, and the problems we still face in achieving our educational aspirations.

As the assessment program has developed, however, some interesting and valuable by-products, not contemplated or foreseen in the early stages, have appeared. This article will deal with these by-products and their potential value for schools and for principals.

It came as a surprise to some of us to discover that the testing programs commonly conducted in the schools do not furnish information about what our pupils have learned. Instead, they indicate (1) how far a student is above or below the average score of the group with which he is compared, and (2)

Ralph W. Tyler was Chairman of the Exploratory Committee on Assessing the Progress of Education and is a member of the Committee on Assessing the Progress of Education.

The article is reprinted with the permission of *The National Elementary Principle.*

how far the average score of a classroom or school is above or below the average of the group with which it is compared. From present test results we cannot obtain such useful information as what percent of our 13-year-old children can read and comprehend a simple newspaper paragraph, or what percent of 17-year-old youth have acquired one or more marketable skills.

Why haven't traditional tests been designed to find out what individuals or groups have learned? Why have they been constructed to report only relative achievements in relation to other individuals or groups?

The approach commonly used in test development in the past can largely be attributed to the assumption that testing is primarily a sorting process. Tests are employed to sort people for courses, for curricular tracks, for admission to college, and the like. They measure individual differences and relative performances of groups; they do not appraise individual and group progress in learning. Using these tests, the schools, then, are largely sorting and selecting agents rather than educational agents.

It was in a society in which most people were unskilled laborers and relatively few people were among the professional, social, and political elite that such a concept of testing developed. Now, however, our society is quite different. Science and technology have freed people from being "hewers of wood and drawers of water." Only 5 percent of the labor force is unskilled. Opportunities for employment in technical, professional, managerial, and service occupations have increased more than 300 percent in one generation. Our society is now seeking to identify potential talents of many sorts and to furnish opportunities for these talents to be developed through education.

Research on the brain and in behavioral genetics indicates that the learning requirements in our schools and colleges place no strain on the basic potential of the vast majority of human beings. Schools can be designed and redesigned to help all students learn. From the standpoint of any student, the way to judge whether or not an institution is an educational one is to find out whether the student gains a wider range of alternatives in his life choices with each year of schooling. An educational institution is one in which a human being is aided to find new doors of opportunity — not trained ever more narrowly to fit into a niche in society. In such a school, new kinds of tests can serve in various ways to promote and guide the development of the student.

One valuable by-product of the national assessment project, therefore, is the clarification of the difference between testing for sorting and testing that can help substantially in the education and guidance of individuals.

A second by-product, useful to the principal, is the demonstration that the educational objectives of a school can be formulated and agreed upon in a way that involves parents, laymen, and school staff members. This greatly increases the common understanding of what schools are trying to do. Because a major purpose of the assessment project is to provide helpful information about the progress of education that can be understood and accepted by lay citizens, the procedures used in the construction of assessment exercises involved laymen. In each field, scholars, teachers, and curriculum specialists formulated statements of the objectives which they believe faithfully reflect the contribution of that field and which the schools are seriously seeking to attain. For each of these major objectives, prototype exercises were then constructed. These were exercises which, in the opinion of scholars and teachers, give students an opportunity to demonstrate the behavior implied by the objective. The lists of objectives and the prototype exercises which help to define them were then reviewed by a series of panels of citizens living in various parts of the country in cities, towns, and villages. The laymen who participated were nominated by national organizations in response to a request for the names of persons interested in education who resided in various sections of the country — in rural, urban, and suburban communities.

Each panel spent two days reviewing the material and making a judgment about each objective. The judgment was made in terms of two questions: "Is this something important for people to learn today? Is it something I would like to have my children learn?"

This process resulted in some revisions of the original listing of objectives and a few eliminations. The procedure was designed to insure that every objective being assessed is: (1) considered important by scholars, (2) accepted as an educational task by the school, and (3) deemed desirable by leading lay citizens. This should help to eliminate the criticism frequently encountered with current tests in which some item is attacked by the scholar as representing shoddy scholarship, or criticized by school people as something not in the curriculum, or labeled by prominent laymen as being unimportant.

This review of objectives by lay panels was useful in constructing assessment exercises; it was also an educational experience for panel members — an experience which they found enlightening and rewarding. A number of the lay panelists reported that these review sessions gave them a much clearer understanding of the purposes of the schools than they had had before.

The sessions also furnished an opportunity for discussing and clarifying some of the common causes of public misunderstanding about such objectives as those in the areas of citizenship, vocational education, biology, social studies, and mathematics. At the request of their local school officials, some of the laymen had earlier participated in formulating objectives for the school or had served on committees to review and criticize the stated educational objectives. They reported that they had not found these experiences fruitful. The difference between the earlier tasks and the work they undertook in the assessment project was largely due to the use of prototype assessment exercises to help clarify the meaning of each statement of objectives. For example, in the field of writing, the material presented to the panels included statements of objectives and prototype exercises such as the following:

> Objective: *Write to communicate adequately in a social situation.*
> This was defined by such exercises as:
> a) Invite your parents to the PTA meeting next Monday at 7:00 p.m. (age 9)
> b) Thank your aunt for the gift she sent you. (age 13)
> c) Write directions for adding cream cheese and other ingredients to make a special treat from a prepared cake mix. (age 17)
> d) Prepare written directions which tell a friend how to get to your home from the nearest highway exit. (adult)
> Objective: *Write to communicate adequately in school situations.*
> This was defined by such exercises as:
> a) Announce the results of the election of crossing guards. (age 9)
> b) Take notes of names, addresses, dates, books, etc., mentioned in a 5-minute taped lecture. (age 17)
> Objective: *Write to communicate adequately in a business or vocational situation.*
> This was defined by such exercises as:
> a) Fill out an application for a driver's license. (age 17)
> b) Write a letter of reference for a neighbor seeking employment. (adult)
> Objective: *Appreciate the value of writing.*
> This was defined by responses to such questions as the following:
> a) Have you written anything during the past week? What was it? Do you think it was worth doing? (age 9)
> b) When you have spare time, do you use some of it to write something? What do you write? Do you do this often? Did you write anything this week? (ages 13 and 17)

When the objectives are defined in this way by prototype exercises, they are likely to be understood by the laymen. Abstract statements alone are often so general that they are meaningless, or they use trite and hallowed terms, like "citizenship," which are commonly approved but mean different things to different people. Discussions of objectives, when guided by examples of this sort, are more easily focused on real issues regarding the aims of the school.

Typically, the public has understood only in very general terms the objectives of a modern educational program. Many people have not really thought of today's objectives as different from those which they perceived when they were children. One result of this limited or distorted perception is evident when we fail to obtain the necessary public support for some of our important educational tasks. The list of objectives developed by the procedure used in the assessment — a procedure involving parents, laymen, and school personnel — should greatly increase public understanding of what the schools are trying to do and gain further appreciation of the importance of these aims. Educators may well find this form of discussion a helpful way to clarify or to modify some of their own views.

A third useful by-product of the assessment project is the demonstration that appraisal exercises can be constructed to provide information about the progress of the entire range of school children, not merely data about the so-called "average" child.

The traditional achievement test is constructed to measure individual differences and to furnish reliable average scores for grades or schools. The test items, therefore, are concentrated on those which are typical of average performance. Exercises which all children or nearly all children can do, as well as those which only a very few can do, are eliminated from such tests.

In reviewing current tests to see whether they could be used in the national assessment, we found that more than 80 percent of the items in the most widely used achievement tests fell between the 40 percent and 60 percent level of difficulty. Only about 5 percent of the items were exercises which could be answered by students in the lower third of the class, another 5 percent represented tasks appropriate for the upper third. For assessing the progress of education, and for informing teachers, principals, and parents in local schools about the achievements of their children, we need to know what *all* children are learning — the disadvantaged or "slow" learners, the most advanced, and the middle or "average." The construction of exercises appropriate for these purposes has been a challenge and a new venture for test constructors. It required the development of exercises in which approximately one-third of the test items represent achievements characteristic of the lower third at that age level, one-third represent achievements characteristic of the middle third at that age level, and one-third represent achievements of the top third.

The contractors found these requirements difficult to meet because their previous experience had not involved appraising the achievements of the upper and lower thirds. In the initial try-outs, we found that many of the exercises made for the lower third used language that could not be understood by the pupils. They did not know what they were being asked to do. It is *extremely* important to distinguish between failure on an exercise *because the child doesn't understand what he is asked to do* and failure *because he is unable to do the task*. In a number of cases, we found that simplification of the instructions opened the way for "slow" learners to demonstrate what they had learned.

A second defect in the first attempt of the contractors to assess the progress of the lower third was the failure to include examples of achievements that represent earlier or lower stages of progress in learning. By consulting with teachers in Head Start programs and with those who had much experience in working with disadvantaged children, the staff was able to construct a sample of exercises appropriate for appraising the progress in learning of "slow" learners. The later try-outs indicate that the final battery of assessment exercises furnishes information about the achievements of the total range of children.

Now that the contractors have learned how to construct batteries of this sort, it should be possible for schools to get tests and other appraisal instruments that will enable teachers, principals, and parents to obtain information about the progress of the entire range of children in the school. This will help to focus attention on (1) the successful efforts of the school, and (2) the problems being encountered that require added efforts or different efforts. This, then, is a third by-product of the national assessment.

A fourth by-product is the demonstration of the feasibility of using a variety of appraisal techniques rather than being limited to the use of paper-and-pencil tests. We have long recognized that many important kinds of educational achievements are not validly indicated by pupil responses on group tests. This is true, for example, of intellectual and aesthetic interests, habits and practices in the areas of citizenship, social attitudes, occupational skills. Experimental projects in evaluation have shown that valid evidence about these kinds of achievements can be obtained by using a variety of devices such as questionnaires, interviews, observation, and performance tests.

These devices have not been considered feasible for use in schools generally, largely because it has been assumed that their use would require too much time. This view of the great amount of time required to make appraisals by means other than paper-and-pencil tests derives from the notion that every pupil must be given every appraisal exercise. Where the purpose is to assess the achievements of groups and subgroups of pupils, sampling methods can be employed as they are in the national assessment. The total battery given this spring is divided into 14 parts, and no one pupil takes more than 1/14th of the total. Some pupils take paper-and-pencil tests; some answer questions about their interests and habits; some show their skills by actual performance tests; and some are involved in a group project where some of their citizenship practices can be observed. By using carefully designed sampling procedures, it is possible to estimate the achievements of a total pupil group from the reactions obtained in the samples of pupils. A single elementary school will probably not have a large enough enrollment to permit dividing the total into 14 samples and still have a sufficient number in each sample to give reliable estimates. But if there were a small number, such as 64 in each grade for example, four samples could be formed and each sample could be given one-fourth of the total list of appraisal exercises. This would permit the use of devices for assessing interests, attitudes, practices, and skills, as well as paper-and-pencil tests. A more comprehensive and useful evaluation of educational progress could thus be conducted.

A fifth by-product of national assessment is the clear indication that appraisal exercises can be constructed to aid teachers in their daily work. At least four kinds of tests or other devices would be helpful to teachers in the classroom:

1. *Placement tests* that help the pupil identify the extent of his progress in each area of instruction and thus indicate in what section of a sequential program he can fruitfully begin his learning. The appropriate section for him to begin would be one in which he can learn things he does not already know and in which his present background should afford an adequate basis for further study. Tests of this sort can be constructed when basic objectives and prototype exercises for different age levels have been formulated, reviewed, and agreed upon. This appraisal does not give the same results as the grade equivalents obtained from traditional tests.

2. *Diagnostic tests* which are based on "work samples" of learning exercises that (1) utilize various appropriate modes of presentation, of problem solving, of practicing, and (2) employ various sensory modalities. Such tests furnish representative samples of the different modes of learning that can be used by the student and enable him to test himself on auditory, visual, and tactile presentations and reactions. These tests should help the pupil to select, at least initially, the means of learning he will find most effective in his own development in this area of the curriculum.

3. *Mastery tests* that sample the pupil's comprehension of basic concepts and his ability to utilize the essential skills that are required to proceed to the next unit in the sequential educational program. The purpose of such tests is not to place him on a scale with relation to his peers but to identify the readiness of the student to move on in his educational development. All, or nearly all, pupils will attain the level of essential mastery; otherwise, the educational program is inappropriate for the students enrolled. The exercises will not be concentrated at the 50 percent

level of difficulty as those in current achievement tests are; each exercise will be an example of the desired skill, knowledge, or the like, at the level in which it is commonly used. Every pupil is expected to perform satisfactorily practically all of the exercises as an indication of mastery. In present experimental and developmental programs, "practically all" is defined as 85 percent of them. Such mastery tests enable the student to recognize when he is ready to move on to the next unit or set of educational experiences.

4. *Tests of generalization* that enable the pupil to determine the extent to which he is able to apply what he has learned in the educational program to the many other situations in his life in which this learning is relevant. These tests will consist of exercises that have not been used in his training but that represent new illustrations of the concepts and skills he has been seeking to master. The tests will include not only simulation and "description of situations" but also actual samples of the situations in other courses, on the playground, and in the wider community where the learning has significant application. The purpose of education is to enable the pupil to gain the competencies he needs in order to continue developing throughout his life — not just the competencies that enable him to get along in school. The student, therefore, needs to appraise his effectiveness in using what he is learning.

Since the beginning of the development of educational achievement tests, educators have recognized the potential value of tests as aids to teaching, but the potential has not been fully realized and the expectations have not been largely fulfilled. We now recognize that there have been two major obstacles: (1) the failure to produce tests that could be effectively used in planning and conducting the instructional program; and (2) the lack of a feasible procedure for incorporating a system of testing into the normal classroom activities. We now can see the elimination of both of these obstacles. Appraisal exercises useful to the teacher can be constructed, and there are practical procedures for their use in normal classroom situations.

A sixth by-product of the national assessment project is the development of ways of reporting the results of educational evaluation that can readily be understood by children, parents, and interested citizens. The results of the national assessment will not be presented in terms of test scores. The following form will be used in reporting: (The statistics are, of course, hypothetical at this point.)

> For the sample of 13-year-old boys of higher socio-economic status from rural and small-town areas of the Midwest region, it was found that:
> 94 percent could read a typical newspaper paragraph like the following: (Note: such a paragraph will be included in the report.)

68 percent could write an acceptable letter ordering several items from a store. (Note: a sample letter will be included.)

57 percent took a responsible part in working with other children in playground and community activities like the following: (A specific illustration will be included.)

You will note that the report presents the actual exercise and gives the percent of each population group that answered the question or performed the task indicated. In the case of writing, samples of what the children have written will be shown, along with the percent of pupils whose compositions were at least as adequate as the samples reproduced.

Parents and other laymen responded enthusiastically to this form of reporting. They believed that seeing the actual examples of the exercises gave them a much clearer idea of the achievements that were being assessed than they got from a test title alone. They also felt that reporting in terms of the "percent" of the group who were able to perform the task indicated was a more understandable figure than a test score or some other abstract measure such as standard scores, percentile ranks, and the like.

The reaction of laymen to this way of reporting the national assessment suggests to me that they would also find this type of reporting results of local school appraisals to be more understandable and thus more helpful than reports presented to the local community in terms of scores. The concrete character of the reports would permit the school administrator to discuss both progress and problems. This results from the fact that the report would not give simply a *single* index of school achievement but would report on different tasks. Some of these would be tasks which most students may have mastered; others would be tasks that might show considerable variation in the proportion of persons who have learned to do them.

Finally, one of the most significant by-products of the national assessment project is to be found in the suggestions it provides for monitoring and studying the outcomes of the school's educational program. At present, the prevailing procedure followed by principals in monitoring the effectiveness of the school programs is the use of standardized tests, comparing the mean test scores in each major subject with similar scores in previous years and with national norms or mean scores of other comparison groups.

When the school population is relatively homogeneous or when the chief community concern is with the education of the "average" child, mean scores on present tests are useful indications of the outcomes of the program. However, as I have pointed out earlier, present tests do not furnish a reliable indication of the achievements of children in the upper and lower parts of the distribution. One may, therefore, be misled by the consistency of mean scores over the year to believe that the school program is continuing to produce desired results when in fact a considerable part of the school population is achieving very differently. Or, conversely, we may be dismayed to note that mean scores are lower when, as a matter of fact, the children in the lower third or the upper third are making greater achievements while the "average" child is achieving somewhat less. Tests which furnish information about the achievements of *all* sections of the school population provide a more helpful basis for focusing efforts toward improvement of learning for all children.

Incidentally, our previous preoccupation with means and with the performance of the "average" child may partly account for the common tendency in our schools to seek *the method, the test, the instructional aids* for each subject field rather than conceiving of the school population as composed of children with different backgrounds, different attitudes, different skills in learning. It is fruitful to view the learning situation as one in which the majority of children will be successful in learning, whatever methods or materials are used. But we must not forget that there are minority groups requiring special attention — children who need procedures and materials geared to their background, their skills, their particular ways of learning.

This appears to be a major conclusion of Jeanne Chall's comprehensive review of research in the teaching of reading.[1] Most children learn to read, whatever method may be used with them, but there are some children who do not successfully cope with the reading tasks. These require special study and the development of or the selection of procedures and materials that are helpful to them in their efforts to learn. As long as present tests are used and a cross section of the school population is involved, the findings regarding reading achievements will continue to show relatively minor differences in the results achieved by different reading methods.

As he monitors the educational program of his school, the principal can obtain data that will furnish more help in recording and analyzing progress and problems by using tests and other assessment exercises designed to indicate what is being learned by the entire range of pupils. By identifying problem areas he can *focus* efforts to improve, rather than scatter energies indiscriminately.

The Exploratory Committee on Assessing the Progress of Education and its successor, the Committee on Assessing the Progress of Education, have reported in some detail the anticipated values to education and educators that are likely to come from the assessment project itself. This article, as indicated earlier, is intended to suggest some things that were not contemplated or foreseen in the original planning of the project. The seven by-products mentioned seem to me to be significant for the school principal and the staff. And as the assessment data are analyzed and reported, we hope that there may be still other ways in which the project will prove helpful to administrators, teachers, and children.

[*ED. NOTE*: Comprehensive information about the assessment program appears in *National Assessment of Educational Progress — Some Questions and Comments* (Revised edition), published by the Department of Elementary School Principals, NEA.]

Note

1. Chall, Jeanne S. *Learning To Read: The Great Debate*. New York: McGraw-Hill Book Co., 1967. (Reviewed in the January 1968 issue of *The National Elementary Principal*.)

V TYLER'S RECENT REFLECTIONS ON HIS WORK

1 OVERVIEW

This section contains a 1981 interview of Ralph Tyler by Jeri Ridings Nowakowski, then a doctoral student at the Evaluation Center of Western Michigan University. During the interview Dr. Tyler reflected on his life's work, his philosophy of education, and the principles that have guided his work. He discusses what he sees as the enduring challenges facing education, and the role of evaluation in addressing these challenges. Based on more than 50 years of experience, he speculates on the future facing education. The exchange is lively, refreshing, optimistic, and spicy. Dr. Tyler's responses are often profound.

Key Points

- Professionals must do their best to serve, but should not dwell on past accomplishments nor take themselves too seriously.
- Effective administrators are both recruiters and facilitators. They must recruit talented people and then help them apply those talents effectively.
- In using evaluation and assessment properly, one must look behind the numbers and try to ascertain what they mean.

- Teachers should not teach until they have something important to say. Their teaching should be grounded in experience.
- Professionals must continually strive to clarify what they are about.
- Educators must be integrally involved in the evaluation process if evaluation results are to contribute to the solution of problems.
- The most important clients of evaluation are not state and federal officials or agencies, but parents and educators.
- Public education is the only viable means of serving the education needs of our pluralistic society.
- The three most important problems facing American education are (1) the education of disadvantaged students; (2) improving the transition of youth into constructive adult life; and (3) rebuilding the total education environment for children and young.
- To advance their field evaluators must engage in a serious study of the ethics of the field. They must address the question of what are the proper ends and means of evaluation work.

2 AN INTERVIEW WITH RALPH TYLER

Preface

This interview will be of interest to those entering the field of education as well as for those who have made their home within the field for some time now. In the interview, Ralph Tyler discusses work in education and educational evaluation that spans over a half a century. He describes issues that were important at the beginning of his career (those related to his work with the Bureau of Accomplishment Testing at The Ohio State University under W. W. Charters, and issues emerging in the Eight Year Study), and issues he thinks are important to education and educational evaluation today.

I asked Dr. Tyler questions about his early career, middle career, and his

This interview was edited from the script of a videotaped conversation between Jeri Ridings Nowakowski, Ed. D., and Dr. Tyler in November, 1981, at The Evaluation Center, College of Education, Western Michigan University, Kalamazoo. It is Paper #13 in the Occasional Paper Series, and is reprinted with permission.

present activities. He discussed the progress he felt was being made, the problems that still exist, and the resources he thinks are available to the field
of education. Throughout, he captures a sense of the history and, perhaps
even the inevitability of public education. He is essentially optimistic — he
sees the gains in public education outweighing the problems, and the prom-
ises still attainable.

Whether the reader is an old or new friend of Ralph Tyler's, the conversation that follows will help him or her get to know this man a little better.
As he discusses a lifetime of efforts and multiple professional responsibilities, a sense of continuity and direction becomes apparent. Here is someone who deliberately chose public education some 60 years ago, and has
spent, and continues to spend most days in pursuit of its improvement. He
is not at all smug, but he seems sincerely to enjoy the idea that his work
has made some important differences.

The interview took place in November 1981 when Dr. Tyler made a
three-day trip to Western Michigan University at the request of Kappa
Delta Pi, an honorary fraternity for students in education. Ralph spent
three days in classrooms and auditoriums, and at luncheons and wine-and-
cheese bashes. Throughout he was approachable — always giving the same
attention and the same quality of response to whomever he was talking.
And whenever anyone began taking Ralph Tyler or the topic at hand too
seriously, you could begin to see his eyes light up as he dropped a saucy joke
or line on an otherwise unsuspecting fan. The interview, I think, gives you
a feel for the combination of levity and seriousness that makes Ralph Tyler
good company as well as an educational legend.

The Appendix contains Dr. Tyler's two-page vitae. It gives the reader
some idea of how Ralph Tyler frames his professional experiences. (It's one
of the few educational documents that is overwhelming in its brevity.)

I am indebted to Dr. Tyler for his willingness to share his thoughts with
me. I am, in turn, pleased to share this interview with other educators. —

JRN

The Interview

RIDINGS: I'd like to begin with some questions about your history and
your education. Were you born in Nebraska?

TYLER: No, I was born in Chicago while my father was in the theo-
logical seminary. And when I was two years old the graduated
and we moved to Nebraska where I was raised.

RIDINGS: You attended Doane College in Nebraska.

TYLER: Yes, I received my bachelor's degree there in 1921 and went to Pierre, South Dakota, the capital of the state to teach science in the high school.

RIDINGS: Did you go from there to the University of Chicago?

TYLER: I first went to the University of Nebraska to get further training in science teaching, and they employed me as a supervisor of practice teachers in science. I was an instructor there for four years until 1926. Then I went back to the University of Chicago and got a doctorate in educational psychology.

RIDINGS: You would have finished your doctorate then, when you were 25 years old. I heard you say the other day that dissertations shouldn't be a student's magnum opus; what was your dissertation study?

TYLER: I was studying educational psychology, but because of my background in mathematics (I had an undergraduate major in mathematics as well as in philosophy), I was employed on the Commonwealth Teacher Training Study as a research assistant, and the title of my dissertation was "Statistical Methods for Utilizing Personal Judgments to Evaluate Teacher Training Curricula." Sounds quite complicated but that was the time when Professor Charters was heading the Commonwealth Teacher Training Study; I had collected some two million cards from each cooperating teacher who wrote down on a card an activity that he was engaged in. We had two million cards. In those days there was no automatic sorting equipment or computers. My role was to classify those two million cards and finally to get statistical methods for identifying what were the important and crucial or what is often called now the "critical incidents" for teachers. That was my dissertation. The classification reduced the two million cards into "The Thousand and One Activities of Teachers in America."

RIDINGS: How do we use that information today?

TYLER: Well, the Commonwealth Teacher Training Study is a report upon which competency-based teacher education in those days was developed. You know about every 20 years or so the uneasy tension between theory and practice in professional education (whether it be doctors or teachers or others) alternates between emphasizing the activities within the profession, or emphasizing the theory that may help to guide the profession. This was one of those times when, as now, the emphasis was on finding the competencies of teachers and trying to focus on them.

RIDINGS: Did you move from the University of Chicago to Ohio State?

TYLER: No, my first position, after I got my degree, was at the University of North Carolina where I worked with teachers in the state on the development of more effective curricula. Because Rex Trabue, who had founded the North Carolina State Testing Program was on leave, I was also in charge of the testing program of North Carolina at that time. Then in 1929, Mr. Charters who had left Chicago and gone to The Ohio State University to head the Bureau of Educational Research asked me to join him there to head the Division of Accomplishment Testing, as it was called, in the Bureau of Educational Research.

RIDINGS: The group of young people who went with Charters to Ohio State turned out to be a pretty exciting group of people. What was it like working at the Bureau at that time?

TYLER: Charters was a very stimulating person to work with. Every other Monday evening beginning at 7:30 the heads of the different parts of the Bureau met at his home. I was in, as it was called, accomplishment testing; there was Edgar Dale in curriculum, W.H. Cowley in personnel, Earl Anderson in teacher education and Tom Holy in buildings and school surveys. We met, with each one of us previously submitting a written report on what we had accomplished during the two weeks, what we saw ahead, and what were the new problems, so that we had a chance continually to see ourselves at the cutting edge in developing new ideas and new research.

RIDINGS: You worked on something called "Service Studies" with professors across campus, didn't you?

TYLER: Yes, my role in the Bureau of Accomplishment Testing was to spend half time or more than that working with the colleges of The Ohio State University to try to increase student retention and improve the teaching. The legislature had become concerned because half of the students that were enrolling in the freshman year never came back for the sophomore year. The legislature appropriated funds to devote to improving teaching and learning in the university. Half my time was devoted to working with faculties there (actually more than half), and the other half of the time with schools in the state.

RIDINGS: What were some of the studies conducted with the schools in the state?

TYLER: Let me begin by describing the public mood at that time. The

Great Depression began in the fall of '29, shortly after I arrived in Columbus. People began to worry about their material losses and blamed much of it on the banks, the government and the schools. A big conference was held in 1933 on "The Crisis in Education: Will the Schools Survive?" The papers were reporting how bad the schools were. Since these accusations included no evidence of school decline, I wrote to the superintendents in Ohio asking them whether they had any of the tests and the papers left that were given 25 or more years before. I offered to get them reproduced if they would give the tests again to see whether the students are really better or worse than those 25 or more years earlier. We found a number of communities where old tests were available, and we gave them again. We found, as was discovered in Indiana a few years ago when they repeated the Stanford Achievement Tests after 25 or 30 years, that the students of today either did the same or better than those of the past. The public acceptance of the notion that in some way things are deteriorating seems to be due not to a presentation of facts but the feeling of people that things are bad because they are not as well off as they expected to be. They are not able to get a second car or to make other purchases that they had planned. So they blame their social institutions, such as the schools, and think they aren't doing their job for the kids are not as submissive as they used to be.

RIDINGS: That's basically an optimistic note, and you feel that's true in 1981 as well?

TYLER: Yes, I do. You've seen it around...people saying it. When you look at the National Assessment, for example, you find that there are more children able to read in 1981 than there were ten years earlier. But the public doesn't pay as much attention to the National Assessment results as it does to the College Board report that the SAT scores were declining slightly, 30 points, which is only 2.4 points in raw score. The standard scores of the SAT are based on a scale in which the mean is 500 and the standard deviation is 100. And the standard deviation of the vocabulary test that fell so much was 8, and so 30 standard score units is 3/10ths of 8 or 2.4 points. This is the extent of the decline in ten years. Now that's not a serious decline, but it looks severe to those who don't know what the SAT standard score means. A more important College Board result was that the subject examination scores were going up. Nor was it generally brought to public attention that the SAT is taken by more and more students in the lower half of the class because they want to get Basic Education Opportunity Grants. And, so, in 1975 no publicity was given to the fact that many more young people from the lower half of the high school classes were taking the test than in 1965. Nothing was reported to the effect that we're testing a larger proportion of students who didn't do very well in high school. The public jumped to the conclusion that the youth of today are not doing as well as those in earlier years. The eagerness with which this conclusion was accepted, I think, is because many people are now not as well off as they hoped to be and they blame their disappointment on the failure of schools and other public institutions.

RIDINGS: You've brought up National Assessment, a project you began working on in the early sixties. Was the National Assessment Project your brainchild?

TYLER: Well, I was asked to design the plans and was chairman of the exploratory committee to develop an effective operation so that it could be taken over by the Education Commission of the States that now operate it.

RIDINGS: Has it turned out to be all that you'd hoped that it could be?

TYLER: Oh nothing is ever all that one hopes for. But certainly it has turned out to provide helpful data about the problems and progress of education in the United States.

RIDINGS: Do you think the change in funding base from a federal to a state nexus is going to have an impact on National Assessment? Will it make national data more important for us?

TYLER: I think it is very important before we spend much money on educational programs to have a picture of where we really are. This is particularly true now when pressure groups are trying hard to get funds for these purposes. So I think the National Assessment is always important — especially in difficult times when funds are rationed and should be focused where they are going to be most needed. However, the National Assessment is being supported by federal funds, and this year they were sharply cut. The Secretary of Education at the annual meeting of the Education Commission of the States in Boston this last August promised that he would do what he could to try to get some of that restored, it hasn't yet been restored. This raises the question of whether the National Assessment can be adequately continued, but I hope it will be.

RIDINGS: Let's move back to the end of your work in accomplishment testing at Ohio State. Was it then that you began to work on the Eight Year Study?

TYLER: I began my work on the Eight-Year Study in 1934. I went to Ohio State in 1929 so it was five years later. Perhaps I should give you the background. When I came to Columbus I worked with faculty members in the university in departments that had a required course for students, e.g., botany, zoology, and agriculture. They were having large numbers of failures and they wanted help, and so it seemed important to find out how much students were learning. The instructors would usually say: "We'll give them a test." Then I would point out the problem: "*What* do you want tested? The typical so-called achievement test is simply a test of what students remember about things that appear in their textbooks, and surely that isn't what you're after...you are not just teaching them to memorize." This conclusion led us to talk about what the instructors' objectives were, that is, what they really hoped their students would be learning. And then they said that a test should provide evidence of whether students were learning those things or not. Because the term "test" usually was interpreted as a collection of memory items, I suggested the use of the term "evaluation" to refer to investigating what students were really learning. As we developed evaluation instruments with those departments and began to use them, we obtained information about what students were learning and were not learning; how permanent some learnings were; how quickly they forgot information; and how long they remembered basic principles. Things of that sort were part of our experimentation. Then we moved on into other subject areas, chemistry, accounting and business, history, and various other departments. This was going on during my first five years at Ohio State. Without going deeply into the background of the Eight-Year Study, one could say that it was a project which developed from a realization on the part of many secondary schools that the depression had brought into the schools many young people that did not plan to go to college; in fact, they didn't really want to go to high school, but they went because there was no place else to go. Youth unemployment was nearly 100 percent. By 1929 we had reached a point where about 25 percent of an age group went to high school. In my day it was only 10 percent of an age group, and suddenly as the Depression went on, 50 percent of an age group were in high school. It doubled the enrollments. Many of these young people didn't find the curriculum for college entrance meaningful to them. And the other common program, the Smith Hughes Vocational Education Program, was highly selective. It enrolled persons who were definitely planning a particular occupation like garage mechanics, or homemaking, or agriculture.

High school principals realized that the schools should have a different program for these new students who were now in the high schools because they couldn't find work. But the course requirements of high schools then were pretty largely determined by, on the one hand, college entrance requirements and on the other hand, the requirements of State Education Departments. These determined what subjects were taught and, how many units were to be taken. Leaders among the principals brought attention to their problems, and the Progressive Education Association, which was interested in innovations, took the responsibility of getting together a conference of school and college people including the state departments to determine what could be done.

Out of that conference emerged the idea that a small number of schools (ultimately 30 schools and school systems), should be encouraged to develop programs that they would design to serve the high school students of that period. These 30 schools were to be given eight years in which to develop and try out new educational programs. During that time they would be freed from meeting the specific requirements of the state and of college entrance subjects in order to provide freedom for experimentation.

But there was a stipulation in the arrangement agreed to by the colleges and the state department; namely, that there would be an evaluation, and the evaluation was to include the following: One, there would be records available about the performance of students that would furnish information to help colleges make wise selections. Second, there would be an appraisal of what students were learning year after year in the high school so that the school would get continuing information as to whether they were learning something important. Third, there would be a followup after graduation to see how well they did in college or in other post-high school arenas employment, marriage, or whatever it might be. This was the three-fold task of evaluation.

The first year of the Eight-Year Study (1933–34) the directing committee expected to use the General Culture Test developed by the Cooperative Test Service for the Pennsylvania Study of School and College relations. But this was just a test of information students recalled about the things presented in widely used textbooks in the various so-called basic subjects. The schools rebelled; that wasn't what they were trying to teach, therefore it would not be a fair measure of their efforts. They threatened to drop out of the study. This produced a crisis in the summer of 1934 at the time of the annual meeting of the participants.

At this point, a member of the directing committee, Boyd Bode, a well-known philosopher of education who had his office across the hall from me in The Ohio State University, said, "We've got a young man in evaluation at Ohio State who bases evaluation on what the schools are trying to do. He works closely with them and doesn't simply take a test off the shelf. Why don't you see if he will take responsibility for directing the evaluation?" I was reached by telephone at Chapel Hill where I was teaching in the summer at the University of North Carolina. I came up to the Princeton Inn where they were meeting. They interrogated me all morning and then I had lunch with them. They went into executive session in the afternoon while I twittled my thumbs and watched people playing golf outside the Inn. At 4:00 p.m. they came and said, "We would like to have you be the director of evaluation for this project." I agreed to do so after making arrangements with The Ohio State University to spend half-time at the University, half-time on the Eight Year Study.

RIDINGS: Would you say that Tylerian Evaluation, as we understand it, was born during the Eight-Year Study?

TYLER: Well I don't know, it depends on what people want to call Tylerian Evaluation.

RIDINGS: That brings up an interesting point. Yesterday I heard you describe the evaluation process in the context of training evaluators, and it sounded a good deal richer than the six or seven steps often used to describe objectives-based evaluation.

TYLER: Oh surely you can't use just the objectives as the basis for comprehensive evaluation. But certainly it was very important for people starting a program to reach new students and find out whether they were accomplishing their purposes. But it is also important to find out many other things in order to understand what's going on in a program and to guide it. I think when people say "Tylerian" as a single process it's like saying Dewey only mentioned child interests; there is no way of summarizing very simply any human being's notions about something complex. But for convenience we are likely to give a procedure a name, rather than describing it more fully.

RIDINGS: As you worked with teachers to produce objectives that reflected their classroom goals, you must have realized that you had an impact on curriculum.

TYLER: I think so. Especially in the areas where there had not been much clarity in the curriculum descriptions and explanations. For example, in the case of literature, the teachers of literature would usually repeat some trite phrase like "the students should learn to appreciate literature." I said, well, that sounds sensible. What do you mean by that? What have you observed that you are trying to help young people learn that you call "appreciation." Is it that they can tell you about who wrote a book? Is it that they can make critical judgments of a literary work in terms of some criteria, such as unity or illusion of reality, or what not. We discussed such things until we began to agree that ultimately with literature we were concerned with comprehension, interpretation and appreciation. They meant by appreciation that the reader responds emotionally to some literary works and thus his life is richer by reason of these emotional reactions. Reading is not just a dull sensing of meaning. All that came out of discussions, and from continuous reminders, "Don't look at some taxonomy to define your objectives. A taxonomy is what someone else states as the meaning of educational objectives. You're a teacher working with students. What have you found students learning that you think is important?"

            We formed a committee of teachers on appreciation of literature from the 30 schools, and their discussions became a very rich way of trying to clarify what one could help students learn with literature. We were aided of course, too, during the Eight-Year Study, by committees of people outside of the schools who had ideas. Louise Rosenblott wrote *Literature as Exploration* and that gave a new vision of what literature could be; or the book written by Alberty and Havinghurst, who was then teacher of Science at the University School in Ohio State, on *Science in General Education* gave new insights into that. So we were trying to help get a vision of what educational objectives could be. These discussions guided both the teaching and the evaluation.

RIDINGS: When we hear criticism of objectives-based evaluation, it's typically that the objectives are not evaluated. Yet in listening to you over the last two days, it's apparent that you have had a good deal of communication with teachers, and respect for their skills. . . .

TYLER: They're the ones who have to do it. Nobody else can tell you what you're trying to do as well as you yourself. Especially, when you try to probe the unconscious intuition of things that teachers are doing that have been sensible, yet they haven't really worded them before.

RIDINGS: So, it's a matter of articulating some things that you think teachers do know how to do, have been doing, but probably need to refine. You approach educational problems with a great deal of common sense.

TYLER: The only problem with common sense is that it's so uncommon.

RIDINGS: One could say that while there might not have been a formal step for assessing the worthwhileness of objectives, that was in fact always going on in the "Tylerian" evaluation process.

TYLER: Yes, of course. The schools were helped not only by the evaluation staff but by a curriculum staff working under Professor Alberty. In 1938, the curriculum staff complained that the schools were saying they were getting more help for the evaluation staff than from the curriculum staff. Alberty explained this by saying: "Tyler has a rationale for evaluation and there isn't any rationale for curriculum. So when we were having lunch, I said to Hilda Taba, my right-hand associate, "Why, that's silly, of course there's a rationale for curriculum." I sketched out on the napkin what is now often called "The Curriculum Rationale." It indicates that in deciding what the school should help students learn, one must look at the society in which they are going to use what they learn and find out the demands and opportunities of that society. To learn something that you can't use means that in the end it will be forgotten. One must also consider the learner — what he has already learned, what his needs are, and what his interests are, and build on them; one

must also consider the potential value to students of each subject. After lunch I said to the curriculum people, "Here's a
rationale you might want to follow," and that kind of outline
of a rationale began to be developed.

RIDINGS: Dr. Tyler, when I was reviewing for this interview, I looked
back at your work, and I looked at Cronbach's piece in 1963
on course evaluation. It was apparent that you really couldn't
talk about evaluation in the early days of educational evaluation without talking about curriculum; that they were in fact
completely intertwined.

TYLER: Well, if you are talking about evaluation of education, of
course.

RIDINGS: It seems, as educational evaluation has grown, in some ways we
have seen the parting of education and educational evaluation;
that is, educational evaluation has taken on a life of its own,
is going in its own direction, and is really not attending to
curriculum.

TYLER: That happens in all professional fields; medical research has
often forgotten the patient, who has become clinical material,
and forgotten the role of the physician as a health counselor.
It was as if in some way, once the physician knew what was
going on in the human body, automatically the patient would
get well; but we know that only the patient can get himself well
— just as only the child can learn. You can't learn for him. So
there is all this evaluation business up here, without considering
what it is the learner is doing. The same problem exists with
social work; they sometimes think of clients as having no minds
of their own. But when, for instance, people discover that
money can be had in the aid to dependent children, some are
tempted to say, "That's the way to make my living. I'll just have
more children and get more money." You've got to consider
the social situation and what it means to the so-called clients.
They're not inert objects out there to be worked on. You can
do that if you're working on plants, but you can't do that with
human beings.

RIDINGS: Ironically the federal dollars that moved evaluation forward
brought us...

TYLER: Has it moved us forward?

RIDINGS: Well, it brought us large funded programs and with them program evaluation which has grown and become more methodo-
logically diverse. I guess the question is whether program

evaluation has co-opted curriculum evaluation in the public school system.

TYLER: Well, I think there will be much less money from the federal government for that kind of evaluation and that may help people to stop chasing dollars and try to consider what is really involved in effective evaluation, and who are the clients for evaluation. One of the problems is that they see the clients as being federal government, the Office of Education, NIE or the Congress, instead of the clients that you're going to improve — the teachers and the people who operate schools, and the parents and children. When you have those clients, you have to have different considerations.

RIDINGS: The evaluation components for many large-scale funded programs are still focused on outcome measures....

TYLER: And often inappropriate ones.

RIDINGS: They don't reflect the literature that we have available in evaluation. Who's in control of educational evaluation in our country? Why don't we see what professionals and academics are doing reflected in evaluation as it's legislated?

TYLER: You're not asking that as a question, are you?

RIDINGS: You mean, it's so apparently government influence.

TYLER: Well, the evaluations that make any difference are those that reach the people that really care about education, the teachers, the parents, the children, and citizens who are concerned with the welfare of the country. Much program evaluation has been directed at Congress which because it's controlled or greatly influenced by high pressure groups doesn't really care as long as it has satisfied its pressure groups. And if it's an act of law, they will not change the law just because something is found not to work — not unless the pressure groups no longer press for it.

RIDINGS: An asbtract of a recent dissertation study on the University of Chicago evaluation group proposed, after looking carefully at you and Bloom and the students that you had touched, that perhaps the most significant aspect of that group is the communication network that was set up and continues between you and your students.

TYLER: How do they determine what is the most significant, what's their criteria for significance?

RIDINGS: I didn't read the whole study. I would speculate that it might mean the characteristic that has been most instrumental in keeping evaluation alive and growing within that group and perhaps influencing the general development of evaluation.

TYLER: Well, that's a theory of history, and there are other theories, such as the need for some things will cause the persons who produce it. The question, for example, of whether it was the automobile industry, as an industry, that made the great use of cars, or the discovery that cars were so helpful to people. It's hard to determine whether it's people with ideas that produce — rather than the need of a time; and, obviously it's some kind of interaction. You can have people pressing for some things and nobody feels the need for it, and it disappears in due time. In some way it's a combination, but it's too simple a theory to talk about. These "networks" haven't changed the world generally when they've been in existence, unless at that time there was a need for one.

RIDINGS: Do you keep in active communication with most of your students?

TYLER: I certainly see them quite often and I live not far from Lee Cronbach. My two right-hand research assistants getting their doctorates in Chicago, in those early days, were Ben Bloom and Lee Cronbach. And then these was Chester Harris, and, of course, Hilda Taba had already finished her doctorate, and I was able to help her stay in this country when she was about to be deported back to Estonia because she came on a student visa.

RIDINGS: In 1938 you made the move from Ohio State back to the University of Chicago where you became the chairman of the Department and later Dean of the Division of Social Science.

TYLER: I came first to do two things. One was to take Mr. Judd's place, who was then retiring, and so to be Head of Education. And the other was to head the Board of Examinations responsible under the Chicago plan for determining the student's completion of his educational program. Under the plan, all the degrees are based on passing various comprehensive examinations. So that I was University Examiner half-time, and half of my salary was paid by the Examiner's Office, and half was paid by the school of education.

RIDINGS: Egon Guba said to me that while people know you as a researcher, a theoretician, and a statesman, you were also a wonderful administrator and a very good dean. Did you enjoy administration?

TYLER: Yes, if you define administration as Lord Acton does, "the art
             of the possible." I like to help people find ways of using their
             talents most effectively and that's usually by giving them an
             opportunity for a time to do what they think is important.
             Then, from that experience thus try to clarify what they really
             feel they can do best in that context.
                 I think that Guba is especially influenced by his own major
             Professor Jacob Getzels. I found Jacob Getzels teaching social
             psychology in the Department of Human Relations at Harvard
             and brought him to Chicago. He said he was a social psychol-
             ogist. He said, "What do you want me to do?" I said, "I want
             you not to teach anything until you feel you've got something
             to teach. I'd like to have you go around to schools, see what
             you see going on in education that could be understood by
             utilizing social psychology," Well, he told me later that he
             didn't really believe me, so when the quarter started he said,
             "What am I to teach?" I said, "Whatever you feel is important
             to people in education." "Well, I don't know." — "Until you
             find that, just go on observing schools and talking to school
             staff." And so this went on until he felt he had something to
             teach teachers. And he also worked with people in administra-
             tion on the theory of organization. I conceive a task of the
             administrator to find what appears to be a bright and able
             young man, then not to put him into a niche, but to help him
             find himself and where he could use his talents and then support
             and encourage that.

RIDINGS: So you were the true facilitator?

TYLER: That's what an administrator should be, a person to help
             people accomplish; it is the art of the possible — helping make
             possible what others dream and hope they can do.

RIDINGS: It's a nice definition.

TYLER: I might name a good many others I tried to help. For example,
             Herb Thelan — I found him teaching chemistry in the univer-
             sity high school in Oakland and again I had him, before he
             taught anything, observe what was going on in teaching. He
             became interested in the interaction of students and teachers.
             He said he wanted to work on that, so I set up a laboratory
             in which interactions in the classroom could be observed and
             recorded; a place in the laboratory school where he could study
             different groups of students. We didn't have video tape in
             those days but we had audio tape and we had ways of looking

through one-way mirrors and so on. So he began to have a chance to do what he had discovered to be interesting after looking at education for awhile. . . and study what he wanted to learn about. Some of his students never went beyond that. Ned Flanders, for example, always wanted to have just interaction — counting. But Herb, if you've seen his recent book just published, has gone a great distance in his understanding of the human influence involved in teaching.

RIDINGS: I'm moving you through your life way too rapidly. I was about to move you into 1953 when you became the Director of the Center for Advanced Studies.

TYLER: But you may want to understand that during the war I was also the Director of the Examinations Staff for the Armed Forces to develop educational testing. The GED Test was originally developed there, guided by Everett F. Lindquist of the University of Iowa.

RIDINGS: Didn't Dan (Stufflebeam) also work on the GED?

TYLER: After I left Chicago, the responsibility was contracted out to Ohio State when Guba was Director of the Bureau of Educational Research, and I believe Dan was working on the GED tests then. We originally developed the examination so that young people who were returning from military service after the Second World War would have a chance to demonstrate what they'd learned and get some credit for it. So we also developed a series of subject examinations and course examinations for that purpose. When the war was over I was asked to serve as Director of the Veterans' Testing Service for the American Council of Education to develop centers where veterans could take the tests, and demonstrate what they had learned in the armed services. Those were some administrative responsibilities to try to make possible something that seemed important.

RIDINGS: You were also instrumental, you and Frank Chase, in beginning Regional Labs in our country.

TYLER: Well, in 1964 Mr. Johnson set up a task force to see what needed to be done in education, if he were elected, as he was in 1964 to the Presidency. The task force was headed by John Gardner and included a number of very able persons like Edwin Land, the inventor and head of Polaroid. He suggested the idea of Supplementary Education Centers in order for children to learn from museums, libraries, and other educative agencies in the community. Unfortunately, this section of ESEA was construed by the educational bureaucracy as another task for the schools, and most projects supported under this title involved school activities, instead of sending kids out where they could learn from other experiences. I was responsible for writing the section on laboratories, the substance of which was included in the Elementary and Secondary Education Act of 1965. We viewed laboratories as the "middleman" between research and schools. We already had the R & D Centers in which educational research and development was supported. What we did need was a way by which the consumers, the schools, could identify problems they had and seek help from research of the past as well as the present. The laboratory was to be based with the consumer, but the laboratories that were actually funded were, with some exceptions, either R & D Centers or oriented toward the producers of research rather than the consumers. The results is that we still lack the "middleman" in most regions.

RIDINGS: Like the National Assessment, it would seem that the regional labs could be jeopardized by lack of funding.

TYLER: Yes, but it is possible that this could be a constructive result. They might then seek to serve the consumer more fully and get support there. For example, the post office looks to Congress, it doesn't worry too much about its consumers; but if the post office were responsible to their consumers then there could be more concern for good service. It is possible that if the federal government doesn't support the labs, they will seek support for their consumers. That may make the labs more responsive to the needs of schools rather than to becoming a sort of second level of R & D Centers.

RIDINGS: From 1953 to 1963 you were the Director for the Center for Advanced Studies. What do you think were the Center's major contributions during that decade before you began work on National Assessment?

TYLER: Providing an opportunity for very able behavioral scientists to spend time to think and to study when they were not responsible for teaching and other services based on their previous work. At the Center they could think about what they needed next and they could get ideas for future development.

The idea of the Center was suggested first by Haus Speier in a communication to the Ford Foundation. The Foundation in the autumn of 1951 appointed a committee to explore the idea.

It consisted of ten leading behavioral scientists. I served as chairman of the committee. We met in New York for Saturday all day and Sunday until noon each weekend from January until June 1952, working out possible ways to help able people to keep growing.

One of our members, Robert Merton, had been studying the careers of Nobel Prize winners and noted that they rarely produced anything new after they were awarded the Prize. We recognized a need for scholars and scientists to get new stimulation and new ideas in mid-career. To this end the Center was founded. Outstanding students of human behavior were invited to come there with no assignments other than their own restless energy. The Center administrations' responsibility is to help each scholar to do what he believes will give him new lines of work. That the Center has been a constructive influence is shown in the visible career lines of those scholars and scientists who have spent a year there. Each year the Center invites about 40 people from the United States and 10 from abroad to be in residence there.

RIDINGS: So once again you played the role of facilitator and nurtured people so they could do good things in education and research.

TYLER: Well, nurture is a term that depends on how suppliant you think they are. And, of course, don't forget the basic political principle that has guided many pressure groups in seeking government funds — when a sow is suckling a pig, the sow enjoys it as much as the pig.

RIDINGS: (Laughing) I like that one. Tell me, when you look back on a career that has already had so many pinnacles...

TYLER: I don't think there are pinnacles.

RIDINGS: Would you buy tiny hills?

TYLER: I don't think of them that way at all. I think about moving along doing the things that seem important.

RIDINGS: Just plodding through with Ralph Tyler. Is there something you feel a greater sense of personal accomplishment over?

TYLER: I never thought of it in those terms.

RIDINGS: If you don't think about accomplishments in a personal sense, what about as contributions to education?

TYLER: I thought they were useful; but I never tried to examine them.

RIDINGS: You don't rank order?

TYLER: No, I certainly don't.

RIDINGS: Okay. I'm going to turn to some specific questions about the field of educational evaluation and start with what I think is the obvious one. You've often been referred to in the literature as the father.

TYLER: I invented the term "evaluation" when applied to educational procedure so if naming the child, as the godfather names babies, makes you father, then I am. And when it began to be a cliche and evaluation meant so many different things to different people, I invented the term "assessment," and that's what we used next.

RIDINGS: Well, that's what I wanted to ask — the amount of paternal responsibility you take for this offspring that is credited to you.

TYLER: You can't take responsibility for what other people do, so the only thing you can do when anything becomes a cliche is to get a new word.

RIDINGS: And that's "assessment"?

TYLER: Right now it's assessment, but that will become a cliche because many people quickly catch on to forms and to labels without understanding the substance of what something is. I was at a meeting yesterday in Chicago for the Board of the Institute of Philosophical Research, and one of the group had been making a study of the influence of the Committee of Ten's report on secondary education. That report was headed by Charles Elliot, the President of Harvard, and it was sponsored by the NEA. It outlined a program of education which in form set the structure of American education for 1893 until at least the Eight-Year Study, or about 1933 — at least 40 years. But what this researcher had discovered, Mrs. VanDoren, was that most of the things that were carried over were forms. The schools offered those subjects named in the committee report, but they did not usually believe in such courses, the aims and the content suggested by the committee. Many of the committee's suggestions are fresh ideas today. I was not surprised. Why was it that PSSC and the other science courses, supported in their preparation by many millions of federal dollars, never really reformed much of the curriculum? Because the people who quickly took it on, took on the form; they were taking PSSC and using the books not as aids to inquiry but as stuff for kids to remember. You may have seen the report of the use of these materials prepared by the University of Illinois committee led by Robert Stake. The problem is that something is labeled, like the Tylerian rationale, and pretty soon it is the form that is in people's minds, not the substance. Forms, like cosmetics, are so much easier to adopt than changing your personality. And that kind of business makes it necessary periodically to change labels because the labels become cliches representing something like Dewey's "Do-I-have-to-do-what-I-want-to-do" sort of cliche — which was not what Dewey said at all, but a way of quickly labeling it. And then it's lost.

RIDINGS: It's also much easier to dismiss an idea after you simplify that greatly.

TYLER: There was a woman, very set in her ways, who taught in the schools of Tulsa during the Eight-Year Study. Every time we had a workshop, she'd say, "We've been doing that for 13 years in Tulsa." Of course, she didn't understand what was being talked about except for the label she could quickly attach and, of course, then dismiss because "We've been doing it for 13 years in Tulsa."

RIDINGS: Speaking of labels, there are a growing number in evaluation. I think Michael Scriven said that, at one count, there were over 50 evaluation models; we have at least two bona fide professional evaluation organizations, and probably more; we have a number of evaluation journals, and a number of sets of standards now. Do you think this is progress?

TYLER: Probably not. It depends on whether evaluation has become so popular that it's a fad and is likely to fade. However, there will be people who really are concerned with finding out what is going on in our educational program and want to understand it. These people will be seeking ways of evaluation. That's what science is about — trying to distinguish between the ideas you have about phenomena, and what's really going on.

RIDINGS: If you were to run a major project tomorrow, would you hire someone called an evaluator to work with you on the project?

TYLER: It depends on whether they could do what needed to be done.

RIDINGS: What kind of a job description would that be?

TYLER: Evaluation is a very broad term — what is it that needs to be done?

RIDINGS: Well, right now you're helping to educate evaluators, working on training programs for professional evaluators, is that right?

TYLER: Well, what I do now, of course, since I have no permanent job, is what's expected of me growing out of my background and where I'm employed. For example, this semester at North Carolina State University I'm employed by the Division of

Adult Continuing Education and Community College Education. Now, for example, the evaluation of general adult education requires the kind of person who understands what learning
and teaching involves and can design a learning system and
evaluate parts of the learning system that are working or not
working. But they need to do this with a good deal of understanding of what that means in the context of the community
college in North Carolina, or adult education that ranges from
the basic education of illiterate adults, of whom there are a lot in
North Carolina, to the adults who have graduated from college.
They need to have gotten well along in a job and understand
what life is really about, or, as Marvin Feldmen says, "Is there
life after work?" Then there are the trainers, people in continuing education whom I meet on Fridays from IBM and a good
many other industries in that area involved in textiles, electronics, and printing. There the problem is identifying what is
be learned and how to evaluate it. Now there are some general
people who can do that, but my own experience in evaluation
is that except for the generalists like you and Dan, most of the
people are going to be in a particular situation where their
understanding of the particular situation is terribly important.
Hence, I would choose someone very familiar with the context
and teach them how to evaluate, or choose an excellent general
evaluator and immerse them in the context. Christine McGuire,
one of my students at the University of Illinois Medical School,
is a good illustration. She is a general evaluator but very
familiar with teaching and learning in the various areas of
medicine, pediatrics, psychiatry, and the like.

RIDINGS: You said yesterday that it was hard for you to believe that
people involved in educational evaluation of schooling would
have much insight or be very productive if they hadn't been in
a public school classroom.

TYLER: Yes, if that's where they're evaluating — or medical schools if
they are there, or training stations if they are there.

RIDINGS: That brought to mind, however, the many new people who are
being graduated and have degrees in evaluation; some are a
new breed of professional with technical skills and quantitative
backgrounds — but they are not necessarily educators.

TYLER: They're like the economists of today who can tell you what's
wrong with the economy, but can't figure out what you're going
to have to do about it.

RIDINGS: In other words, such evaluators are playing a role in finding problems, but not in solving them.

TYLER: Well, it depends on what the purpose is; there's a place for finding problems. There's a place for the diagnostician or the person who runs the blood tests in the clinic, but he is not the one who is going to tell you what to do with the information.

RIDINGS: Let me ask you about the *Standards*. As you know, the Project to Develop Standards for Educational Evaluation is housed here at Western Michigan at the Evaluation Center and has been chaired by Dan Stufflebeam. That group dedicated their *Standards* to you.

TYLER: That was nice of them.

RIDINGS: Certainly it was a sign of respect. What do you think about the quality of the *Standards*? Do they hit the mark now? Do we need them?

TYLER: I think it's very helpful for the kinds of program evaluation that have been done under federal support to have this set of standards. Standards for anything have to be in light of the context and where the problems lie. There are different problems if you're talking about the evaluation of medical school curriculum in order to produce general practitioners, rather than people who are primarily research people in medicine.

RIDINGS: Do you think the *Standards*, or a profession searching for standards, will bring up some issues that will have to be resolved?

TYLER: Oh, I think that anything that causes you to look critically at what's going on will help you to identify places that have to be examined very carefully. Put another way, a professional occupation is one where there is continuous effort in the research of the profession to identify both the proper ends and the effective means of that profession. Research on the proper ends is concerned with the ethics of the profession relating the professional's work to the common good rather than the notion that what's good for General Motors is good for the country.

For example, there needs to be a continuing study of the nature of medical ethics as new ways are developed for keeping people alive a long time at a great cost. The ethical issue is: How much can society spend, if it has limited resources, on keeping some person of age 65 alive for ten years at a cost that would cover the health services to children for perhaps 20 or 30 times that many children? This is an ethical question not easily answered, and should be a matter of continuing study. Correspondingly, for the profession of evaluating the questions of who are the clients and what proper service can be given clients are raised. Is it proper for some people to get information that might be wrongly used? These are kinds of questions in evaluation that are continually gong to come up, and they change with time.

One role of the research profession, the important one, is the continuing study of ethics in the light of changing situations. The second is trying to understand the processes and trying to characterize them in ways that others can understand so they can do more than simply follow what the "master" does. They need to understand what goes on and be able to solve new problems as they arise. Evaluation needs to continually try to examine the appraisal process and to find principles rather than setting up models to be followed. If you look at science, it has not benefited by structural models alone except as an illustration of principles in which the models keep changing as new situations and applications of the principles require.

RIDINGS: Whether you look at medicine, or fields like accounting and auditing that deal with information, if those fields don't revisit their principles and the impact of those principles on their audiences, instead of a guiding set of principles they end up with a very restrictive set of expectations.

TYLER: And with limited time and resources, an important question for applied research in evaluation is to discover how far a further refinement of evaluation data is justified in terms of the cost, and how much difference it would make in the actions to be taken. A number of researchers seek more refinement but, because they think only of general group data, are happy to talk about a correlation say of .6. Many testers were jubilant when they found a correlation of .6 between the SAT and first-year grades. But they did not examine the question as to whether this correlation was a sign that college teachers should change their ways of teaching so that they could reach students who had not learned to study before, or whether they select only students who have already learned to study. That's an ethical problem in connection with testing for admission. Testers did not consider another question. What does the admissions committee do about the SAT score when the correlation is only .6. How many individuals are misplaced, and does the college care about the misjudged individuals? If one only cares about the institution getting its share of good students, one can disregard the errors which individual students suffer. What is the ethical responsibility of testers? Don't they need to learn more about the person than is provided by an instrument giving a correlation of .6? This ethical question is the one on which the Communists and Fascists differ most from avowed democracies. Communists and Fascists say, we don't care as long as we get what we need to keep the state going. It's too bad that an individual suffers; but people serve the state. However, we believe in the individual; we believe in equality, and what right have we to say that we're satisfied to be guided by a .6 when we could go and try to learn more about the individual and get to a point where we could make fairer decisions. These are ethical questions that arise from a statistical method which applies only to groups. Don't we have a responsibility to learn more about the individual's within the group?

(*Interruption for a photo session*)

RIDINGS: During the photo session, we were talking about statesman. I made the statement that you were, if not the premiere educational statesman, one of our most important educational statesmen.

TYLER: Well, flattery doesn't get you everywhere. Let's go on with the questions.

RIDINGS: Let's talk about the necessity of statespersons and how to groom them in education.

TYLER: Well, of course, there are different history theories, too. One is the necessity of statesmen, and the other is the English theory, during the time of the First World War, that you can muddle through without statesmen some way and the civilization survives. But, in any event, it's nice to have them. Whether they're necessary is another question.

RIDINGS: We mentioned a few; Frank Chase was one of the people we were talking about, and Horace Mann. You also included Hilda Taba. These are all people who are or have been national and sometimes international leaders in education. We were talking about the problems of why sometimes we seem to lack statespersons in education and suggesting that it might be, in fact, the educational process or training process. Could you talk a little bit about what makes a statesperson and what kind of activities they're involved in?

TYLER: You might want to talk first about why some situations produce more statesmen than others, and that, of course, has been a concern of religious writing for many many years. Amos advanced a theory in his book of the Bible that in periods of affluence (he described vividly how women flaunted their jewelry), people were no longer interested in God because they could satisfy their wants easily. The great ethical period for the Jews was in their Babylonian captivity. The general theory, which is hard to refute because it seems to fit so many historic periods, is that the human being is both an animal that, like other animals, depends upon various physical things, food, for example, and is greatly attracted to material possessions but also is capable of immense efforts to attain goals that are non-material (concern for others, unselfishness, altruism, and so on). In times when it's easy to satisfy the material wants, people generally become greatly attached to material things so that in affluent times people spend more than they need, they're satisfied and get happy about all the things they can get, and they pay little attention to the nonmaterial because they spend little time in reflection when enjoying physical gratifications. In difficult times, when the physical gratifications are not easily obtained, more time is spent in thinking about seeking non-material goals.

John Dewey pointed out that man as a human being is essentially a problem solver. He's not a cow that chews its cud after a nice meal in the pasture and just enjoys that. Men and women are essentially made to deal with problems, and that's why civilization advances. People have been able to meet new environmental problems when other organisms have often perished because they couldn't adapt. Which suggests that the environment in which people can continue to develop is one where goals require effort and problems must be solved and not one of relative ease. Now that's a theory of history that I think may be useful in this connection. Look back at the times that we've had people that we call statesmen. For example, in the case of Horace Mann, it was when there was a great expansion in the elementary school system of Massachusetts. They didn't have enough teachers, and he had to solve the problem of how to educate teachers. He invented the normal schools, and he did a number of other things. But during the periods before that, when there wasn't a great expansion and when there weren't problems in educating teachers, they didn't have any demands in that sense for persons to lead them in new ways.

RIDINGS: If times are getting bad, are we about to see the emergence of some new statesmen?

TYLER: If they're viewed as bad by those for whom the measure is money and physical satisfactions, then the times ahead are likely to be austere times. But that has nothing to do at all with the question of whether there will be good times for education or for people who care about others, who are concerned with some sense of satisfaction in serving others as well as being served, and those who care about a closely knit family. Those are things that can become better during periods of austerity.

RIDINGS: So the funding hiatus in education might in fact help us?

TYLER: It's probably going to produce better education. You might ask yourself, if you got 25 percent more salary would you do a better job than you do now?

RIDINGS: No.

TYLER: So really money has nothing to do with how well you do, does it? Money helps because it provides for your physical satisfactions and it may be nice for you to have other clothes or other physical things. But if it causes you to be so interested in such things that it distracts you from thinking about your work, then it can be distracting. The point is, when is physical well-being such that you don't worry about it? People who are starving certainly can't think about things because in some way they have to get food. So there's some line between which a situation is so devastating that people can't rise to it, or so satisfying that they don't worry about anything else. There is some line which promotes the problem-solving characteristic that we should try to attain.

RIDINGS: You have seen a number of crises or what people characterized as crisis periods in public education. You've also seen enormous amounts of gain made in education, and probably experienced some disappointing losses. . . .

TYLER: That's life.

RIDINGS: Something must have motivated you all those years to stay active in public education, to still look forward to another decade or more of active work in education. What keeps you going?

TYLER: Well, I think like all people if you feel your experience and your training gives you a chance to make contributions to important things you want to be right in there fighting.

RIDINGS: And you're optimistic and believe in the public education system.

TYLER: There isn't any alternative. Public education didn't come first,
you know. When we first really had formal education it was
supported by the family. You remember that in the English law
from which our English ancestors came in the 1600s, the family
was responsible. Every person had to be with a family; if someone had no relatives, he had to be attached to a family under
law, or bound over, if he was a child, to somebody or to an
orphanage. And the family was responsible for seeing that the
person respected the law and obeyed it, for deciding which
occupation to carry on to make his living, for his religious
duties, and all those things that followed the requirements of
the state for citizenship — that was all left to the family. People
who came from upper classes were destined to be the rulers so
they were sent to secondary schools in England, Eaton and
Harrow, and so on, and then those of them who were going
to be scholars and intellectuals were sent on to Oxford and
Cambridge Universities.

But what happened with this group who first came to
the New England Colonies? They were Congregationalists.
They did not believe that a priest could lead them to salva-
tion; they thought you had to read the Bible and understand
what Christianity meant and make a voluntary decision to be
Christian. Now that was a new conception; a view that a person
had to make himself good meant they had to teach the children
to read the Bible. It became a community responsibility because
they were a religious community. So the first schools founded
in New England were not just families tutoring children. The
first schools were based on the need to have everybody learning
to read.

Now we've got the same corresponding business. Less than
5 percent of the population can work at unskilled labor; that's
the present proportion of the labor force that is unskilled. All
the other jobs require some education. The people who don't
have some education are typically on welfare and they can't get
jobs. So that makes another requirement and reason for why
public schools are important. The largest percentage of private
schools we ever had in my time was just before the Depression
hit — we had around 20 to 22 percent of our students in private
schools. Now we've got about 11 percent, about half that num-

ber. In those days, the parochial schools were the largest; nuns belonged to orders in which they had taken a vow of poverty and so it didn't take very much tuition to go to a parochial school. Now, of course, fewer young people are going in the orders so that most of the parochial schools have to pay higher salaries and they are more expensive for the family than the public schools. And, then, also the people who were moving up in social class felt their kids should have a better education than the public could provide so they had private schools for them.

When it came to secondary education, the last state to have public secondary schools adopted them in 1912, so public high schools were relatively rare. They started out as the Latin grammar school so most learning was in Latin. Then when Benjamin Franklin recommended that the time for a person to be educated was while carrying on business activities of that sort, they established academies. Still they were usually private academies. And finally public schools began to be adopted after the Civil War, and the first public high schools were around 1870.

This evolution is not likely to go backwards because the requirements of managing a system privately, making it capable of accomplishing or getting along, is too great for people to handle. When I was Director of the laboratory schools at the University of Chicago and later when I was helping to put the Dalton School back on its feet, it was hard to find people who could manage it, get good teaching, satisfy parents, and be able to make it go with the money required. So that the notion that in some way private schools are going to take over all education seems very improbable. Private schools are going to be hanging in there, but they are not going to expand very much.

RIDINGS: I've got a few phrases, and I thought we would end with them.

TYLER: Cliches, I hope?

RIDINGS: Yes, your favorite cliches; cliches that will make me vulnerable to all your one-liners. I thought if you would give a couple of sentences, whatever comes to mind. First, the most promising development in educational evaluation.

TYLER: I always believe the most promising developments are people with vision and dedication to education who get some additional technical skills to handle it. Developments in human things are the persons — the ideas are only guiding persons.

RIDINGS: Okay. How about the major problem in American education K–12?

TYLER: The most obvious one that we are still struggling with is reaching the proportion of the population that is now here. The civil rights movement has made us conscious of a lack of adequate service for the minority groups of various sorts, and that's still with us. And it is likely to be with us for some time because of the increased number of illegitimate children born to teenage mothers who won't be able to provide a background for their children unless their grandparents bring them up. We're going to have a lot of children coming in that do not have the background in the home that we've been accustomed to teaching, so that's certainly a problem that we must keep working on — the so-called education of disadvantaged children.

The second problem that we've got to work on more effectively is the transition of youth into constructive adult life — which means being able to move easily from school to work, being able to accept and carry on effectively the responsibilities of citizenship, of adults in all aspects of life. We have continually tried to keep youth off the labor market, and we've continually tried to lengthen their period of childhood without allowing them to gradually assume more responsibilities. Kids have to learn to take responsibility and take the consequences when they make a mistake; that's the way they learn. The transition to adult life is terrible now, and we've become so concerned with it that there have been four commissions publishing reports on the importance of that transition. I think we're going to work more on that.

And the third problem, greatly related to it, is the problem of rebuilding the total education environment for children. What's happened with the changes in the home, with mother's employment? What's happened with television taking the place of recreational things in which there's more constructive activity for the child? We've got to rebuild that environment because the demands of education are far greater than the school time of five or six hours a day for five days a week for perhaps nine or ten months a year. There is far too little to do, and that's a big problem. Why don't we stop with those three. I could add some more if you wish; there's enough to keep us busy and happy for some time.

RIDINGS: You've put in more than your share of time on this; why don't we conclude now. Let me thank you, I've enjoyed it.

TYLER: Now, fine, can we make a date for a later time....

RIDINGS: Sure....

TYLER: And a different place....

3 APPENDIX: VITA OF RALPH WINFRED TYLER

RALPH WINFRED TYLER
Director Emeritus
Center for Advanced Study in the Behavioral Sciences

Born, Chicago, April 22, 1902

Education	Doane College, A.B., 1921
	University of Nebraska, A.M., 1923
	University of Chicago, Ph.D., 1927
Occupational	High School Teacher, Pierre, S.D., 1921–1922
Career	University Faculty Member:
	Univeristy of Nebraska, 1922–1926
	University of North Carolina, 1927–1929
	Ohio State University, 1929–1938
	University of Chicago, 1938–1953
Administrative	Chairman, Department of Education, University of
Positions	Chicago, 1938–1948
	University Examiner, University of Chicago, 1938–1953

Dean, Division of Social Sciences, University of Chicago, 1948–1953

Director, Center for Advanced Study in the Behavioral Sciences, Stanford, California, 1953–1967

Acting President, Social Science Research Council, 1971–1972

Vice President, Center for the Study of Democratic Institutions, 1975–1978

President, System Development Foundation, 1969–

Special Projects

Director of Evaluation, Eight-Year Study, 1934–1942

Director, Cooperative Study in General Education, 1939–1945

Director, Examinations Staff, U.S. Armed Forces Institute, 1943–53

Chairman, Exploratory Committee on Assessing the Progress of Education, 1964–1968

Senior Consultant, Science Research Associates, Inc., 1967–

Associations and Affiliations

Member, U.S. National Advisory Mental Health Council, 1959–1963

Chairman, National Commission on Resources for Youth, 1964–1979; Vice Chairman, 1979–

Chairman, National Commission for Cooperative Education, 1962–1975; Honorary Life Chairman, 1975–;

President, National Academy of Education, 1965–1969; Secretary-Treasurer, 1969–1971

Chairman, Research Advisory Council of the U.S. Office of Education, 1967–1970

Member, National Science Board, 1962–1968; Vice Chairman, 1966–1968

Member, National Advisory Council on the Education of Disadvantaged Children, 1965–1972

VI A
CHRONOLOGICAL
BIBLIOGRAPHY

This chronological bibliography lists the writings of Ralph W. Tyler in the period from 1929 through 1974. The materials listed are available, for the most part, in periodicals, books, and published reports. Unpublished writings are not listed except in a few instances where the materials are known to be available from the Ralph W. Tyler Collection at the University of Chicago Library.

The chronological presentation makes it possible to identify some of the basic concerns of educators and of society in general at different times throughout the past 45 years.

Much of the material written by Ralph W. Tyler has appeared in more than one publication. Articles that have been reprinted have been designated with an asterisk in the bibliography that follows. Reprinted materials are also listed separately in the last two sections of the bibliography.

Periodicals

"New Tests." *Educational Research Bulletin*. VIII (September 25, 1929) p. 310.

"Books to Read." Review of *The Objective or New Type of Examination* by G.M. Ruch. *Educational Research Bulletin.* VIII (October 9, 1929), p. 330.

"New Tests." *Educational Research Bulletin.* VIII (October 9, 1929), p. 332.

"New Tests." *Educational Research Bulletin.* VIII (October 23, 1929), p. 354.

"Books to Read." Review of *The Psychology of Elementary School Subjects* by S. C. Garrison and K. C. Garrison. *Educational Research Bulletin.* VIII (November 6, 1929), p. 375.

"New Tests." *Educational Research Bulletin.* VIII (November 6, 1929), p. 376.

"The Choice of Tests." *Educational Research Bulletin.* VIII (November 20, 1929), pp. 386–87.

"In Paper Covers." *Review of Scientific Method in Supervision* by National Conference of Supervisors and Directors of Instruction. *Educational Research Bulletin.* VIII (November 20, 1929), p. 394.

"Books to Read." Review of *Elementary Statistics* by J.H. Williams. *Educational Research Bulletin.* VIII (November 20, 1929), pp. 396–97.

"New Tests." *Educational Research Bulletin.* VIII (November 20, 1929), pp. 397–98.

"The Need for Adequate Data." *Educational Research Bulletin.* VIII (December 4, 1929), pp. 404–6.

"A Course in History of Education." *Educational Research Bulletin.* IX (February 5, 1930), pp. 57–65.

"A Course in History of Education." *Educational Research Bulletin.* IX (March 5, 1930), pp. 133–35.

"Evaluating the Importance of Teachers' Activities." *Educational Administration and Supervision.* XVI (April, 1930), pp. 287–92.

"Statistics Needed by Readers." *Educational Research Bulletin.* IX (April 16, 1930), pp. 205–11.

"A Plea for Scientists in Education." *Educational Research Bulletin.* IX (April 16, 1930), pp. 222–23.

"Training Teachers in Service through Investigations in Teaching." *The High School Journal.* XIII (May, 1930), pp. 205–10.

"The Relation Between the Frequency and the University of Teaching Activities." *Journal of Educational Research.* XXII (September 10, 1930), pp. 130–32.

"Unsuccessful Efforts in Supervision." *Educational Research Bulletin.* IX (September 10, 1930), pp. 330–38.

"High-School Pupils of Today." *Educational Research Bulletin.* IX (October 22, 1930), pp. 409–11.

"Measuring the Ability to Infer." *Educational Research Bulletin*. IX (November 19, 1930), pp. 475–80.

"What High School Pupils Forget." *Educational Research Bulletin*. IX (November 19, 1930), pp. 490–92.

"Test of Skill in Using a Microscope." *Educational Research Bulletin*. IX (November 19, 1930), pp. 493–96.

"Editorial Comment." *Educational Research Bulletin*. IX (November 19, 1930), p. 497.

"The Master-List as a Device." *Educational Research Bulletin*. X (January 7, 1931), pp. 1–11.

"Nature of Learning Activities." *Review of Educational Research*. I (January, 1931), pp. 22–29.

"New Tests." *Educational Research Bulletin*. X (January 21, 1931). pp. 55–56.

"What is Statistical Significance?" *Educational Research Bulletin*. X (March 4, 1931), pp. 115–18, 142.

"New Tests." *Educational Research Bulletin*. X (March 4, 1931), pp. 141–42.

"New Tests." *Educational Research Bulletin*. X (April 1, 1931), pp. 197–98.

"A Generalized Technique for Constructing Achievement Tests." *Educational Research Bulletin*. X (April 15, 1931), pp. 199–208.

"New Tests." *Educational Research Bulletin*. X (April 15, 1931), pp. 225–26.

"New Tests." *Educational Research Bulletin*. X (April 29, 1931), pp. 253–54.

"New Tests." *Educational Research Bulletin*. X (May 13, 1931), pp. 281–82.

"New Tests." *Educational Research Bulletin*. X (May 27, 1931), pp. 309–10.

"Testing the Ability to Use Scientific Method." *The Ohio State University Bulletin*, Proceedings of the Ohio State Educational Conference Eleventh Annual Session. XXXVI (September 15, 1931), pp. 157–58.

"Division of Accomplishments Tests." *Educational Research Bulletin*. X (September 16, 1931), pp. 322–24.

"New Tests." *Educational Research Bulletin*. X (September 30, 1931). pp. 364–66.

"New Tests." *Educational Research Bulletin*. X (October 14, 1931), p. 394.

"New Tests." *Educational Research Bulletin*. X (October 28, 1931), pp. 421–22.

"New Tests." *Educational Research Bulletin*. X (November 25, 1931), pp. 477–78.

"More Valid Measurements of College Work." *The Journal of the National Education Association.* XX (December, 1931) pp. 327–28.

"Ability to Use Scientific Method." *Educational Research Bulletin.* XI (January 6, 1932), pp. 1–9.

"New Tests." *Educational Research Bulletin.* XI (January, 6, 1932), pp. 27–28.

"New Tests." *Educational Research Bulletin.* XI (January 20, 1932), pp. 55–56.

"The Interest Questionnaire." *Educational Research Bulletin.* XI (February 3, 1932), pp. 71–72.

"New Tests." *Educational Research Bulletin.* XI (February 17, 1932), pp. 111–12.

"Training Courses for Research Workers." *Educational Research Bulletin.* XI (March 30, 1932), pp. 169–79.

"New Tests." *Educational Research Bulletin.* XI (April 27, 1932), pp. 251–52.

"Measuring the Results of College Instruction." *Educational Research Bulletin.* XI (May 11, 1932), pp. 253–60.

"Making a Co-operative Test Service Effective." *Educational Research Bulletin.* XI (May 25, 1932), pp. 287–92.

"New Tests." *Educational Research Bulletin.* XI (May 25, 1932), pp. 307–8.

"Division of Accomplishment Tests." *Educational Research Bulletin.* XI (October 12, 1932), pp. 329-33.*

"New Tests." *Educational Research Bulletin.* XI (October 26, 1932), pp. 363–64.

"Improving Test Materials in the Social Studies." *Educational Research Bulletin.* XI (November 9, 1932), pp. 373–79.

"Assumptions Involved in Achievement Test Construction." *Educational Research Bulletin.* XII (February 8, 1933), pp. 29–36.

"Permanence of Learning." *Journal of Higher Education.* IV (April, 1933), pp. 203–4.

"Tests in Biology." *School Science and Mathematics.* XXXIII (June, 1933), pp. 590–95.

"Prevailing Misconceptions." *Journal of Higher Education.* IV (June, 1933), pp. 286–89.*

"Formulating Objectives for Tests." *Educational Research Bulletin.* XII (October 11, 1933), pp. 197–206.

"New Tests." *Educational Research Bulletin.* XII (October 11, 1933), pp. 225–26.

"Division of Accomplishment Tests." *Educational Research Bulletin.* XII (November 15, 1933), pp. 230–31.

"Education and Research at a Mechanics Institute: VII Measuring Individual Accomplishment." *Personnel Journal*. XII (December, 1933), pp. 213–21.

"Techniques for Evaluating Behavior." *Educational Research Bulletin*. XIII (January 17, 1934), pp. 1–11.

"New Tests." *Educational Research Bulletin*. XIII (April 18, 1934), p. 94.

"Evaluating The Achievement of College Students." *Junior College Journal*. IV (May, 1934), pp. 389–96.

"A Study of the Factors Influencing the Difficulty of Reading Materials for Adults of Limited Reading Ability." *Library Quarterly*. IV (July, 1934), pp. 384–405 (with Dale, Edgar).

"Some Findings from Studies in the Field of College Biology." *Science Education*. XVIII (October, 1934) pp. 133–42.*

"Testing Ability to Apply Chemical Principles." *Journal of Chemical Education*. XI (November, 1934), pp. 611–13 (with Hendricks, B. C., and Frutchey F. P.).

"Testing for a Mastery of the Principles of Chemistry." *Science Education*. XVIII (December, 1934), pp. 212–15 (with Hendricks, Bernard C.).

"Evaluation: A Challenge and an Opportunity to Progressive Education." *The Educational Record*. XVI (January, 1935), pp. 121–31.

"Achievement Tests in Colleges and Universities." *Review of Educational Research*. V (December, 1935), pp. 491–501 (with Frutchey, F. P.).

"Defining and Measuring Objectives of Progressive Education." *Educational Record*. XVII (January, 1936 supplement), pp. 78-85.*

"Measuring the Ability to Interpret Experimental Data." *Journal of Chemical Education*. XIII (February, 1936), pp. 62–64 (with Frutchey F. P., and Hendricks, B. C.).

"Appraising Progressive Schools." *Educational Method*. XV (May, 1936), pp. 412–15.

"Division of Accomplishment Tests." *Educational Research Bulletin*. XV (October 14, 1936), pp. 181–82.

"The Significance of a Comprehensive Testing Program." *Journal of Chemical Education*. XIV (April, 1937), pp. 158–60.

"Evaluation of Student Achievement in the Physical Sciences." *American Physics Teacher*. V (June, 1937), pp. 102–7 (with Smith, Alpheus, and Hell, Louis M.).

"The Objective Examination: Its Development and Application to Nursing Education." *The American Journal of Nursing*. XXXVII (October, 1937), pp. 1131–38.

"The Division of Accomplishment Tests." *Educational Research Bulletin*. XVI (November 10, 1937), pp. 198–200.

"An Invitation to Teachers of Science." *School and Society.* XLVII (June 4, 1938), pp. 735–36 (with Taylor, Lloyd W., and Kinsey, A. C.).

"Division of Accomplishment Tests." *Educational Research Bulletin.* XVII (September 21, 1938), pp. 146–48.

"Secondary Curriculum Improvements." *Curriculum Journal.* X (February, 1939), pp. 64–65.

"Cooperation in the Education of Teachers and Administrators." *The North Central Association Quarterly.* XIV (January, 1940), pp. 261–67.

"Educational News and Editorial Comment." *The Elementary School Journal.* XLI (September, 1940), pp. 1–7.

"State Program for Education in Citizenship." *School Review.* XLVII (November, 1940), pp. 653–55.

"Workshops at The University of Chicago." *The Bulletin of the National Association of Secondary School Principals.* XXV (January, 1941), pp. 45–50.

"Progress Report of the Evaluation Staff." *Progressive Education.* XVIII (January, 1941), pp. 54–56, 59–60.

"Education in Defense of Democracy." *The Educational Screen.* XX (March, 1941), pp. 112–13.

"The Future of American Colleges." *Journal of the American Association of Collegiate Registrars.* XVI (April, 1941), pp. 322–24.

"Place of the Textbook in Modern Education." *Harvard Educational Review.* XI (May, 1941), pp. 329–38.*

"Schools and Public Libraries." *Elementary School Journal.* XLII (September, 1941), pp. 10–11.

"Educational News and Editorial Comment." *The School Review.* XLIX (December, 1941), pp. 721–34.

"Educational News and Editorial Comment." *The School Review.* L (February, 1942), pp. 81–83.

"General Statement on Evaluation." *Journal of Educational Research.* XXXV (March, 1942), pp. 492–501.

"Educational News and Editorial Comment." *The Elementary School Journal.* XLIII (September, 1942), pp. 1–12.

"Some Techniques Used in the Follow-Up Study of College Success of Graduates of the Thirty Schools Participating in the Eight-Year Study of the Progressive Education Association." *Journal of the American Association of Collegiate Registrars.* XVIII (October, 1942), pp. 23–28.

"The Importance in Wartime of Co-operation between Schools and Parents." *The Elementary School Journal.* LXIII (February, 1943), pp. 330–35.

"The Role of Education in Our Present Emergency." *School Science and Mathematics.* XLIII (February, 1943), pp. 99–104.

"Trends in the Preparation of Teachers." *The School Review.* LI (April, 1943), pp. 207–12.

"Appraisal of Educational Achievement Gained in the Armed Forces." *Educational and Psychological Measurement.* III (Summer, 1943), pp. 97–104.*

"Educational News and Editorial Comment." *The School Review.* LI (June, 1943), pp. 319–33.

"College Credit for Men in Service." I. *The North Central Association Quarterly.* XVIII (October, 1943), pp. 165–70.

"Evaluation of Educational Growth During Military Service." *Public Personnel Review.* V (April, 1944), pp. 95–100 (with Lily Detchen).

"Educational News and Editorial Comment." *The School Review.* LII (June, 1944), pp. 321–34.

"Educational News and Editorial Comment." *The School Review.* LII (November, 1944), pp. 511–23.

"Placement Tests as a Means of Determining Advanced Standing at The University of Chicago." *Journal of the American Association of Collegiate Registrars.* XX (July, 1945), pp. 520–26.

"Extension of Responsibilities for Counseling and Guidance in Higher Institutions." *The School Review.* LIII (September, 1945), pp. 391–400.

"Educational News and Editorial Comment." *The Elementary School Journal.* XLVI (October, 1945), pp. 59–70.

"Trends in Safety Education at the Elementary Level." *Safety Education.* XXV (November, 1945). pp. 5–7.

"Charles Hubbard Judd, 1873–1946." *The Elementary School Journal.* XLVI (September, 1946), pp. 1–2.*

"Major Issues in Education Today." *Ohio Schools.* XXV (February, 1947), pp. 58–59, 86–87.

"Adult Education Is for Teachers, Too." *Ohio Schools.* XXV (November, 1947), pp. 358–59, 392–93.*

"A Place Where Teachers Learn." *Montana Education.* XXIV (November, 1947), pp. 16–17.*

"The Cooperative Study in General Education." *Higher Education.* IV (January 1, 1948), pp. 97–100.

"Should Every High School Develop a Core Curriculum?" *The North Central Association Quarterly.* XXII (January, 1948), pp. 301–5.

"Cooperation and Conflict in the Mental Development of the Child." *Mental Hygiene.* XXXII (April, 1948), pp. 253–60.

"How Can We Improve High-School Teaching?" *The School Review.* LVI (September, 1948), pp. 387–99.*

"Words That Do Not Educate." *School and Community.* XXXIV (November, 1948), pp. 413–14.*

"The Need for a More Comprehensive Formulation of Theory of Learning a Second Language." *The Modern Language Journal*. XXXII (December, 1948), pp. 559–67.

"Educability and the Schools." *The Elementary School Journal*. XLIX (December, 1948), pp. 200–12.*

"Trends in Professional Education." *The American Journal of Nursing*. XLIX (January, 1949), pp. 50–53, 55–56.

"Better Teachers are Coming." As Told to Mary Tomancik. *The Nation's Schools*. XLIII (May, 1949), pp. 27–28.

"The Road to Better Appraisal." *NEA Journal*. XXXVIII (May, 1949), pp. 336–37.

"How to Improve High School Teaching." *Wisconsin Journal of Education*. LXXXII (November, 1949), pp. 3–4.*

"Trends in Teaching — How Research is Affecting Our Understanding of the Learning Process." *The School Review*. LIX (May, 1951), pp. 263–72.*

"Evolving a Functional Curriculum." *The American Journal of Nursing*. LI (December, 1951), pp. 736–38.

"The Distinctive Attributes of Education for the Professions." *Social Work Journal*. XXXIII (April, 1952), pp. 55–62, 94.

"Next Steps in Improving Secondary Education." *The School Review*. LX (December, 1952), pp. 523–31.

"Facing Up to the Big Issues." As told to Emma Scott. *Ohio Schools*. XXXI (January, 1953), pp. 11–13, 38.*

"The Leader of Major Educational Projects." *Educational Research Bulletin*. XXXII (February 11, 1953), pp. 42–52.

"Helen is Smarter than Betsy." *NEA Journal*. XLII (March, 1953), pp. 165–66.

"The Core Curriculum." *NEA Journal*. XLII (December, 1953), pp. 563–65.

"Leadership Role of the School Administrator in Curriculum and Instruction." *The Elementary School Journal*. LIV (December, 1953), pp. 200–9.

"Modern Aspects of Evaluation." *California Journal of Secondary Education*. XXIX (November, 1954), pp. 410–12.

"Human Behavior," *NEA Journal*. XLIV (October, 1955), pp. 426–29.

"Study Center for Behavioral Scientists." *Science*. CXXIII (March 9, 1956), pp. 405–8.

"Recent Research Sheds Light on School Staff Relationships." *The Elementary School Journal*. LVI (May, 1956), pp. 395–99.

"Clarifying the Role of the Elementary School." *Elementary School Journal*. LVII (November, 1956), pp. 74–82.

"The Individual in Modern Society." *The National Elementary Principal*. XXXVI (February, 1957), pp. 50–54.

"The Place of the Social Sciences in the Liberal Arts Curriculum." *The Journal of General Education*. X (April, 1957), pp. 114–20.

"Scholarship and Career Education for the Correctional Service." *California Youth Authority Quarterly*. X (Fall, 1957), pp. 3–11.

"Meeting the Challenge of the Gifted." *The Elementary School Journal*. LVIII (November, 1957), pp. 75–82.*

"Six Kinds of Tasks for High Schools." *The School Review*. LXVI (March, 1958), pp. 43–46.

"The Education of Teachers: A Major Responsibility of Colleges and Universities." *The Educational Record*. XXXIX (July, 1958), pp. 253–61.

"Emphasize Tasks Appropriate for the School." *Phi Delta Kappan*. XL (November, 1958), pp. 72–74.

"Conditions for Effective Learning." *NEA Journal*, XLVIII (September, 1959), pp. 47–49.

"Do We Need a 'National Curriculum?'" A Conference Report. *The Clearing House*. XXXIV (November, 1959), pp. 141–48.*

"Policies and Strategy for Strengthening the Curriculum." *The Bulletin of the National Association of Secondary School Principals*. XLIV (February, 1960), pp. 76–85.

"Science and the Seeking Mind." *National 4-H News*. XXXVIII (May, 1960), pp. 18–19.

"The Teaching Obligation." *Junior College Journal*. XXX (May, 1960), pp. 525–33.

"The Evaluation of Teaching." *Journal of Engineering Education*. L (June, 1960), pp. 863–65.

"Health Education implications from the Behavioral Sciences." *Journal of Health, Physical Education, Recreation*. XXXI (May-June, 1960), pp. 17–18, 44.

"The Teaching Obligation and Typewriting." *Business Education Forum*. XV (November, 1960), pp. 9–11.

"The Learning Process." *Oregon Higher Education*. IV (Spring, 1961), pp. 3–9.

"Educational Measurement — A Broad Perspective." *The National Elementary Principal*. XLI (September, 1961), pp. 8–13.

"Specific Contributions of Research to Education." *Theory Into Practice*. 1 (April, 1962), pp. 75–80.

"Where We Came Out." *Technology and Culture*. III (Fall, 1962), pp. 651–58.

"Education in a World of Change." *Journal of Home Economics.* LIV (September, 1962), pp. 527–33.

"Social Forces and Trends." *NEA Journal.* LI (September, 1962), pp. 26–28 (with Miller, Richard I.).

"Implications of Behavioral Studies for Health Education." *The Journal of School Health.* XXXIII (January, 1963), pp. 9–15.

"America Needs the Experimental College." *Educational Forum.* XXVIII (January, 1964), pp. 151–57.

"Evaluation in Teaching for Creativity." *Creativity & College Teaching, Bulletin of the Bureau of School Service.* XXXV (June, 1963), pp. 92–106.

"The Interrelationship of Knowledge." *The National Elementary Principal.* XLIII (February, 1964), pp. 13–21.

"Evaluating the Elementary School." *The National Elementary Principal.* XLIII (May, 1964), pp. 8–13.

"What Should the High Schools Accomplish?" *The PTA Magazine.* LIX (November, 1964), pp. 22–24.

"The Knowledge Explosion: Implications for Secondary Education." *The Educational Forum.* XXIX (January, 1965), pp. 145–53.

"Assessing the Progress of Education." *Phi Delta Kappan.* XLVII (September, 1965), pp. 13–16.

"Let's Clear the Air on Assessing Education." *Nation's Schools.* LXXVII (February, 1966), pp. 68–70.

"Importance of Innovations in Schools and Colleges." *Educational Perspectives.* V (March, 1966), pp. 24–27.

"Reactions." *NEA Journal.* LV (March, 1966), pp. 28–29.

"The Objectives and Plans for a National Assessment of Educational Progress." *Journal of Educational Measurement.* III (Spring, 1966), pp. 1–4.

"Assessing the Progress of Education." *Science Education.* L (April, 1966), pp. 39–42.

"Frontiers in Industrial Arts Education." *The Journal of Industrial Arts Education.* XXV (May-June, 1966), pp. 28–31.

"A Program of National Assessment." *Educational Forum.* XXX (May, 1966), pp. 391–96.

"New Trends in Education." *The American Journal of Psychiatry.* CXXII (June, 1966), pp. 1394–98.

"Assessing the Progress of Education in Science." *The Science Teacher.* XXXIII (September, 1966), pp. 11–14.

"New Dimensions in Curriculum Development." *Phi Delta Kappan.* XLVIII (September, 1966), pp. 25–28.

"How Can Engineering Education Increase Student Learning?" *Engineering Education.* LVII (September, 1966), pp. 20–24.

"What the Assessment of Education Will Ask." *Nation's Schools.* LXXVIII (November, 1966), pp. 77–79 (with co-author Jack C. Merwin).

"National Educational Assessment — Pro and Con." *School Board Notes.* XII (January, 1967), p. 12.

"A.A.S.A. Confuses Assessing with Testing, contends Ralph Tyler." An Interview with Ralph W. Tyler. *Nation's Schools.* LXXIX (March, 1967), pp. 43–44.

"Resources, Models, and Theory in the Improvement of Research in Science Education" *Journal of Research in Science Teaching.* V (May, 1967), pp.43–51.

"Analysis of Strengths and Weaknesses in Current Research in Science Education." *The Journal of Research in Science Teaching.* V (May, 1967), pp. 52–63.

"The Current Status of the Project on Assessing the Progress of Education." *Educational Horizons.* XLV (Summer, 1967), pp. 184–90.

"National Assessment of Educational Progress." *Art Education.* XX (September, 1967), pp. 15–17.

"Instructional Technology and the Behavioral Sciences." *Educational Broadcasting Review.* I (October, 1967), pp. 35–40.

"Critique of the Issue on Educational and Psychological Testing." *Review of Educational Research.* XXXVIII (February, 1968), pp. 102–7.

"Purposes for our Schools." *The Bulletin of the National Association of Secondary-School Principals.* LII (December, 1968), pp. 1–12.*

"National Assessment — Some Valuable By-Products for Schools." *The National Elementary Principal.* XLVIII (May, 1969), pp. 42–48.

"Curriculum for a Troubled Society." *National Catholic Education Association Bulletin.* LXVI (August, 1969), pp. 32–36.

"The Education of Health Personnel to Meet the Needs of the Child in Contemporary Society." *Canadian Journal of Public Health.* LXI (January, 1970), pp. 31–36.

"Curriculum Improvement in the University." *The Medical School Curriculum,* edited by William N. Hubbard, Jr., John A. Gronvall, George R. DeMuth. *Journal of Medical Education.* XLV (November, 1970), Pt. 2, pp. 42–48.

"Testing for Accountability." *Nation's Schools.* LXXXVI (December, 1970), pp. 37–39.*

"Recommendations for Action." *The Bulletin of the National Association of Secondary-School Principals.* LV (January, 1971), pp. 205–12.

"First Reports from the National Assessment." *Educational Leadership.* XXVIII (March, 1971), pp. 577–80.

"Theory and Practice: Bridging the Gap." An interview with Ralph W. Tyler. *Grade Teacher.* LXXXVIII (May-June, 1971), pp. 46–49, 52–54, 56, 58–60, 62, 65.

"Why Evaluate Education?" *Compact.* VI (February, 1972), pp. 3–4.

"Conditions for Learning Religion." *Religion and Public School Curriculum.* Edited by Richard U. Smith. *Religious Education.* LXVII (July-August, 1972, Part 2), pp. 31–34.

"Assessing the Potential of Vicarious Experience in the Development of Children." *Journal of Educational Research.* LXVI (October, 1972), inside front and back covers.

"What if the School Doesn't Have an Oil Well?" *Compact.* VI (December, 1972), pp. 31–32.

"Assessing Educational Achievement in the Affective Domain." *Measurement in Education.* IV (Spring, 1973), pp. 1–4.

"Father of Behavioral Objectives Criticizes Them: Interview." Edited by J. M. Fishbein. *Phi Delta Kappan.* LV (September, 1973), pp. 55–57.

"Ralph Tyler Discusses Behavioral Objectives." Interviewed by June Grant Shane and Harold G. Shane. *Today's Education.* XII (September-October, 1973), pp. 41–46.

"The National Assessment of Educational Progress." *New York University Education Quarterly.* V (Spring, 1974), pp. 13–18.

"Educational Supply and Manpower Needs in the Coming Decades." *CASC Newsletter.* XVII (March, 1974), pp. 4–8.

"The Federal Role in Education." *The Public Interest*, No. 34 (Winter, 1974), pp. 164–87.

"Research in Science Teaching in a Larger Context." *Journal of Research in Science Teaching.* XI (Issue 2, 1974), pp. 133–39.

"Utilizing Research in Curriculum Development." *Theory into Practice.* XIII (February, 1974), pp. 5–10.

Books

Tyler, Ralph W., and Waples, Douglas. *Research Methods and Teachers' Problems: A Manual for Systematic Studies of Classroom Procedure.* New York: Macmillan, 1930.

_____, et al. *Service Studies in Higher Education.* Columbus, Ohio: The Bureau of Educational Research, Ohio State University, 1932.

_____, and Waples, Douglas. *What People Want to Read About.* Chicago: The University of Chicago Press, 1932.

Constructing Achievement Tests. Columbus, Ohio: Ohio State University, 1934.

_____, and Judd, Charles H.; Breslich, E. R.; and McCallister, J. M. *Education as Cultivation of the Higher Mental Processes.* New York: Macmillan, 1936.

_____, and Ryan, Will Carson. *Summer Workshops in Secondary Education*: *An Experiment in the In-service Training of Teachers and Other Educational Workers.* New York: Progressive Education Association, 1939. (pamphlet)

_____, Smith, E. R., and the Evaluation Staff. "Purposes and Procedures of the Evaluation Staff." *Appraising and Recording Student Progress* Vol. III. Adventure in American Education. New York: Harper & Bros., 1942, pp. 3–34.

"Foreword." *The Cooperative Study in General Education*: *A Final Report of the Executive Committee of the Cooperative Study in General Education.* Washington, D.C.: American Council on Education, 1947, pp. v–xi.

Basic Principles of Curriculum and Instruction. Chicago: The University of Chicago Press, 1950.*

"The Organization of Learning Experiences." *Toward Improved Curriculum Theory.* Compiled and edited by Virgil E. Herrick and Ralph W. Tyler. Chicago: The University of Chicago Press, 1950, pp. 59–67.

_____, and Mills, Annice L. *Report on Cooperative Education.* Summary of the National Study. New York: Thomas Alva Edison Foundation, 1961. (pamphlet)

Some Reflections on Soviet Education. Rochester, New York: Rochester Institute of Technology, 1962. (pamphlet)

_____, and Gagné, Robert M., and Scriven, Michael. *Perspectives of Curriculum Evaluation.* Chicago: Rand McNally & Company, 1967.

The Challenge of National Assessment. Columbus, Ohio: Charles E. Merrill Publishing Company, 1968.

_____, and Lessinger, Leon M., editors. *Accountability in Education.* Worthington, Ohio: Charles A. Jones, 1971.

_____, and Mangum, Garth L.; Wolbein, Seymour L.; and Matthews, Howard A. *Functional Education for Disadvantaged Youth.* Edited by Sterling M. McMurrin. New York: Committee for Economic Development, 1971.

_____, and Wolf, Richard M., editors. *Crucial Issues in Testing.* Berkeley, California: McCutchan, 1974.

Contributing Author

"Identification and Definition of the Objectives to be Measured." *The Construction and Use of Achievement Examinations.* Herbert E. Hawkes, E. F. Lindquist, and C. R. Mann, Editors. Boston: Houghton Mifflin, 1936, pp. 3–16.

"Examinations in the Natural Sciences." *The Construction and Use of Achievement Examinations.* Herbert E. Hawkes, E.F. Lindquist, and C. R. Mann, Editors. Boston: Houghton Mifflin, 1936, pp. 214–63 (with Frutchey, Fred P.).

"The Study of Adolescent Reading by the Progressive Education Association." *Library Trends.* Louis R. Wilson, Editor. Chicago: The University of Chicago Press, 1937, pp. 269–285.

"Basic Assumptions which Guide My Work in Educational Measurement." *Research on the Foundations of American Education.* American Educational Research Association — Official Report. Washington, D.C.: American Educational Research Association, 1939, pp. 139–41.

"Evaluation in Teacher Education Programs." *Bennington Planning Conference for the Cooperative Study of Teacher Education.* Reports and Addresses. Washington, D.C.: Commission on Teacher Education, American Council on Education, 1939, pp. 194–99.

"An Appraisal of Technics of Evaluation — A Critique." *Official Report of the 1940 Meeting.* Washington, D.C.: American Educational Research Association, 1940, pp. 72–77.

"Contribution of Tests to Research in the Field of Student Personnel Work." *Report of the 18th Annual Meeting.* Washington, D.C.: American College Personnel Association, 1941, pp. 98–105.

"The Relation of the Curriculum to American Democratic Ideals." *Education in a Democracy.* Newton Edwards, Editor. Chicago: The University of Chicago Press, 1941, pp. 80–93.

"Putting Life Values Into Science Education." *The Science Teacher Yearbook Supplement.* American Council of Science Teachers. Washington, D.C.: National Education Association, 1942, pp. 1–2.

"Admission and Articulation Based on Study of the Individual." *New Directions for Measurement and Guidance.* American Council of Education. Series I — Reports of Committees and Conferences. Washington, D.C.: American Council on Education, 1944, pp. 1–15.

"Sound Credit for Military Experience." *Higher Education and the War.* Philadelphia, Pa.: The Annals of the American Academy of Political and Social Science CCXXXI (January, 1944), pp. 58–64.

"What Rural Schools Can Learn from the Training Programs of the Armed

Forces." *Education for Rural America*. F. W. Reeves, Editor. Chicago: The University of Chicago Press, 1945, pp. 107–18.*

"The Accomplishments and the Promise of Educational Research in Sharpening the Tools of Educational Science." *Improving Educational Research*. American Educational Research Association — Official Report. Washington, D.C.: American Educational Research Association, 1948, pp. 84–89.

"The Significance of this Investigation to School Administrators, to Teachers and to Students of Education." *How Well Are Indian Children Educated?* Shailer Alvarey Peterson, Editor. Washington, D.C.: United States Indian Service, 1948, pp. 113–17.

"Achievement Testing and Curriculum Construction." *Trends in Student Personnel Work*. E.G. Williamson, Editor. Minneapolis: The University of Minnesota Press, 1949, pp. 391–407.

"Educational Problems in Other Professions." *Education for Librarianship*. Bernard Berelson, Editor. Chicago: American Library Association, 1949, pp. 22–38.

"The Functions of Measurement in Improving Instruction." *Educational Measurement*. E. F. Lindquist, Editor, Washington, D.C.: American Council on Education, 1951, pp. 47–67.

"Can Intelligence Tests be Used to Predict Educability?" *Intelligence and Cultural Differences*. Kenneth Eells, *et al.*, Editors. Chicago: The University of Chicago Press, 1951, pp. 39–47.

"What Will Be the Emerging Curricular Implications for Colleges and Universities of the New Social and Technological Concepts? Analyst's Statement." *Current Issues in Higher Education: A Bold New Look at the Not-Too-Distant Future*. G. Kerry Smith, Editor, Washington, D.C.: National Education Association, 1957, pp. 78–80.

"Educational Values of Cooperative Education." *Highlights of the Conferences on Cooperative Education and the Impending Educational Crisis, Dayton, Ohio, May 23–24, 1957*. New York: Thomas Alva Edison Foundation, 1957, pp. 35–38.

"The Evaluation of Teaching." *The Two Ends of the Log*. Russell M. Cooper, Editor, Minneapolis: The University of Minnesota Press, 1958, pp. 167–76.

"New Criteria for Curriculum Content and Method." *The High School in a New Era*. Francis S. Chase and Harold A. Anderson, Editors, Chicago: The University of Chicago Press, 1958, pp. 170–182.

"Changing Horizons in Nursing Education." *New Dimensions of Learning in a Free Society*. Pittsburgh, Pa.: The University of Pittsburgh Press, 1958, pp. 177–89.

"A Behavioral Scientist Looks at Medicine." *Report of the First Institute on Clinical Teaching.* Helen Hofer Gee and Julius B. Richmond, Editors. Evanston, III.: Association of American Medical Colleges, 1959, pp. 136–43.

"The School Librarian's Boss." *The Climate of Book Selection, Social Influences on School and Public Libraries.* J. Periam Danton, Editor, Berkeley, California: University of California, 1959, pp. 35–40.

"The Contribution of the Behavioral Sciences to Educational Research." *First Annual Phi Delta Kappa Symposium on Educational Research.* Frank W. Banghart, Editor. Bloomington, Indiana: Phi Delta Kappa, Inc., 1960, pp. 55–70.

"Educational Objectives of American Democracy." *The Nation's Children.* Vol. II: *Development and Education.* New York: Columbia University Press, 1960, pp. 70–92.

"Psychological Knowledge and Needed Curriculum Research." *Research Frontiers in the Study of Children's Learning.* James B. MacDonald, Editor. Milwaukee: University of Wisconsin Press, 1960, pp. 36–45.

"Social Trends, and Problems for Tomorrow's Schools." *New Teaching Aids for the American Classroom.* Stanford, California: The Institute for Communication Research, 1960, pp. 3–9.

"The Educational Potential of 4-H." *Selected Readings and References in 4-H Club Work.* Madison, Wis.: National Agricultural Extension Center for Advanced Study, 1961, pp. 12–16.

"Mental Health and National Survival: Mr. Tyler's Analysis." *Official Report, American Association of School Administrators for the Year, 1960–61.* Washington, D.C.: American Association of School Administrators, 1961, pp. 45–54.

"Some Guiding Principles for Decision-Making." *Measurement and Research in Today's Schools.* Arthur E. Traxler, Editor. Washington, D.C.: American Council on Education, 1961, pp. 20–31.

"The Study of Campus Cultures." *The Study of Campus Cultures.* Papers presented at Fourth Annual Institute on College Self Study, University of California, Berkeley, July 24–27, 1962. Terry Lunsford, Editor. Boulder, Colo.: Western Interstate Commission for Higher Education, February, 1963, pp. 1–10.

"An Assessment: The Edge of the Future." *The Social Studies: Curriculum Proposals for the Future.* C. Wesley Sowards, Editor. Chicago: Scott, Foresman, 1963, pp. 120–32.

"Forces Redirecting Science Teaching." *Revolution in Teaching: New Theory, Technology and Curricula.* Alfred de Grazia and David A. Sohn, Editors. New York: Bantam Books, 1964, pp. 187–192.*

"National Planning and Quality Control in Education." *Modern Viewpoints in the Curriculum.* Paul C. Rosenbloom, Editor. New York: McGraw-Hill, 1964, 11–18.

"Some Persistent Questions on the Defining of Objectives." *Defining Educational Objectives.* C. M. Lindvall, Editor, Pittsburgh: The University of Pittsburgh Press, 1964, pp. 77–83.*

"Future Prospects of the Behavioral Sciences." *The Behavioral Sciences: Problems and Prospects.* Boulder, Colorado: Institute of Behavioral Science, University of Colorado, August, 1964, pp. 27–40.

"Innovations in Our Schools and Colleges." *White House Conference on Education: A Milestone for Educational Progress.* Committee Print, Subcommittee on Education of the Committee on Labor and Public Welfare, United States Senate, 89th Congress, 1st Session, 1965, pp. 185–90.*

"Vice Chairmen's Reports." *White House Conference on Education: A Milestone for Educational Progress.* Committee Print, Subcommittee on Education of the Committee on Labor and Public Welfare, United States Senate, 89th Congress, 1st Session, 1965, pp. 201–203.

"The Field of Educational Research." *The Training and Nuture of Educational Researchers.* Egon Guba and Stanley Elam, Editors. Bloomington, Indiana: Phi Delta Kappa, Inc., 1965, pp. 1–12.

"A Program of National Assessment." Address and panel reactions. Official Report. *American Association of School Administrators, 1966.* Washington, D.C.: American Association of School Administrators, 1966, pp. 8–30 (with others).

"An Overview of American Higher Education." *Higher Education in a Changing World.* Addresses selected from the 1965 Conferences for the Visiting Fulbright-Hays Scholars in the U.S. Washington, D.C.: Department of State, 1966, pp. 62–68.

"The Social Sciences: Major Problems and Challenges of the Future." *Expanding Horizons of Knowledge About Man.* New York: Yeshiva University Press, 1966, pp. 25–33.

"Purposes, Scope and Organization of Education." *Implications for Education of Prospective Changes in Society.* Denver, Colo.: Designing Education for the Future Project, January, 1967, pp. 34–46.

"Investing in Better Schools." *Agenda for the Nation.* Kermit Gordon, Editor. Washington, D.C.: The Brookings Institution, 1968, pp. 207–36.

"Charge to the Conference." *Teaching Psychiatry in Medical School.* The working papers of the Conference on Psychiatry and Medical Education, 1967. Washington, D.C.: American Psychiatric Association, 1969, pp. 1–6.

"Education Must Relate to a Way of Life." *Automation and Society*. E. L. Scott and R. W. Bolz, Editors. Athens, Ga.: The Center for the Study of Automation and Society, 1969, pp. 91–106.*

"Educational Effects of Examination in the United States." *Examinations — The World Year Book of Education 1969*. Joseph A. Lauwerys and David G. Scanlon, Editors. New York: Harcourt, Brace & World, 1969, pp. 342–46.

"The Field of Educational Research." *Essays on World Education: The Crisis of Supply and Demand*. George Z. F. Bereday, Editor. New York: Oxford University Press, 1969, pp. 167–79.

"Impact of Testing on Student Development." *Impact of Testing on Student Development*. Ann Arbor, Mich.: Michigan School Testing Service, 1969, pp. 3–6.

"The Changing Structure of American Institutions of Higher Education." *The Economics and Financing of Higher Education in the United States*. A Compendium of Papers submitted to the Joint Economic Committee, Congress of the United States, 91st Congress, Washington, D.C.: U.S. Government Printing Office, 1969, pp. 305–320.

"The Problems and Possibilities of Educational Evaluation." *The Schools and the Challenge of Innovation*. New York: Committee for Economic Development, 1969, pp. 76–90.

"The Purposes of Assessment." *Improving Educational Assessment and an Inventory of Measures of A*ffective Behavior. Walcott B. Beatty, Editor. Washington, D.C.: Association for Supervision and Curriculum Development, 1969, pp. 2–13.

"Changing Responsibilities of Higher Education." *Academic Change and the Library Function*. Compiled by C. Walter Stone. Pittsburgh: The Pennsylvania Library Association, 1970, pp. 7–26.

"Epilogue: Academic Excellence and Equal Opportunity." *Issues of the Seventies: The Future in Higher Education*. Fred F. Harcleroad, Editor. San Francisco: Jossey-Bass, 1970, pp. 166–83.

"In-Service Education of Teachers: A Look at the Past and Future." *Improving In-Service Education: Proposals and Procedures for Change*. Louis J. Rubin, Editor. Boston: Allyn and Bacon, 1971, pp. 5–17.

"National Assessment: A History and Sociology." *New Models for American Education*. James W. Guthrie and Edward Wynne, Editors. Englewood Cliffs, New Jersey: Prentice-Hall, 1971, pp. 20–34.*

"Education: Balancing Conditioned Response and Responsible Claims." *Annals of the New York Academy of Sciences*, Vol. 184, June 7, 1971, pp. 297–307.

"Concepts and the Teaching-Learning Process." *Selected Concepts from*

Educational Psychology and Adult Education for Extension and Continuing Educators. Publications in Continuing Education. Syracuse, New York: Syracuse University, November, 1971, pp. 1–8 (with Leagans, J. Paul; Copeland, Harland G.; and Kaiser, Gertrude E.).

"Values and Objectives." *The Handbook of Cooperative Education.* San Francisco: Jossey-Bass, 1972, pp. 18–25 (with Knowles, Asa A., and Associates).

"Purposes for Our Schools." *Educational Issues of the 70's: Foundations of Education.* Richard J. Kraft, Editor. MSS Information Corp., 655 Madison Avenue, New York, N.Y. 10021. 1973.*

"The Autonomous Teacher." *Facts & Feelings in the Classroom.* Louis J. Rubin, Editor. New York: Walker and Company, 1973, pp. 33–59.

"Educational Evaluation in the Revolutionary Age." *Educational Communication in a Revolutionary Age.* Compiled by I. Keith Tyler and Catharine M. Williams. Worthington, Ohio: Charles A. Jones, 1973, pp. 101–18.

"The Right Student, the Right Time and the Right Place." *College/Career Choice: Right Student, Right Time, Right Place.* Kenneth J. McCaffrey and Elaine King, Editors. Iowa City, Iowa: The American College Testing Program, 1973, pp. 1–13.

"Schools for Young Children — The Recent American Past." *Education in Anticipation of Tomorrow.* Robert H. Anderson, Editor. Worthington, Ohio: Charles A. Jones, 1973, pp. 7–27.

"Education: An Optimistic View." Chapter 3, *Social Psychiatry*, Volume I. Jules H. Masserman, John J. Schwab, editors. New York: Grune & Stratton, 1974, pp. 33–42.

Yearbooks

National Society for the Study of Education

"Characteristics of a Satisfactory Diagnosis." *Educational Diagnosis.* Thirty-fourth Yearbook of the National Society for the Study of Education. Bloomington, Illinois: Public School Publishing, 1935, pp. 95–111.

"Elements of Diagnosis." *Educational Diagnosis.* Thirty-fourth Yearbook of the National Society for the Study of Education. Bloomington, Illinois: Public School Publishing, 1935, pp. 113–29.

"The Specific Techniques of Investigation: Examining and Testing Acquired Knowledge, Skill and Ability." *The Scientific Movement in Edu-*

cation. Thirty-seventh Yearbook of the National Society for the Study of Education, Part II. Bloomington, Illinois: Public School Publishing, 1938, pp. 341–55.

"Introduction." *American Education in the Postwar Period*. Forty-fourth Yearbook of the National Society for the Study of Education, Part I. Chicago: The University of Chicago Press, 1945, pp. 1–4.

"Implications for Improving Instruction in the High School." *The Education of Exceptional Children*. Forty-ninth Yearbook of the National Society for the Study of Education, Part I. Chicago: The University of Chicago Press, 1950, pp. 304–35 (with Thelen, Herbert A.).

"The Functions of Graduate Departments and Schools of Education." *Graduate Study in Education*. Fiftieth Yearbook of the National Society for the Study of Education, Part I. Chicago: The University of Chicago Press, 1951, pp. 10–21.

"Graduate Programs in Education at The University of Chicago." *Graduate Study in Education*. Fiftieth Yearbook of the National Society for the Study of Education, Part I. Chicago: The University of Chicago Press, 1951, pp. 150–57.

"Translating Youth Needs into Teaching Goals." *Adapting the Secondary School Program to the Needs of Youth*. Fifty-second Yearbook of the National Society for the Study of Education, Part I. Chicago: The University of Chicago Press, 1953, pp. 215–29.

"Curriculum Organization." *The Integration of Educational Experiences*. Fifty-seventh Yearbook of the National Society for the Study of Education, Part III. Chicago: The University of Chicago Press, 1958, pp. 105–25.

"The Behavioral Scientist Looks at the Purposes of Science-Teaching." *Rethinking Science Education*. Fifty-ninth Yearbook of the National Society for the Study of Education, Part I. Chicago: The University of Chicago Press, 1960, pp. 31–33.

"The Purpose and Plan of this Yearbook." *Social Forces Influencing American Education*. Sixtieth Yearbook of the National Society for the Study of Education, Part II. Chicago: The University of Chicago Press, 1961, pp. 1–7.*

"The Impact of Students on Schools and Colleges." *Social Forces Influencing American Education*. Sixtieth Yearbook of the National Society for the Study of Education, Part II. Chicago: The University of Chicago Press, 1961, pp. 171–81.

"Understanding Stability and Change in American Education." *Social Forces Influencing American Education*. Sixtieth Yearbook of the National Society for the Study of Education, Part II. Chicago: The University of Chicago Press, 1961, pp. 230–46.

"The Impact of External Testing Programs." *The Impact and Improvement of School Testing Programs.* Sixty-second Yearbook of the National Society for the Study of Education, Part II. Chicago: The University of Chicago Press, 1963, pp. 193–210.

"The Behavioral Sciences and the Schools." *The Changing American School.* Sixty-fifth Yearbook of the National Society for the Study of Education, Part II. Chicago: The University of Chicago Press, 1966, pp. 200–14.

"Introduction." *Educational Evaluation: New Roles, New Means.* Sixty-eighth Yearbook of the National Society for the Study of Education, Part II. Chicago: The University of Chicago Press, 1969, pp. 1–5.

"Outlook for the Future." *Educational Evaluation: New Roles, New Means.* Sixty-eighth Yearbook of the National Society for the Study of Education, Part II. Chicago: The University of Chicago Press, 1969, pp. 391–400.

"Curriculum Development in the Twenties and Thirties." *The Curriculum: Retrospect and Prospect.* Seventieth Yearbook of the National Society for the Study of Education, Part I. Chicago: The University of Chicago Press, 1971, pp. 26–44.

The American Association of Colleges for Teacher Education

"The Evaluation of Professional Training." *The Sixteenth Yearbook of the American Association of Teachers Colleges*, 1937. Washington, D.C.: The American Association of Colleges for Teacher Education, 1937, pp. 75–82.

"Social Forces Influencing American Education." *Unity in Diversity.* The Fourteenth Yearbook of the American Association of Colleges for Teacher Education. Washington, D.C.: The American Association of Colleges for Teacher Education, 1961, pp. 42–52.

Encyclopedia

"Testing and Assessment Programs, National." *The Encyclopedia of Education.* First edition. Vol. 9, pp. 175–179, Crowell-Collier Educational Corp., 1971.

Proceedings

Conference for Administrative Officers of Public Private Schools

"Training Administrative Officers for Democratic Leadership." *Democratic Practices in School Administration*. Edited by William C. Reavis. Proceedings of the Eighth Annual Conference for Administrative Officers of Public and Private Schools. Chicago: The University of Chicago Press, 1939, pp. 63–72.*

"The Place of Evaluation in Modern Education." *Evaluating the Work of the School*. Edited by William C. Reavis. Proceedings of the Ninth Annual Conference for Administrative Officers of Public and Private Schools. Chicago: The University of Chicago Press, 1940, pp. 3–11.*

"Educational Adjustments Necessitated by Changing Ideological Concepts." *Administrative Adjustments Required by Socio-Economic Change*. Edited by William C. Reavis. Proceedings of the Tenth Annual Conference of Administrative Officers of Public and Private Schools. Chicago: The University of Chicago Press, 1941, pp. 3–13.*

"Relations of the Urban Community and the Modern School." *The School and the Urban Community*. Edited by William C. Reavis. Proceedings of the Eleventh Annual Conference for Administrative Officers of Public and Private Schools. Chicago: The University of Chicago Press, 1942, pp. 3–13.*

"The Role of the Schools in the Nation's War Efforts." *War and Post-War Responsibilities of American Schools*. Edited by William C. Reavis. Proceedings of the Twelfth Annual Conference for Administrative Officers of Public and Private Schools. Chicago: The University of Chicago Press, 1943, pp. 2–12.

"The Responsibility of the School for the Improvement of American Life." *Significant Aspects of American Life and Postwar Education*. Edited by William C. Reavis. Proceedings of the Thirteenth Annual Conference for Administrative Officers of Public and Private Schools. Chicago: The University of Chicago Press, 1944, pp. 1–7.*

"The Role of University Departments of Education in the Preparation of School Administrators." *Educational Administration: A Survey of Progress, Problems and Needs*. Edited by William C. Reavis. Proceedings of the Fifteenth Annual Conference for Administrative Officers of Public and Private Schools. Chicago: The University of Chicago Press, 1946, pp. 31–45.*

"Characteristics of a Modern Educational Program: Proposals for Adults." *Administrative Planning for School Programs and Plants*. Edited by Dan H. Cooper. Proceedings of the Sixteenth Annual Conference for Administrative Officers of Public and Private Schools. Chicago: The University of Chicago Press, 1947, pp. 14–24.*

Institute for Administrative Officers of Higher Institutions

"The Development of Examinations at Ohio State University." *Recent Trends in American College Education*. Proceedings of the Institute for Administrative Officers of Higher Institutions. Edited by William S. Gray. Chicago: The University of Chicago Press, 1931, pp. 228–38.

"Methods Used in Improving Tests and Examinations at the Ohio State University." *Tests and Measurements in Higher Education*. Proceedings of the Institute for Administrative Officers of Higher Institutions. Chicago: The University of Chicago Press, 1936, pp. 146–154.

"Needed Research in the Field of Tests and Examinations." *Tests and Measurements in Higher Education*. Proceedings of the Institute for Admininstrative Officers of Higher Institutions. Edited by William S. Gray. Chicago: The University of Chicago Press, 1936, pp. 230–37.

"Co-operation in the Study of Institutional Problems." *The Outlook for Higher Education*. Proceedings of the Institute for Administrative Officers of Higher Institutions. Compiled and edited by John Dale Russell. Chicago: The University of Chicago Press, 1939, pp. 230–43.

"Principles Involved in Evaluating Student Personnel Services." *Student Personnel Services in Colleges and Universities*. Proceedings of the Institute for Administrative Officers of Higher Institutions. Edited by John Dale Russell. Chicago: The University of Chicago Press, 1940, pp. 291–300.

"A Summary of Trends in the Attack on College Instructional Problems." *New Frontiers in Collegiate Instruction*. Proceedings of the Institute for Administrative Officers of Higher Institutions. Edited by John Dale Russell. Chicago: The University of Chicago Press, 1941, pp. 237–48.

"Acceptance of Military Experience Toward College Credit." *Higher Education Under War Conditions*. Proceedings of the Institute for Administrative Officers of Higher Institutions. Edited by John Dale Russell. Chicago: The University of Chicago Press, 1943, pp 107–16.

"Situations Requiring an Extension of Institutional Responsibilities for Counseling and Guidance." *Emergent Responsibilities in Higher Education*. Proceedings of the Institute for Administrative Officers of Higher Institutions. Edited by John Dale Russell and Donald M. Mackenzie. Chicago: The University of Chicago Press, 1945, pp. 1–14.

"The Evaluation of Faculty Services." *Problems of Faculty Personnel*. Proceedings of the Institute for Administrative Officers of Higher Institutions. Compiled and edited by John Dale Russell. Chicago: The University of Chicago Press, 1946, pp. 124–133.

Conference on Reading

"Newer Techniques in Evaluating Growth." *Reading and Pupil Development.* Compiled and edited by William S. Gray. Proceedings of the Conference on Reading held at The University of Chicago, Vol. II. Chicago: The University of Chicago, 1940, pp. 275–81.

"Wartime Interests and Needs and Their Relation to Reading Programs." *Adapting Reading Programs to Wartime Needs.* Compiled and edited by William S. Gray. Proceedings of the Conference on Reading held at The University of Chicago, Vol. V. Chicago: The University of Chicago, 1943, pp. 14–19.

"Summary of Criteria for Appraising a School's Reading Program." *The Appraisal of Current Practices in Reading.* Compiled and edited by William S. Gray. Proceedings of the Conference on Reading held at The University of Chicago, Vol. VII. Chicago: The University of Chicago, 1945, pp. 222–30.

"What is Evaluation?" *Evaluation of Reading.* Compiled and edited by Helen M. Robinson. Proceedings of the Conference on Reading held at The University of Chicago, Vol. XX. Chicago: The University of Chicago, 1958, pp. 4–9.

"The Importance of Sequence in Teaching Reading." *Sequential Development of Reading Abilities.* Compiled and edited by Helen M. Robinson. Proceedings of the Conference on Reading held at The University of Chicago, Vol. XXII. Chicago: The University of Chicago, 1960, pp. 3–8.

"What is Evaluation?" *Reading: Seventy-Five Years of Progress.* Compiled and edited by H. Alan Robinson. Proceedings of the Conference on Reading held at The University of Chicago, Vol. XXVIII. Chicago: The University of Chicago Press, 1966, pp. 190–98.

Conference on Business Education

"Evaluation of Business-Education Criteria." *Business Education in School Situations.* Proceedings of the Sixth University of Chicago Conference on Business Education. Chicago: The University of Chicago Press, 1939, pp. 13–18.

Schoolmen's Week — University of Pennsylvania

"Techniques for Evaluating Behavior." *Educational Responsibilities of*

Today and Tomorrow. Proceedings of Twenty-Second Annual School-men's Week. Philadelphia: The University of Pennsylvania Press, 1935, pp. 348–57.

"Evaluation as a Function of Supervision." *Challenges to Education: War and Post-War.* Proceedings of Thirtieth Annual Schoolmen's Week. Philadelphia: The University of Pennsylvania Press, 1943, pp. 104–16.*

"Appraisal of Military Training and Experience." *Challenges to Education: War and Post-War.* Proceedings of Thirtieth Annual Schoolmen's Week. Philadelphia: The University of Pennsylvania Press, 1943, pp. 346–52.*

Annual Forum — National Conference on Social Welfare

"Implications of Research in the Behavioral Sciences for Group Life and Group Services." *Social Welfare Forum, 1960.* Official Proceedings, 87th Annual Forum, National Conference on Social Welfare, Volume 87. New York: Columbia University Press, 1960, pp. 113–26.

The Abington Conference

"New Directions in Individualizing Instruction." *Proceedings of The Abington Conference '67 "New Directions in Individualizing Instruction."* Willow Grove, Pa.: April 23–25, 1967.

Third Invitational Conference on Elementary Education

"Schools for the 70's." *Individualized Curriculum and Instruction.* Proceedings of the Third Invitational Conference on Elementary Education, Banff, Alberta, October 1969. Edited by K. Allen Neufeld. Edmonton, Alberta: University of Alberta, 1970, pp. 7–16.

National Education Association

"A Survey of Present Training Courses for Research Workers." *Proceedings of the Seventieth Annual Meeting of the National Education Association of the United States,* Volume LXX. Washington, D.C.: National Education Association, 1932, pp. 368–69.

The Conference of Foundations

"New Areas for Foundation Initiative." *Proceedings of the Conference of Foundations.* Claremont, California: The Associated Colleges, 1960, pp. 14–22.

National Committee for Support of the Public Schools

"Assessing the Progress of Education." *Education and Social Change.* Proceedings of the Fourth Annual Conference, National Committee for Support of the Public Schools. Washington, D.C.: National Committee for Support of the Public Schools, 1966, pp. 82–85.*

The Association of Land Grant Colleges and Universities

"Measuring the Effectiveness of Instruction." *Proceedings of the Forty-Seventh Annual Convention of the Association of Land Grant Colleges and Universities.* Washington, D.C.: Association of Land Grant Colleges and Universities, 1934, pp. 130–33.

The Council on Social Work Education

"Distinctive Attributes of Education for the Professions." *Proceedings of the 1952 Annual Meeting, American Association of Schools of Social Work.* New York: Council on Social Work Education, 1952, pp. 3–11.
"Scholarship and Education for the Professions." *Education for Social Work.* Proceedings of the 1957 Annual Meeting, Council on Social Work Education. New York: Council on Social Work Education, 1957, pp. 13–22.

Invitational Conference on Testing Problems

"Curriculum: Then and Now." *Proceedings of the 1956 Invitational Conference on Testing Problems.* Princeton, N.J.: Educational Testing Service, 1957, pp. 79–94.*
"What Testing Does to Teachers and Students." *Proceedings of the 1959 Invitational Conference on Testing Problems.* Princeton, N.J.: Educational Testing Service, 1960, pp. 10–16.
"The Role of Machines in Educational Decision-Making." *Proceedings of the 1962 Invitational Conference on Testing Problems.* Princeton, N.J.: Educational Testing Service, 1963, pp. 102–13.

"The Development of Instruments for Assessing Educational Progress." *Proceedings of the 1965 Invitational Conference on Testing Problems.* Princeton, N.J.: Educational Testing Service, 1965, pp. 95–105.

Reports

The Fact Finding Study of the Testing Program of the United Stated Armed Forces Institute. Madison, Wis.: The U.S. Armed Forces Institute, 1 July 1954.

Analysis of the Purpose, Pattern, Scope, and Structure of the Officer Education Program of Air University. Maxwell Air Force Base, Ala.: Officer Eduation Research Laboratory, 1955.

Report of the Chairman, Air University Board of Visitors. Chancellor Alexander Heard, Chairman. Maxwell Air Force Base, Ala.: Air University, 1970, pp. 12–13.

Report of the Chairman, Air University Board of Visitors. Dr. Sanford S. Atwood, Chairman. Maxwell Air Force Base, Ala.: Air University, 1971, pp. 2–3, 6–8.

Report of the Chairman, Air University Board of Visitors. Dr. Ralph W. Tyler, Chairman. Maxwell Air Force Base, Ala.: Air University, 1972, p. 1, 18–20.

Theses

"A Test for High School Science." Unpublished Masters's Thesis, University of Nebraska, 1923.

"Statistical Methods for Utilizing Personal Judgments to Evaluate Activities for Teacher-Training Curricula." Unpublished Ph.D. Dissertation, The University of Chicago, 1927.

"Statistical Methods for Utilizing Personal Judgments to Evaluate Activities for Teacher-Training Curricula." *Abstracts of Theses.* The University of Chicago: Humanistic Series. Vol. VI, 1927–1928. Chicago: The University of Chicago Press, 1928.

Radio Scripts

Chicago Round Table

Education for Freedom. The University of Chicago Round Table Series #261. NBC Radio Discussion by Alvin C. Eurich, Richard P. McKeon, and Ralph W. Tyler. Introduction by Robert Maynard Hutchins. March 21, 1943.

When Johnny Comes Marching Home. The University of Chicago Round Table Series #285. NBC Radio Discussion by S. H. Nerlove, Floyd Reeves, and Ralph W. Tyler. September 15, 1943, 16 pp.

G.I. Education. The University of Chicago Round Table Series #410. NBC Radio Discussion by C. E. Hostetler, Floyd Reeves, and Ralph W. Tyler, January 27, 1946.

Education and the G.I.s. The University of Chicago Round Table Series #432. NBC Radio Discussion by Clarence Faust, Henry Heald, and Ralph W. Tyler, June 30, 1946.

Equality of Educational Opportunity. The University of Chicago Round Table Series #562. NBC Radio Discussion by George Stoddard, Louis Wirth, and Ralph W. Tyler. December 26, 1948, pp. 1–17.

What Should Society Expect from a University? The University of Chicago Round Table Series #574. NBC Radio Discussion by Laird Bell, Arthur Holly Compton, and Ralph W. Tyler, March 20, 1949, pp. 1–11.

Love is Not Enough. The University of Chicago Round Table Series #695. NBC Radio Discussion by Bruno Bettelheim, Ralph W. Tyler, and Ethel Verry. July 22, 1951, pp. 1–11.

What Makes a Good Public School? The University of Chicago Round Table Series #815. NBC Radio Discussion by G. Lester Anderson, James Lewis, and Ralph W. Tyler. November 22, 1953, pp. 1–11.

The Teacher Crisis. The University of Chicago Round Table Series #858. NBC Radio Discussion by Robet J. Havighurst, Ralph W. Tyler, and Benjamin C. Willis. September 19, 1954, 12 pp.

Voice of America

Institutional Organization of the Behavioral Sciences. Lecture Broadcast on Voice of America (No. 2 in Forum Lectures, Behavioral Science Series) first aired September 21, 1959, then September 24, 1959, revised slightly and aired August 7 and 10, 1961.

The National Committee on Education by Radio

Why Give Examinations? Education Series Talk No. 1, 1938, W.O.S.U. (Ohio State University).

How Do Present Measuring Instruments of the School Compare with the

Old? Education Series Talk, August 20, 1938, W.O.S.U. (Ohio State University).
(Texts for both of the above scripts will be found in the Ralph W. Tyler Collection, housed in the University Archives in the Special Collections Department of the Joseph Regenstein Library at the University of Chicago. The first is in Box XXIII, folder 7; the second in Box XXIII, folder 3.)

Newspaper

"From School to College — Curriculum Experiment in the United States." *The Times Educational Supplement*, No. 1577 (July 21, 1945), p. 340.

ERIC Entries

"Report of the Postdoctoral Educational Research Training Program of the Center for Advanced Study in the Behavioral Sciences." ED 021 817. August, 1967, p. 15.
"A Viable Model for a College of Education." ED 059 961. October 30, 1971, p. 14.
"Research in Science Teaching in a Larger Context." ED 076 426. March, 1973, p. 18.

Reprinted Articles

The articles listed below are Tyler articles that have appeared in more than one publication, sometimes under a different title. The article, as it appeared first, is listed elsewhere in this bibliography with complete identifying data. In the following list, the title of the first article is repeated and immediately after it, in parentheses, is the heading in the bibliography under which the complete entry appears; for example: (Periodicals), (Proceedings), etc. Immediately following the heading is the complete bibliographical data for the reprinted publication.
"Division of Accomplishment Tests" (Periodicals). Renamed "Research in the University," *Journal of Higher Education*, III (November, 1932), pp. 439–42.
"Prevailing Misconceptions" (Periodicals). Excerpts, *American Association of University Professors Bulletin*, X (October, 1933), pp. 367–69.

"Evaluation: A Challenge and an Opportunity to Progressive Education" (Periodicals). *Educational Research Bulletin*, XIV (January 16, 1935), pp. 9–16. *Progressive Education*, XII (December, 1935), pp. 552–56.

"Some Findings in the Field of College Biology" (Periodicals). Summary, *Journal of Higher Education*, VI (January, 1935), pp. 40–42.

"*Defining and Measuring Objectives of Progressive Education*" (Periodicals). *Educational Research Bulletin*, XV (March 18, 1936), pp. 67–72.

"Needed Research in the Field of Tests and Examinations" (Proceedings). *Educational Research Bulletin*, XV (September 16, 1936), pp. 151–58.

"Training Administrative Officers for Democratic Leadership" (Proceedings). *American Teacher*, XXIV (February, 1940), pp. 14–17.

"The Place of Evaluation in Modern Education" (Proceedings). *The Elementary School Journal*, XLI (September, 1940), pp. 19–27.

"Educational Adjustments Necessitated by Changing Ideological Concepts" (Proceedings). *The Elementary School Journal*, XLII (September, 1941), pp. 17–26.

"Place of the Textbook in Modern Education" (Periodicals). *Ohio Schools*, XIX (December, 1941), pp. 428–9+. *Texas Outlook,* XXVII (November, 1943), pp. 27–29.

"Relations of the Urban Community and the Modern School" (Proceedings). *The Elementary School Journal*, XLIII (September, 1942), pp. 14–22.

"Appraisal of Military Training and Experience" (Periodicals). *American Association of Collegiate Registrars Journal*, XVII (July, 1943), pp. 345–52. *North Central Association Quarterly*, XVIII (October, 1943), pp. 165–70. *Illinois Education*, XXXI (May, 1943), pp. 261–62+.

"The Responsibility of the School for the Improvement of American Life" (Proceedings). *The School Review*, LII (September, 1944), pp. 400–5.

"Evaluation as a Function of Supervision" (Proceedings). *The Elementary School Journal*, XLIV (January, 1944), pp. 264–72.

"What the Schools can Learn from the Training Programs of the Armed Forces" (Contributing Author). *The Elementary School Journal*, XLV (May, 1945), pp. 495–502.

"Charles Hubbard Judd, 1873–1946" (Periodicals). *The School Review*, LIV (September, 1946), pp. 375–76.

"The Role of University Departments of Education in the Preparation of School Administrators" (Proceedings). *The School Review*, LIV (October, 1946), pp. 451–61.

"Characteristics of a Modern Educational Program: Proposals for Adults" (Proceedings). *The Elementary School Journal*, XLVIII (November, 1947), pp. 127–36.

"Adult Education is for Teachers, Too" (Periodicals). *Wisconsin Journal of Education*, LXXX (November, 1947), pp. 140–42. *Kentucky School Journal*, XXVI (February, 1948), pp. 10–12. *Texas Outlook*, XXXI (February, 1948), pp. 8–9. *Illinois Education*, XXXVII (October, 1948), pp. 56–57. *Education Digest*, XIII (February, 1948), pp. 44–46.

"A Place Where Teachers Learn" (Periodicals). *Nebraska Education Journal*, XXVIII (January, 1948), pp. 22–23. *Virginia Journal of Education*, XLI (March, 1948), pp. 297–98.

"Words That Do Not Educate" (Periodicals). *Secondary Education*, XIV (November, 1948), pp. 13–14.

"How Can We Improve High School Teaching?" (Periodicals). *Education Digest*, XIV (December, 1948), pp. 34–37.

"Educability in the Schools" (Periodicals). *Education Digest*, XIV (April, 1949), pp. 5–8.

"How to Improve High School Teaching" (Periodicals). *School and Community*, XXXV (December, 1949), pp. 423–24. *Kentucky School Journal*, XXVIII (January, 1950), pp. 32–34. *Ohio Schools*, XXVIII (January, 1950), pp. 10–11. *Virginia Journal of Education*, XLIII (March, 1950), pp. 23–24.

"Trends in Teaching: How Research is Affecting our Understanding of the Learning Process" (Periodicals). *Education Digest*, XVII (December, 1951), pp. 22–26.

Basic Principles of Curriculum and Instruction (Books). "How Can Learning Experiences Be Selected Which Are Likely to Be Useful in Attaining Objectives?" *Contemporary Thought on Public Schools Curriculum: Readings*. Edited by Edmund C. Short and George D. Marconnit. Dubuque, Iowa: William C. Brown, 1968, pp. 268–90.

"Facing up to the Big Issues" (Periodicals). *Montana Education*, XXIX (January, 1953), pp. 10–11. *Maryland Schools*, LXVII (March, 1953), pp. 18–19. *Pennsylvania School Journal*, CII (March, 1954), pp. 254–56.

"The Curriculum — Then and Now" (Proceedings). *The Elementary School Journal*, LVII (April, 1957), pp. 363–74. *Education Digest*, XXIII (October, 1957), pp. 13–16. *Contemporary Thought on Public Schools Curriculum: Readings*. Edited by Edmund C. Short and George D. Marconnit. Dubuque, Iowa: William C. Brown, 1968, pp. 250–57.

"Meeting the Challenge of the Gifted" (Periodicals). *Education Digest*, XXIII (February, 1958), pp. 5–8.

"Do We Need a National Curriculum? A Conference Report" (Periodicals). *National Association of Secondary School Principals Bulletin*,

XLIV (February, 1960), pp. 76–85. *Social Studies*, L (October, 1959), pp. 187–92.

"The Purpose and Plan of this Yearbook" (Yearbooks). Renamed and adapted as "Social Forces Influencing American Education...Education and Change." *Minnesota Journal of Education*, XLII (September, 1961), pp. 11–13.

"Forces Redirecting Science Teaching" (Contributing Authors). *The Science Teacher*, XXIX (October, 1962), pp. 122–25.

"Innovations in our Schools and Colleges" (Contributing Authors). *SDC Magazine* (Systems Development Corporation), VIII (Winter, 1965–66), pp. 2–8.

"Assessing the Progress of Education" (Proceedings). *Teachers College Record*, LXVIII (December, 1966), pp. 233–35. *Contemporary Thought on Public Schools Curriculum: Readings*. Edited by Edmund C. Short and George D. Marconnit. Dubuque, Iowa: William C. Brown, 1968, pp. 187–89.

"Some Persistent Questions on Defining of Objectives" (Contributing Author). *Contemporary Thought on Public Schools Curriculum: Readings*. Edited by Edmund C. Short and George D. Marconnit. Dubuque, Iowa: William C. Brown, 1968, pp. 279–83. Abridged. "Considerations in Selecting Objectives." *Curriculum Evaluation: Commentaries on Purpose, Process, Product*. Edited by David A. Payne. Lexington, Massachusetts: D. C. Heath, 1974, pp. 64–68.

"Purposes for our Schools" (Periodicals). Edited version. *California Elementary Administrator*, XXXII (March, 1969), pp. 9–14.

"Education Must Relate to a Way of Life" (Contributing Author). *Education Digest*, XXXVI (October, 1970), pp. 8–11.

"National Assessment: A History and Sociology" (Contributing Author). *School and Society*, XCVIII (December, 1970), pp. 471–77.

"Testing for Accountability" (Periodicals). *Educational Digest* XXXVI (March, 1971), pp. 112–14.

Reprinted Book

Basic Principles of Curriculum and Instruction. This book has recently been translated into the following languages: Dutch, German, Norwegian, Portuguese, and Spanish.

Index